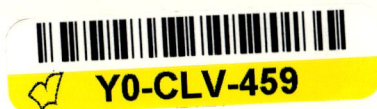

The Germans:
an Englishman's notebook

Alan G Jones
is also editor of the
Anglo-German Songbook

The Germans:
an Englishman's notebook

Alan G Jones BA FIL

POND PRESS
46 St Augustine's Avenue
Ealing   London W5

1st edition 1968   SBN: GB 85375 020 3

Text and Hatherall photos copyright © Alan G Jones 1968

Made in England
for Pond Press

Set in 10/11 point Times
and printed offset-litho by
Unwin Brothers Limited
Woking and London

Bound by Kemp Hall Bindery Ltd
Oxford

For BMJ

"There can be no question of nations thinking alike, but they should at least become aware of each other and comprehend each other. Even if they cannot love each other, they should at least learn to tolerate each other." — Goethe

About people

Many books have been written about Germany: books about its history and politics and economics, official handbooks bristling with statistics, illustrated guidebooks, and so on. Each usually has its dominant theme and its specialist readership.

This book does not attempt to specialise. Instead, it tries to give a broad view of a nation's life. A look at almost everything, sometimes a glance, sometimes a stare. If there is a theme, it is people: the people of Germany, East and West, what they are doing and saying and thinking.

It began as a research paper undertaken at York University for the German Section of the Nuffield Foreign Language Teaching Materials Project. The aim at that stage was ambitious enough: to bring together background material on life in Germany for use by teachers of German in secondary schools. With encouragement from Pond Press, the note-taking continued after the Nuffield paper was finished, with the more ambitious aim of expanding the material into a comprehensive survey that would be useful not only to teachers and students but also to tourists, businessmen, writers, politicians and anyone else with an interest in Germany.

No claim is made that all or even most of the material in this book is now seeing print for the first time. Nearly all of it has appeared in books, periodicals or newspapers in English or in German. Wherever it seems relevant, the facts are supplemented with my own experience in Germany — but all the time I have been conscious of the need to let the facts speak for themselves and to avoid the all-too-easy pitfall of turning a subjective experience into a sweeping generalisation.

There are so many people to thank for help. In the early stages of the work, considerable help and advice was given by Peter Green, lecturer at York University and joint author of "German — a Structural Approach", and also by the members of the Nuffield German team. Jenny Leftwich provided much of the information on German art, and an East Berlin publishing house, Volk und Wissen, kindly supplied detailed answers to a series of questions about life in East Germany. The German-British Society in the GDR supplied books and newspapers, the German Tourist Information Bureau in London a variety of printed matter, and Inter Nationes eV in Bad Godesberg a selection of books and leaflets which they obtained for me from many sources.

So that the book would contain information of interest to readers on both sides of the Atlantic, it was decided to enlist the help of some American collaborators. Dale S Cunningham, head of the Into English translating and language information service in Camden, New Jersey, helped here, as did Adrian Di Cyan, editor of the Chicago Mensa magazine "Chime". On the home front, Christopher Monro, whose depth of knowledge on many aspects of German culture and history has always amazed me, kindly agreed to read the manuscript form of several chapters, and offered helpful suggestions for additional material. Elaine Lively, tutor in Philosophy at Manchester College, Oxford, checked the chapter entitled "A nation of thinkers", and Rolf Tonndorf, former President of the Association of German Translators, supplied information on the German legal system. Martin Walker, a British graduate now lecturing at the University of California, allowed me to use some of his research as a source for the chapter on sport, and the Export Services Branch of the (British) Board of Trade helped with information on the new German Turnover Tax Law. And all the while my publisher not only coped with a barrage of questions about technicalities, but also supplied ideas for paragraphs and whole chapters.

Glyn Hatherall, while lecturing at the University of Münster, found time to take several photographs in different parts of Germany in response to a list of detailed requests, including the sausage-and-sauerkraut picture on the cover. Other photos were provided by David Kedgley of Hemel Hempstead and James G Maguire of Dublin (the latter took the top picture on the cover). The German Tourist Information Bureau in London kindly allowed me to raid their stocks of photographs, as did Lex Hornsby & Partners, public relations agents for the East German tourist and trade representatives in London. Further sets of prints were sent by the Press and Information Office of the West German government and by ADN-Zentralbild, the East German state news agency.

The cartoons in this book come from two sources. Those indicated by the wording "Desch collection" are taken from the book "Ohne Worte — Deutschland" published by the Kurt Desch Verlag, Munich. The remainder are reproduced by permission of the newspaper "Junge Welt", East Berlin. The maps were drawn by Les Bawden, a former Ordnance Survey artist.

The final typescript went to the publishers at the end of February, 1968. I am most grateful to the Federal Statistical Office in Wiesbaden, and to the Editor of "Democratic German Report" for digging out the latest available statistics just before the book went to press.

There may be criticism from some quarters for my over-reliance on the results of opinion polls. My defence is that whatever the failings of opinion polls, they are likely to be more reliable than impressions gained by an individual. The poll results given in these pages come from two reputable institutes, the Institut für Demoskopie at Allensbach, and the EMNID Institute (the German branch of the Gallup chain).

Although this book does not aim to present any particular political viewpoint, I make no claim to complete objectivity. There is much I admire in both parts of Germany, and I have been greeted on both sides of the Iron Curtain with hospitality and kindness. But I also see faults on both sides, and make no attempt in this book to conceal them.

In accordance with current English usage, I have occasionally used the word "Germany" where "West Germany" or "West Germany and Berlin" would be a more accurate description. I hope that, in these cases, the meaning will be clear.

Any writer who tries to deal with both West and East Germany is really taking on the whole subject of east and west Europe. The work of compiling this book has therefore acquired a measure of idealism, a desire to help promote better understanding of the two viewpoints as exemplified by the two parts of Germany. Fortunately, the very nature of this book, its deliberately wide scope, keeps the emphasis on people rather than politics. And the differences between people are insignificant compared with their similarities.

Contents

How they live	Eighty million individuals	10
	A home of their own	12
	Happy families	17
	Dress and fashion	21
	On the menu	26
	To wash it down	31
	Good manners	36
	Going shopping	38
	Growing up	43
— and work	Men and machines	50
	Exports and imports	55
	In the office	60
	The ad-men	65
— and play	A night out	70
	Sport	76
	On holiday	81
	Excuses for a celebration	89
Their government and institutions	Government and politics	97
	Schools for young and old	102
	The Church past and present	108
	Law and lawbreakers	113
	Post and telephone	116
	The printed word	122
	Radio and television	129
	Money and banking	133
	Road users	136
	Quicker by rail	141
	The sick and the needy	145
	Armed forces	147
Germans of the past	A little history	151
	A nation of thinkers	160
	The literary heritage	164
	Art and architecture	170
	Music and musicians	176
	Men of science	181
The foreigner and Germany	Language problems	184
	Looking at a map	187
	Places worth seeing	197
	Serious and not-so-serious museums	212
	Question time	217
	Germany and the world	220
Appendices	The value of money	222
	How to get there	223
	Further reading	225
	Some useful addresses	229
Index		232

HOW THEY LIVE

Eighty million individuals

On returning from a stay in Germany, I am sometimes asked "How do you get on with the Germans?" This is a careful way of saying "Are the Germans as inhuman as they are sometimes portrayed in Britain, or has this stereotype now become inaccurate?"

The question also implies that the stereotype was accurate at some time in the past. Since I have known Germany and her people for only the last ten years of her existence, I am unable to judge this. But sticking to the present, let us see how some British ideas about the Germans match the facts.

The mythical "average German" is above all believed to be a hard worker. The main virtue in his code of ethics is ruthless efficiency. He eats sauerkraut at every meal, and washes it down with four pints of strong beer. He is supposed to be priggishly arrogant, and always insists that he is in the right. He takes his dachshund and his collapsible umbrella with him wherever he goes. He loves philosophy, and is well educated. But he is so serious about everything that he is quite incapable of letting his hair down.

Now the facts. Certainly, many Germans start work earlier than we do in Britain, but most of them are surprised when the "hard-working" epithet is taken seriously by foreigners. Germans have longer holidays, and many office workers — particularly in senior positions — do not adhere rigorously to the house rules about knocking-off times at midday or in the evenings. I even knew one office in Germany where the boss frequently seemed to be "at lunch" from eleven in the morning until five in the afternoon. On the other hand, punctuality is a form of thoroughness for which most Germans have much regard. And when two thousand German women were asked what qualities they looked for in a man, diligence took second place in their lists (only faithfulness being considered more important).

One German in three, according to the pollsters, drinks no beer. Those who do, choose mostly the rather weak varieties in preference to the stronger brews. As to sauerkraut, this appears on average only once a fortnight on the table of the German family with whom I stay for most of my visits. However, the foreign tourist visiting Germany is well advised to try sauerkraut, a peculiarity of German cooking for which it is worth acquiring a taste.

Strangely, German arrogance is a phenomenon you encounter less within Germany's boundaries than outside. It is certain German tourists abroad who tend to act in a bombastic manner — a fact noticed by other Germans as well as by foreigners. Apart from some reckless driving habits and a reluctance to queue in an orderly fashion for a bus, the supposedly-traditional arrogance rarely surfaces in everyday life. On the other hand, I do sometimes get the impression that many Germans are unable to accept contradiction in argument. But I would not wish to go on record as saying that they were generally worse in this respect than other nationalities.

According to the latest poll results, only one German in eight keeps a dog as a pet, and these dogs are not all dachshunds! The collapsible umbrella is far more popular.

Germany has contributed much to the world of philosophy, but this has been the work of individuals rather than the result of a national interest in the subject.

Indeed, I find no evidence to suggest that, as a race, they are exceptionally interested in philosophy. Although very few (in the West, at least) get a university education, many Germans appear knowledgeable on a wide range of subjects from geography to ancient history. Their ability to unravel geographical and historical crossword clues has often intrigued me.

The final attribute of the German stereotype, his constant straight face and inability to enjoy himself, is the one I feel most misses the point. Certainly, the North German tends to take his work seriously, and to reserve his laughter for when he is off-duty. But his countrymen in the Rhineland and the south are particularly good-natured, not only at Carnival time (when they really let go) but in everyday situations too. And the Berliners have a reputation for being able to make a joke out of any predicament.

The main objection to the stereotype is that the Germans are not all alike. The blonde, nordic German you often see in Kiel is quite different from the thick-set, dark Bavarians or the dapper Berliners. Moreover, the different social and economic structure in East Germany (which a leading British politician once called the "Belgianisation" of East German life) has resulted in a different attitude towards youth, towards the State and towards commercial organisations.

However, there are some aspects of German life which first strike the foreigner as different from normal practice in Britain and the USA. Even if we discount as over-generalised any idea of a "German character" it is quite feasible to talk with reservations of a "German way of life", meaning the customs and mores generally adopted by German Society. Though even here we will have to distinguish at many points between East and West, and occasionally between North and South.

A good starting point is to look at the homes in which the Germans live.

Fig 1 Flat-dwelling has its problems. Cartoon by Grabbert, reproduced from "Junge Welt".

Zeichnung: Grabbert

A home of their own

Most German families live in flats (or, to use the American term, apartments). The 1961 census revealed that West Germany contained ten million leasehold flats, as compared with five million freehold and owner-occupied dwellings. This prevalence of flats is even more marked in the cities, where houses for one family only are the exception. Of the ten million flats mentioned above, seven million were in buildings containing more than two dwellings.

The average German family, it has been calculated, spends 8% of its income on rent or on its house. The cost of building a house in Germany in 1968 was roughly double that of a house in the Midlands of England — the absolute minimum is 100,000 Mark. Rents, however, seem to be about the same as in Britain — though this statement is based on personal experience, not on statistical averages.

In multi-dwelling houses, the main door is usually opened by remote control from any of the flats — a feature beginning to appear in Britain. A visitor presses a bell by the main door, and waits for a buzzing sound which is the signal that if he pushes the door it will open. Sometimes there is also an intercom system, so the visitor will first hear his host's voice asking who is there. Just outside the main door — or in some houses just inside — is a row of letter-boxes, one for each family. They are opened by individual keys, and to open someone else's letter-box counts as "breaking and entering".

Houses in Germany do not have names, as so many do in Britain. Thus there is no German equivalent for "Fiftyone" or "Fredanethel". But where the Germans do build individual houses, they take great care over an impressive exterior, with the result that each house in the street looks different from all its neighbours. The row of identical estate-built houses, such a common sight in Britain, is rare in Germany.

Many German flats have balconies, and the owners take great pride in these. Frequently they are used as miniature gardens, and the result is most impressive when looking up from the street.

Most houses and flats have either double glazing or even double windows — and German visitors sometimes seem astonished that England, with a more unpleasant climate, lags behind the Continent in this respect. In Bavaria, wooden shutters are the order of the day; in winter they keep out the snow.

Germans tend to leave their curtains open, even in the evening. The window normally has a net curtain in addition to the main heavy curtains. This net curtain is usually short, for the window-sill is a favourite place for pot plants.

Modern small flats tend not to have a separate dining room. No German flat is complete, however, without a small hallway from which the other rooms lead off. This is called the "Flur", and seems to serve no useful purpose.

The Allensbach Institute did a survey on homes in September 1967. 75% of those questioned were happy in their present home (as compared with 59% in a similar poll in 1950). 67% had their own bath or shower, 11% shared one, and 22% had no access to either bath or shower.

On the same occasion, the Institute's interviewers were asked to make their own assessment of the dwellings concerned. 10% were described as "luxurious, comfortable", 53% as "bourgeois, normal", 34% as "rather simple, but nothing lacking" and 3% as "poor, miserable". As to the cleanliness — again in the eyes of the interviewer — 18% were "spotless", 63% "neat and tidy", 16% "reasonably well-kept" and 3% "rather untidy".

Furniture

In the main lounge or living-room, there is no fire-place around which the furniture can be set. Thus the room is arranged in a manner different from that customary in Britain, where almost every piece of furniture faces the hearth. (Most houses in Germany have central heating, though some older buildings use tiled stoves, kept in a corner of the room). In a German home, the furniture is usually arranged around a central low table.

There is a tendency towards dark wood for all furniture, and everything looks substantial. Very heavy furniture, however, is dying out. In many families, piano lessons are "the done thing" for the children, and in such families the living room will contain a piano. Of recent years, black leather chairs have become popular, particularly if they look imposing. They are often expensive.

Book-shelves are more prominent than in Britain, and look impressive because the Germans go in for leather-bound collections. The book clubs sell complete collections of classical authors in leather or half-leather bindings; these are frequently bought because they are "a good thing to possess", but rarely read.

In the dining-room the visitor will find a long sideboard with several sections, and also a tall cupboard for crockery. Dining-room furniture of huge proportions is still fashionable in Germany, though in England it lost favour decades ago.

Beds in Germany are also huge, particularly double beds, which always have two single-bed mattresses. Instead of blankets, Germans prefer a large feather pillow (called a "Plumeau"); in Winter, this is remarkably effective. Many Germans use their Plumeau all the year round, but others use a quilt in Summer.

Fig 2   In South Germany many families keep the old style of furniture, including tiled stoves (left). Photo: Glyn Hatherall.

Fig 3   A rubber plant is found in many German homes, reminding British visitors of their grandparents' aspidistra. Photo: Glyn Hatherall.

By the side of each of the beds, near the headboard, there is likely to be a small night-table, often combined with a cupboard. Clothes and bed-linen are kept in a huge wardrobe, often taking up a whole wall. (Most German women receive several sets of bed-linen as wedding presents).

Smaller items

There are several small features about a German home which the foreign visitor may find confusing. The front door key, for example, is turned twice for a complete lock — a rare device in Britain. If the foreign visitor tries to be helpful by drawing the curtains, his host will be horrified if he pulls at the curtain material itself — there are nearly always rods attached to the top of the curtain which make sliding the curtains easier.

Water is often heated with a gadget called a "Tauchsieder", an electric heater in the form of a spiral metal tube. It is important to put it in the water before you switch on — otherwise it gets red hot. No German home is complete without its coffee grinder and coffee filter. The grinder is usually electrically operated.

Bread is sliced with a large circular bread saw. For cucumber and tomato slicing, the Germans use a wooden or metal board which has a knife-edge half way down.

The Englishman who is used to identifying the salt by the single hole in the top of the salt-pot will be confused in Germany, because German salt-pots have several holes in the top.

The German housewife has several small kitchen gadgets not often seen in Britain. One is a "Quirl", a handle with a number of hooked prongs used for beating eggs or whipping other liquids. Cutlets, steaks and "Schnitzel" are beaten with a special little wooden hammer. Kidney beans can be sliced with a gadget that looks like a mincer. One of the taps on the kitchen sink will probably be fitted with a spray for vegetables.

A German housewife, particularly of the older generation, is proud of her dinner service and tea service, usually of tall, straight china thinner than most English porcelain. Many ladies in Germany collect special sets called "Sammeltassen", each set consisting of cup, saucer and plate, and often expensive.

Fig 4   An excellent example of modern German china design — the "Studio Line" by Rosenthal AG, 8672 Selb, Postfach 104.

East Germany

House building in East Germany has lagged behind the progress made in the West. In 1965, East Germany built 41 dwellings per thousand population; West Germany 102. Thus new flats are difficult to get, and only one East German family in ten lives in a post-war home. Many of the families now living in new flats had to help build them in their spare time. But living in a pre-war flat in East Germany has one big advantage: the rent is fixed at its 1938 level. And although many houses in East Germany look rather dilapidated from the outside, they are often comfortable inside. Thus a walk round slum areas in East Berlin (which, despite newspaper reports to the contrary, are no worse than some areas of West Berlin) can give a false impression of the standard of living. The houses are communally owned, so the individual has less incentive to improve the outside appearances.

Happy families

Brick walls, furniture and gadgets do not really make a home. More important is the harmony of the people living in the home, the family. Our short look at family life in present-day Germany begins with German engagement customs.

Engagements are more formal affairs in Germany than in Britain. When an Englishman wrote to his English friends, "We've bought the ring", congratulation cards arrived by return of post. He wrote the same to his German friends, who then asked "When are you getting engaged?" In Germany, the couple send all their friends and relations a printed card announcing their intention of getting engaged on such and such a date (normally a Sunday), so that engagement congratulations and gifts can arrive on time. Engagement parties are normally family affairs, though a few friends are also invited. There are two engagement rings, for the couple wear one each. They are plain gold rings engraved with the initials of the other partner and are worn on the left hand during the engagement and on the right hand after the wedding (usually engraved with the date of the wedding).

In the 1964 EMNID survey, young people aged between 18 and 21 were asked their views on premarital intercourse. 20% thought premarital experience was

Fig 5 Bavarian lovers are supposed to take a ladder to their sweetheart's window and visit her for the night. But — as cartoonist Kurt Weber shows here — you need to be sure you are welcome. Reproduced from the Desch collection.

B

right, and a further 34% felt it was only right "with the future marriage partner". 20% thought it was mostly wrong, but only 11% rejected it outright.

A German boy may not marry until he has reached the age of 18. Weddings do not necessarily involve visits from all possible relations, as they normally do in Britain. The only legal ceremony is the civil ceremony, and all couples must go through this; a church ceremony can be an addition, but no substitute. On the night before the wedding the couple throw a party (known as a "Polterabend") which traditionally includes breaking china against the wall for good luck — rather hard on the downstairs neighbours if the party goes on late into the night.

If the wedding is accompanied by a ceremony in a Catholic church, there will be children in white carrying candles for the couple. In a Protestant church, the children carry flowers which are thrown after the couple as they walk down the aisle to the church door. In some areas, when the couple reach the church door other children bar the way with a rope; the bridegroom must throw them some money (it must be silver) before they will remove the rope.

For every thousand inhabitants, there are in West Germany each year 8·3 weddings (Britain 7·5, USA 9) and 0·95 divorces (Britain 0·61, USA 2·3). Divorce is easier in Germany than in Britain, as it is not necessary for either party to be found guilty; a couple may have a divorce if they have been living apart for three years. Adultery is a less common ground for divorce than in Britain, because it is not permissible in Germany for the guilty party in such a divorce to marry the co-respondent. Thus even if adultery is the real reason for the divorce, it is seldom entered as the official grounds. German law is quite vague as to the circumstances under which a partner can claim nullity of a marriage on the grounds that he was under a misapprehension as to his partner's qualities at the time of the marriage; English law is far more specific in this respect.

The "average German" of the statisticians marries when he is 28 years of age, and his wife is 25. Every fifth marriage is childless; 21% have one child, 30% two children, 17% three and 15% four or more.

Fig 6 Live births per 1,000 population 1964

Although the father in a German household is not the god-like figure he used to be, he is still more the head of the family than his British or American counterpart. Particularly among the older generation, the tradition persists that the father does no housework at all. The mother's place was traditionally in the kitchen, and the Germans often talk of the three K's, meaning "Küche, Kirche, Kinderstube" (kitchen, church and nursery) as the mother's domain. Nowadays, however, the number of working mothers is increasing rapidly; every third German woman now goes out to work — and the remaining two-thirds includes schoolgirls and pensioners!

The EMNID interviewers asked over two thousand young people in 1964 if they had anyone with whom they could talk over personal problems. 89% said that they did, and of these 29% named their parents as the people with whom they could talk things over. Here there was a marked difference between the two parents; 28% could discuss problems with their mothers, and only 6% with their fathers. The strength of the German family as a unit is demonstrated by the fact that 73% of the young people believed that a working teenager should live with his or her parents.

The influence of the home on the German child is stronger in comparison with Britain, because from 1 pm onwards the child is at home. German visitors to Britain have noted a tendency in this country to leave more of the social education to the school — in Germany it is definitely the role of the home. German children are trained to show greater respect for older people in general. A German child is taught to give up his seat to an older person in a bus or tram; many observers agree that this gesture is seen more often in Germany than in Britain.

German children are kept on a tighter rein by their parents than are their English and American counterparts. This is noticed particularly by English girls of 14 or 15 years of age who visit German families; they resent the discipline which seems to them "too strict", particularly in the matter of having to return home by a fixed time after an evening out. Parties where parents tactfully "go out for the evening" are almost unheard-of in Germany. At meal times, many German parents insist that the children shall not leave any food on their plates. In short, German discipline is imposed from above, whereas English parents hope their children will develop self-discipline (though German visitors sometimes question the success of this!).

The family in its wider sense, meaning all grandparents, second cousins and great-aunts, has been admirably described by the German humorous writer Tucholsky: "It consists of a collection of people of different sexes, who consider their main task to be that of poking their nose into your affairs."

The division of Germany after the war led to the division of many families; an EMNID survey in 1967 showed that 35% of the participants had relations or close friends in East Germany. Those living in the West may visit relatives in the East, and pensioners in the East may visit relatives in the West — but such visits are complicated with paper-work and formalities. For relations able to visit each other without formality (i.e. those living in the same part of the country) family visiting is a national ritual. Such visits mean white table-cloths, huge flans and gallons of coffee. The favourite day for such visits is Sunday, and a particularly important family occasion is confirmation or first communion (which I shall describe more fully in a chapter on the Church).

East Germany

Young people in East Germany must wait until they are both eighteen years of age before they may marry. Many marriages — an unofficial estimate puts it at 70% — are "accelerated" by pregnancy. Illegitimacy is higher than in Western countries; in East Germany 10% of all live births are illegitimate, and according to UN statistics East Berlin has the second highest illegitimacy rate in the world (the highest, ironically enough, is that of the Virgin Islands). These figures, however, are probably due to the inclusion of East Berlin as a separate entity in UN statistics, whereas other cities such as Hamburg and London are merged with statistics for the whole country concerned. Illegitimate children in East Germany have the same legal position vis-a-vis their parents as do legitimate offspring.

Per thousand population the annual marriage rate in East Germany is 8·0, and the divorce rate 1·63. Divorce courts do not allocate blame, but merely decide whether the marriage is devoid of meaning for the individuals concerned and for society.

The percentage of working mothers in East Germany is particularly high; over 70% of the female population between 16 and 60 years of age is gainfully employed. The state proclaims full equality for women, and when a couple marry they are asked which surname they wish to adopt! The same equality also affects divorced women, who have fewer rights than their Western counterparts. Only if the woman is unable to earn her own living will alimony be awarded.

In 1964, 820 East German girls between 14 and 22 years of age were asked about their attitudes towards marriage and work. The answers were anonymous, so they had no need to conform to "politically acceptable" attitudes. Just under half (49%) said that when they had children they would give up work for a short time, and 18% announced an intention to give up permanently after the birth of the first child. But 28% said they would try to carry on work throughout marriage, and only 2% that they would give up as soon as they got married. (These figures were first published in "Der Schüler von zehn bis sechszehn" by Wiedemann and Forst, 1965.)

Two factors have helped strengthen the East German family unit. One is the restriction on movement from one place of work to another (hindered by a chronic shortage of single-room accommodation) which has made more young people stay at home. The other is the fact that if a family occupies more than a fixed amount of living space, it can be made to take in lodgers. Many families prefer to have distant relatives staying with them rather than take in a paying but non-related sub-tenant.

Dress and fashion

From the German family we turn our attention to the German as an individual, and look first at the way he dresses.

Men's clothing
In general, it is probably fair to say that the German is more dress-conscious than the Englishman. The English tourists, so often seen in a shabby tweed jacket, grey shirt and baggy trousers, contrast with the ever-elegant German. Moreover, most Germans will insist on dressing for the occasion; a mountaineering holiday calls for different clothes than a seaside holiday. And few Germans will wear their office suits on Sundays.

Men's clothing in Germany is subject to rapidly-changing fashions, but within any given fashion there is considerable conformity. The eccentric in dress is less

Fig 7 Always dress for the occasion! Cartoon by Werner Kruse, reproduced from the Desch collection.

common than in Britain; in general, the German sticks to what he feels is expected of him.

This is particularly noticeable on Sundays, when the German puts on his best bib and tucker whether he is going to Church or not. Many eye-witnesses record that, in the immediate post-war years, Berlin families could be seen taking a Sunday afternoon walk amid the ruins of their city, all in their Sunday best. A German does not feel well dressed without a suit. This can be grey (particularly in summer), black (on festive occasions) or navy blue. The style is what an Englishman would describe as "continental" and the trousers will not have turn-ups (US: cuffs). Part of Sunday best is a white shirt; I have long been an admirer of German shirt styles, and at around 20 Mark each they are excellent value.

The German is far more conservative in his choice of tie than the Briton or American. Tie shops tend to have less variety than their equivalents elsewhere — perhaps an indication that the customer is less likely to risk being an "odd-man-out" with a gaudy tie. There is no "old school tie" in Germany.

The pointed Italian-style shoe reached Germany long before it came to Britain but, at the time of writing, this fashion is already no fashion any more; it is definitely "out". Shoes are expensive in both parts of Germany, particularly in the East.

There is something very German-looking about German overcoats, but it is difficult to define. They tend to make the wearer look much stockier than he really is, and the coat itself looks heavy. The material is usually a thick weave. Hats tend to be more common than in Britain, particularly with older men. In the South, the Alpine hat with a feather is popular. Bowlers are almost unknown — except through the imported television series, "The Avengers".

In summer, the German frequently wears a light nylon raincoat; the most popular colour is navy blue, and the belted style is common. Typically German is the folding umbrella; the best known make is the Knirps, which has given its name to the whole type (of umbrella). A genuine Knirps costs around forty Mark, but there are many cheaper imitations. My personal experience with cheap folding umbrellas, however, has not been encouraging.

Also in summer, the visitor will notice many blazers in Germany, particularly blue blazers. These are worn without badges on the breast pocket, and are accompanied by grey trousers (again without turn-ups). Many German men wear jackets without lapels; these are normally grey in colour, frequently with green binding. British tweeds are fashionable, though they must be made into a German-style jacket. Germany spends four times as much on importing textiles as on importing ready-made clothes.

Ladies' clothes

It seems to be generally agreed among those who visit Germany that the German ladies go in for duller colours than their counterparts in Britain. Dark greens and browns are more popular than pastel or vivid colours. On the other hand, young ladies in Germany manage to look very smart. The motto of many clothes advertisements is "sportingly elegant", and this seems to sum up the general attitude to fashion. A German lady takes more care over selecting the style of her clothes than over the colour of the material.

English girl students who have been shopping in Germany tell me there is less tendency there to go into dress shops and try on various items, only to emerge empty-handed. This has been attributed to the greater attentiveness of the sales staff. There are fewer shops in Germany where dresses are cheap.

There are no occasions in Germany where it is compulsory for ladies to wear hats, even in church. In general, hats tend to be duller than those worn in Britain; a particularly popular type is what one might uncharitably call the flower-pot-style.

Cosmetics Until the end of the Second World War, cosmetics were frowned on in Germany; it was claimed that German women did not need them. In the post-war era, when nationalism became a dirty word, such arguments lost their force, but even today the German woman wears less make-up than her neighbours in other European countries. In general, the type of make-up used is similar to that in other countries; but few German women wear coloured eye-shadow during the day. Popular brands of cosmetics in Germany are Revlon, Juventa, Arden and Margaret Astor.

Fig 8 "What cosmetics did you use last week?" Figures are percentages, from Allensbach survey 1965.

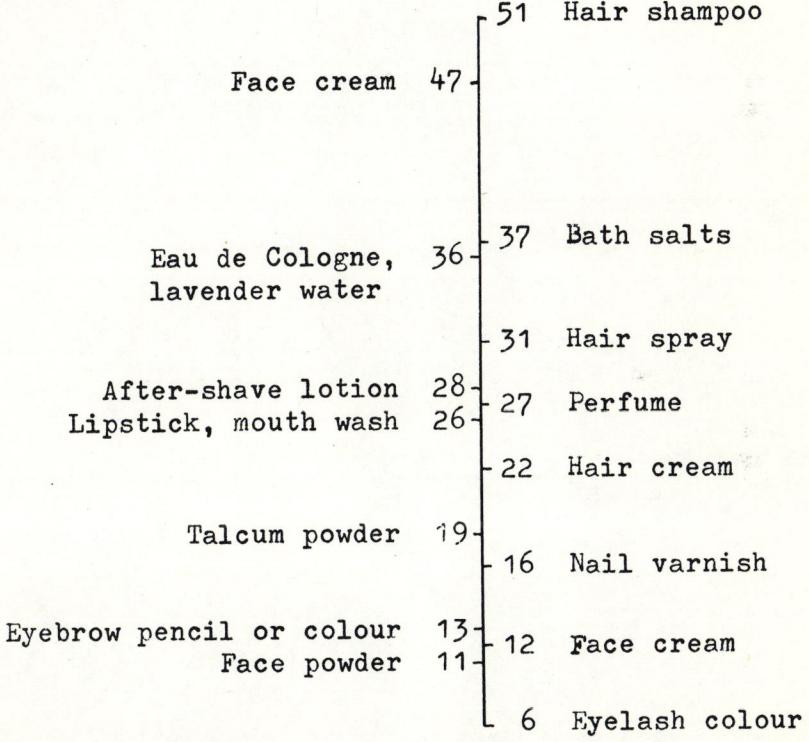

Young people and children

School uniforms, worn by most children in Britain when they reach the secondary school, are unknown in Germany. This has a big effect on the dress sense of German teenagers; they need normal, everyday clothes whereas the English pupil needs school uniform and something else to wear on special occasions. German girls, particularly, feel the need for elegant everyday wear much earlier. "Gimmicky" fashions are unpopular in Germany, where teenagers prefer "sporty" wear. A year after their introduction in Britain, mini-skirts were still a rarity in Germany,

24 HOW THEY LIVE

and the start of the "hippy" cult in some German cities was many months behind the same trend in Britain, let alone the USA.

Many German teenagers have no "scruffy" clothes. They throw clothes away long before they are completely worn out.

In South Germany young people often wear traditional Bavarian costume: leather shorts for the boys and check dresses with aprons for the girls. Leather

Fig 9 Despite the generally conservative attitude of their customers, East German fashion designers move with the times. These trouser suits were first shown to the public in December 1967. Photo: Lex Hornsby & Partners.

shorts are now less of a regional speciality, and there must be few German men and boys who have not possessed a pair at some time in their lives.

For reasons explained in the section on "cosmetics" above, German girls wear little make-up. They do not normally start until about fifteen or sixteen. Make-up may first be used when the girl's class begins dancing lessons at school.

East Germany

Most of the above also applies to East Germany. The visitor notices a certain "shabbiness", but on examination this is seen to be the result of ultra-conservatism in the choice of colours, rather than lack of taste or style. Although many East German suits have an appearance of "cheapness", they are quite expensive in the shops. Nylon raincoats are less common than in the West — hardly surprising when one realises that they cost 200 Mark each.

On the menu

It always puzzles me that although the countries of Western Europe are so close together, and although travellers from each country have been visiting the others for centuries, their national cuisines should nevertheless be so different. I can think of only one meal that Britain and Germany have in common: boiled eggs. Apart from this, every dish is different in some way.

But before considering individual dishes, a word about the quantity of food that is eaten. The German, in general, is capable of eating more at a single meal than his English counterpart. This is, probably, conditioned by habit. The Englishman eats until he knows he has had enough; the German is not satisfied until he feels he could not eat any more. One should bear in mind, however, that the German normally only has three meals a day. Mid-morning coffee is almost unknown, and afternoon tea (or its German equivalent, coffee and cakes) is usually reserved for Sundays or when visitors come.

Breakfast

The German eats a small breakfast, usually rolls and coffee. The rolls are crisp and often fresh; many families still have them delivered early in the morning. They are eaten with butter and jam; strawberry, raspberry and plum jam are favourites, and apply jelly.

Fig 10 Typical German breakfast — rolls, jam, cheese and coffee — in an East German home. Photo: Zentralbild/Spremberg.

There are generally no cereals and no "bacon and egg". Occasionally a boiled egg is eaten. Cheeses and cold meats are an alternative to jam, and in good hotels catering for foreign visitors there is a wide choice of cold meats.

The coffee is made black and tinned milk is added. The most popular method of coffee-making is with a filter, and most families grind their coffee freshly. Foreign visitors often admire the well-roasted varieties of coffee in Germany. Except for a small tea-drinking area in the coastal region, coffee is the national drink. This is hardly surprising in view of the way Germans make tea; this drink is so expensive that it is made very weak. The German will often hang a metal tea-bell in a pot of hot water for a few minutes, then pour out the resulting yellowish liquid and call it tea. An Englishman's comment: "You can read a newspaper through it!"

Many Germans distinguish between weekday breakfast and Sunday breakfast. On Sundays, the usual breakfast is supplemented by cold meats, boiled eggs and many different varieties of cheese and cake. Some families like to talk around the Sunday breakfast table, and discussion often extends until mid-morning.

Lunch

For most families, lunch is the main meal of the day. The main meal is taken in the evening only when the family cannot be at home for lunch or cannot get a good hot meal at work. (The children will be home from school by 2 pm, in time for a late lunch.)

The table is laid much the same as in England, except for the fact that small dishes are used for salads, or for water if the meal involves something eaten with the fingers.

The fork is used "upside down", and vegetables are cut with a fork, not with a knife. (This includes potatoes, even chipped potatoes!) Few things look funnier to a German than an Englishman trying to push peas on to a fork with his knife.

Soup The Germans drink soup with a pointed spoon, which is always held with the tip towards the mouth. When the plate is nearly empty, it is raised slightly from the front (i.e. tip it away from you).

The Germans drink more soup than the English, and it rarely comes out of a tin. The German housewife often takes great pride in making soups and flavouring them correctly. Popular soups include spring vegetable soup (including tomatoes, asparagus and parsley), potato soup, oxtail soup (using a recipe similar to that used in Britain, but cooked for two hours) and white wine soup.

A German speciality is cold soup made from any variety of stewed soft fruit, diluted with sugar syrup or fruit juice and thickened into a soup by stirring in some corn flour, semolina, sago or arrow root. These soups are chilled before serving.

Meat Veal is more popular than in Britain, while lamb is almost unknown. All sorts of poultry are popular, also pork and beef. Foreign visitors are attracted by the habit of frying escallops or cutlets in egg and breadcrumbs; this is how the famous Wiener Schnitzel is prepared. Fricassee is more popular in Germany than in Britain, as is goulash. The latter is eaten with a fork only. "Eisebein" (boiled salted pigs' knuckles) used to be a Berlin speciality, but is now popular everywhere. Also to be recommended is "Roulade", a delicious meat roll held together by a skewer. Englishmen tend to wince when they see a German eating raw mince and egg, but this dish (known as "Tartar") is worth trying, for it is very tasty.

Sausages Germany is renowned for its sausages, and justifiably so. A sausage in Germany is no half-meat-half-bread mixture; it is pure meat. Including regional specialities, there are over three hundred varieties. Liver sausage and blood

Fig 11 Cooking sausages and Sauerkraut in the kitchen of a well-known restaurant in Regensburg. Photo: Glyn Hatherall.

sausage (black pudding) are the best-known outside Germany, but for the German worker a sausage often means a fried or boiled sausage bought for a Mark at a snack-bar or pavement stand and eaten with a dry roll and a generous helping of mustard. Cold sausages are eaten sliced, the most popular being salami and "Servalatwurst".

Fish Because Germany has only one coast, in the north, the habits in fish-eating differ widely according to region. In the north, far more fish is eaten; in the south, comparatively little except (for religious reasons) on Fridays. The varieties of fish are much the same as in England. One big difference, however, is in the popularity of herrings, which are something of a national dish. Inland they are sold in tins, like sardines in Britain. Eels and trout are also popular, and mussels, though the latter are a seasonal dish.

Stew Stew first became popular with the farmers, because it is easy to prepare and cheap. Popular types include "Labskaus" (a northern dish, related to the Liverpool "scouse") and "Heaven and earth", a stew made from apples and potatoes.

Vegetables The most typically German vegetable is, of course, Sauerkraut. This is simply salt-pickled white cabbage, shredded and fermented in wooden barrels for several months. It is often eaten with "Eisbein", the pig's knuckles mentioned above. Spinach and red cabbage are more popular in Germany than in Britain, the red cabbage being eaten hot and not pickled. Salads in Germany are served ready mixed with a sweet or sour salad dressing. Sometimes a salad using only one vegetable will make a delightful addition to a meal — my own favourite in Germany is cucumber salad. A salad is served on a separate dish, and should not be taken on to the main plate before eating. This also applies to stewed fruit, which — strange as it may seem to Englishmen — is also served cold as an accompaniment to the main course.

Sweets Popular sweets in Germany are cold stewed fruit (without custard), fresh fruit, ice cream and blancmange. The ice creams are often elaborate and — in hotels and restaurants — expensive.

Mid-afternoon

As mentioned earlier, the Germans do not normally have anything to eat in the afternoon, except when they have visitors or on Sundays. Then they have "coffee and cakes". The coffee is made the same way as at breakfast — freshly ground. Fruit flans are the most popular type of cake and are eaten with piles of whipped cream. (This may explain why so many German women are overweight.) Waffles are also popular, as are cheese cakes and Apfelstrudel; the latter is eaten as cake, not as a sweet with the main meal. On the whole, the Germans prefer a slice of cake to a small individual cake.

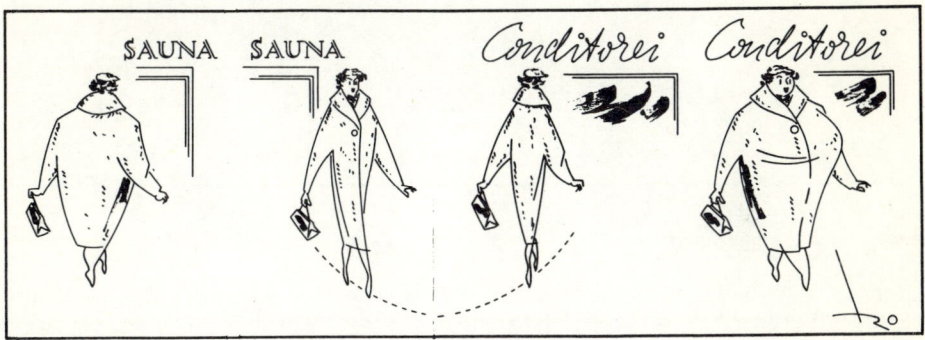

Fig 12 Going to a "Conditorei" for afternoon coffee and cakes can play havoc with your figure. Cartoon by Joachim Rohnstein, reproduced from the Desch collection.

Supper

The German word for supper literally means "evening bread", and bread forms the main part of the meal. German white bread is much drier than that eaten in Britain, and in any case most Germans prefer other varieties. These include "grey bread", a heavy grey-brown loaf, and black bread made from rye meal. A special variety of black bread is Pumpernickel. With the bread (and butter, of course) the Germans eat cold meat or cheese. The meat can be one of the cold sausages mentioned above, or cold ham, either boiled or raw. Cold roast beef is also popular, but expensive. In addition to imitating French cheeses, the Germans produce several national varieties, notably Limburger, Harzer and Romadour; the latter, despite its French name, is a German variety. Normally each member of the family serves himself at supper, and the bread with cheese or meat is eaten with a knife and fork. Only if visitors are present will the housewife prepare the meal beforehand and cut the bread into pieces small enough to be picked up without knife and fork.

Regional specialities

Every region in Germany takes pride in its own special dishes. Some have become known all over the country and have lost their original regional character, but many others are still purely regional. In the area around Kassel, for instance, you can find "Weckewerk", a sort of mince with pork, veal, and white rolls. Farmers in the Black Forest have a mid-morning snack of smoked bacon and dark rye

Fig 13 German supper: cheese, cold meat, rolls and different types of bread, with beer and "Schnaps" (see next chapter). Photo: Glyn Hatherall.

bread, while in Nuremberg you can try bread soup with apples. Cologne is renowned for its potato fritters, and Westphalia for its ham. Finally — to put a mouth-watering end to a list which could go on for pages — Bremen is noted for its special ragout, containing sweetbreads, spring chicken, tiny veal balls, asparagus, clams and fresh peas, all cooked in a white sauce.

East Germany

On the whole, the food in East Germany is similar to that in the West. The only thing the tourist may miss is chipped potatoes, which are less common — this is attributed, as so many deficiencies in the restaurant service are, to a shortage of kitchen and serving staff. In the summer of 1966, the magazine "Neue Berliner Illustrierte" did a survey of regional specialities and found that they were rapidly dying out. They are being replaced by dishes from other Eastern Bloc countries, which are becoming more popular. From the Soviet Union, a soup called Soljanka has been imported; this contains meat, meat stock, salted cucumber and many spices, and has quite a sharp taste. Another popular imported habit is the Hungarian dish of paprika shoots with rice.

Coffee in East Germany is expensive, and not always of good quality. A pot of coffee in a restaurant can cost up to 2 Mark, and the visitor who is watching his budget may have to accustom himself to German weak-tea-drinking habits.

In case the above comments should appear too critical, I would hasten to point out that on the whole, food in East German restaurants is good. Moreover, one can go into the most expensive-looking restaurant or hotel without dreading the bill; in a luxury hotel, a normal meal will cost around 7 Mark.

Housewives in East Germany frequently complain about a lack of choice at the butcher's. If you want liver, you have to become a hospital patient or go to a restaurant. Whipped cream is also quite a rarity.

To wash it down

German families drink less at meal times than do the French, but more than the English. The choice of wine or beer is a matter of taste, for Germany produces many excellent varieties of both. So many, in fact, that the following notes are restricted mostly to those I have tried myself on visits to Germany.

Wine

For the purposes of a general survey, German red wine can be ignored. There is some red wine made in Germany, particularly in the Nahe valley, but it cannot compare with that produced in France.

In Britain, German wine is generally known as "Hock", because it was from Hochheim that much wine was imported in the last century. In the trade, Hock now means "a Rhine wine" — ironic, because Hochheim, though still in the Rhineland area, actually lies on the River Main. There are three main subdivisions of the Rhine area: the Palatinate, the Rheingau and Rheinhessen. Among the best-known villages whose names appear on wines are Rüdesheim, Nierstein, Oppenheim and Deidesheim. It is a vintners' tradition to sell Rhine wine in tall, brown bottles — though only the best firms stick rigidly to this.

A somewhat sharper wine comes from the Moselle area. In theory, the Moselle area includes the Saar and Ruwer valleys, but most of the wine is grown on the banks of the Moselle itself. Bernkastel and Traben-Trabach are the best-known wine-producing villages in this region. Moselle wine is sold in tall, green bottles.

If wine-drinkers were to pay more attention to the shape of the bottle than to its contents, then Franconian wine would be the most popular of all German wines. It is sold in green flagons known as "Bocksbeutel", similar in shape to the brown flagons used for Mateus Rosé. The wine itself is a dry, white wine, less popular than those produced on the Rhine and Moselle. The main centres in the Franconian region are Würzburg, Escherndorf and Iphofen.

The finest grape used in Germany is the riesling, used for Moselle and the best of the Rhine wines. Its small yield results in a fairly high price, so the name riesling is usually stated on the label. A sweeter wine comes from the traminer grape, most common in the Palatinate and in Baden wines. Between the two, a light soft wine is produced by the sylvaner grape, a prolific yielder found everywhere except the Moselle region.

German wines come in different qualities and at different prices. To guarantee that his wine has no artificially added sugar, the customer should look for the word "Naturrein" on the label, though this is taken for granted in "Auslese" (wine from selected grape bunches), "Spätlese" (from late-picked grapes) and "Beerenauslese" (from individually picked rotten-ripe grapes). The most expensive wine is "Trockenbeerenauslese", made from dried, raisiny grapes and only possible in exceptionally dry summers. This can cost anything up to 100 Mark per bottle.

The foreign visitor should avoid the mistake of telling his German host that he knows something about wine. The German likes to think he knows best what to give his guest, and he will often be quite an expert. I well remember the twelve-year-old who, on my second visit to Germany, asked me if I preferred a '58 or a '59 vintage; he knew the difference, of course, and had his own preferences. For

Fig 14 Vineyards on the banks of the Moselle. Photo: German Tourist Information Bureau.

Fig 15 Wine label from the firm of "Count Schwarzburg" showing the family coat of arms. "Rheinhessen" is the region, "Oppenheim" the town of origin (though not all wine that claims to be Oppenheimer comes from Oppenheim). "Spätlese" indicates the wine was made from late-picked grapes.

the record, and for those who have to choose wine in a German shop or hotel, the best vintages in recent years have been 1957, 1959 and 1964. The latter year was outstanding in the Moselle area.

Finally a word about Liebfraumilch. Originally, this name (or rather the proper German spelling Liebfrauenmilch) came from the Liebfrauenkirche, the Church of Our Lady near Worms. But the name has no legal protection, and is now given to other mild Rhine wines. Connoisseurs despise it, and at least one high-class British importer refuses on principle to use the name. But in foreign countries where German wine is expensive, a cheap Liebfraumilch can often be a "best buy". It may not be a guarantee of quality, but does give an indication of the type of wine to be expected.

Beer

Most German towns have their own breweries and make their own particular type of beer. The best known is "Pils", a type of beer named after the Czech town Pilsen; most breweries, in addition to local specialities, produce their own Pils. It is similar to lager and has somewhat more taste than Danish lager.

The simplest way to order a beer in Germany, apart from simply saying "beer", is to ask for a light ("helles") or dark "(dunkles") beer. The dark beers vary considerably. Dark beer in the north means a sweet malt beer, low in alcohol content; in the south it means a different brew, more bitter in taste and very potent. Many

Fig 16 Heaving crates of beer about can be hard work. The man doing so here is Herr Müller, whose family has been brewing in Münster for a century and a half. Photo: Glyn Hatherall.

Bavarian dark beers have Latin names; "Maximator" and "Salvator" are among the best known. The strongest of all the dark beers is "G'frornes" ("frozen beer"). At the opposite end of the scale, Cologne's "Kölsch" is comparatively harmless, a doubly-fermented bitter beer supposed to be good for the kidneys and even recommended by some doctors. In Berlin, the local speciality is a white beer, which can be served with a dash of raspberry juice; on its own, it is rather bitter.

Spirits

Many Germans drink spirits and beer together, so the demand is less for a high-grade product than for one which is cheap. The German word "Schnaps" can be applied to any clear, strong distilled drink. The best known are Korn (made from maize) and a gin called Steinhäger.

German brandy is generally of poorer quality than the French cognacs; but Asbach, the best-known name, is tasty and mild, and can be recommended to the visitor. The Black Forest is noted for its eaux-de-vie, particularly Kirschwasser, made from cherries. In Bavaria, a local speciality is Enzian (gentian), which comes from the Alpine foothills.

Soft drinks

Coca-cola is as popular in Germany as it is everywhere else in the world. Orangeade is also popular, but known as "Limonade", much to the annoyance of English-speaking visitors, who order orangeade and are served with an expensive pure orange juice. There is a tasty, still apple-juice and a delightful, but expensive, blackcurrant juice. Germans do not normally drink diluted fruit drinks. With a meal, they often drink plain soda-water, known in German as "Selters".

In general

An interesting feature of drinking habits is that after saying "cheers" ("Prost" in German), a German will take a sip and then salute with his glass a second time. If he is pouring beer into a glass, he will ensure that it has a good froth on it — much to the annoyance of English visitors. An English schoolboy visiting Germany for the first time was delighted when his hosts took him out to a local inn. The waiter brought him a bottle and a glass, and he was able to pour his beer in true English style, leaving no "head" at all. But his pleasure was short-lived for the waiter, seeing the beer with no froth, assumed it must be flat. He quickly removed the glass and, with profuse apologies on behalf of the management, replaced it with a ready-filled glass — complete, of course, with froth.

However, the thirsty tourist has one consolation: he can get alcoholic drinks in Germany at any time of day, and until the early hours of the morning.

East Germany

Despite nationalisation, many East German breweries have kept their old names and reputations; the best-known (and to my mind quite justifiably so) is Radeberger. Particularly in Berlin, many hotels and restaurants serve original Pils from Pilsen, at reasonable prices.

Far less wine is drunk in East Germany than in the West; this is because the country produces almost no wine of its own, except for a small wine-growing area near Dresden. Some French wine is imported, together with large quantities of Hungarian and Bulgarian wine. In the best hotels, West German wines can be obtained but at extortionate prices. Thus it is hardly surprising that the average East German drinks only one-third of the quantity consumed by the average West German. East Germany produces its own brandy (including "Edel", "Auslese" and "Grand mit Dreien") and more cognac is imported from other Eastern Bloc countries. Vodka is more popular than in the West, the most expensive variety being Russian vodka.

Good manners

Many foreigners visiting Germany make the mistake of thinking that if they stick to the same code of good manners that they are used to at home, they will offend nobody. Some even go so far as to believe that, as foreigners, they have a right to offend against all the conventions of the host country, and that nobody will take it amiss if various minor do's and dont's of German etiquette are overlooked. To a certain extent, this is true, because most Germans are willing to make allowances for a foreigner not knowing how to behave. But to make no effort at all to conform is a short-sighted policy on the part of a tourist, because following the minor rules of conduct is often regarded as a sign of consideration for others. Unfortunately, many Germans are too polite to tell a foreigner how to behave, so the rules of conduct have to be learnt for the most part by trial and error.

The Germans are meticulous in matters of etiquette, and seem to base their code of behaviour largely on the writings of Adolf Freiherr von Knigge, a landlord and member of court society in the late 18th century. Ask any German today which is the best book on German etiquette, and he will probably refer you to Knigge. Most of Knigge's writing is concerned less with the rules of etiquette than with general words of wisdom as to how to get along with your fellow men; nevertheless he is regarded as the father of German etiquette.

Some of the most important rules of behaviour have already been given in the chapter entitled "On the menu", for they refer to table manners. What follows is a small selection of other rules that a foreigner would do well to observe, and which the Germans normally observe themselves.

When walking along, the German used to let a lady walk on his right, but modern traffic conditions are changing this habit and it is now good manners to walk on the outside of the pavement, as in Britain. If a gentleman and a lady meet in the street, it is the gentleman's duty to raise his hat and bow slightly; but the decision as to whether to stop and talk is the lady's privilege.

The Germans are the world's greatest hand-shakers. Even when you meet a German friend whom you have known for years, and whom you saw the previous day, he will expect you to shake his hand — and to shake it again when you say goodbye. In some German offices everyone shakes everyone else's hand both morning and evening.

Even in offices where they don't shake hands, everyone is expected to say "Guten Morgen" when he arrives. Failure to do so is a serious offence against etiquette and will not go unnoticed, as it would in Britain. I worked for a few months in a German office, and only later discovered that my lack of greeting in the morning had not only been noticed, but actually held against me by my colleagues. I have also had to get used to saying "Guten Morgen" to the members of the family with whom I always stay in Germany. This, too, is a strictly-kept rule in Germany.

Young children in Germany often amuse foreigners with their bows and curtsies. They will make a low bow (a "Diener") or a curtsy (a "Knicks") when introduced to an adult, and young girls sometimes curtsy when meeting each other! Even teenage girls will sometimes do a slight "Knicks" when being introduced to an older woman.

There is a general order of precedence in German etiquette. Top of the list come highly-respected ladies and elderly ladies. Second are highly-respected or elderly gentlemen. Ladies not covered by the first category take third place, and other gentlemen fourth. When people are being introduced to each other, the person lower on the list is always presented to the person higher in order of precedence. Thus if Herr Schmidt is an elderly gentleman, and Herr Meier a younger man, whoever is introducing them should say "Herr Schmidt, may I introduce Herr Meier?" A gentleman may also, if necessary, introduce himself by giving his surname. Thus Herr Meier would introduce himself by saying "Guten Tag, Meier". A lady may introduce herself to another woman but not to a man.

When visiting a family for the first time — or for the first time after a long absence — it is customary to take some flowers for the hostess. These should be an odd number; the Germans believe that an odd number looks better in a vase. The flowers are presented without the wrapping paper, which you remove as you wait for the hostess to open the door. (If the host opens the door and tells you his wife will be back from the hairdresser's in half an hour, you are in a bit of a fix — but rules are rules!) Pot plants may be presented only by a lady, not by a gentleman. The choice of flowers is important, for mistakes can be embarrassing. Red roses and dark red carnations are a symbol of love, and should be given only to a sweetheart. White flowers — especially lilies, asters and white carnations — are associated with the cemetery, particularly with the graves of children, so they would hardly be suitable as a gift for a hostess! However, a bridegroom will often give his bride white myrtles or roses to match her wedding dress. "Safe" flowers to suit any occasion are light pink carnations or assorted tulips.

If you are staying with a family for any length of time, you should give the hostess a small present when you arrive rather than — or, of course, as well as — when you leave. Chocolates, small pieces of china and glass are suitable, as are flowers. In East Germany, it is a good idea to buy something from the "Intershop" where you can get luxury articles the East German housewife could not buy for herself. (You will have to pay in Western currency: dollars, sterling or DM.) I shall give more details in the next chapter.

When a German couple enter a restaurant, the man goes first in order to find a suitable table. He helps the lady on and off with her coat, and does not leave this to the waiter. Indeed, this helping a lady with her coat is something Germans tend to take to extremes.

Contrary to the practice in France, you need not give a tip to the lady who shows you your seat in a theatre. One thing an Englishman must watch, however, when taking his seat, is that Germans consider it impolite to turn your back on the people you have to pass as you make your way along the row. Always face them. This also applies in cinemas.

Finally, a cardinal rule for foreigners in Germany: don't complain when you find things differ from what you are used to. Far too many foreigners behave as though whatever is the practice in their own country must be better than what they find abroad. Even if you do miss your ham and eggs, fish and chips or hot dog, there's really no need to say so to every German you meet.

Going shopping

It is when shopping that many foreign tourists first notice the Germans' attention to courtesy. Most German shop assistants are courteous, and make a point of, saying "Auf Wiedersehen!" to a customer as he leaves. (If they are not too busy they will even open the door for him.) German shop assistants serve proper apprenticeships to learn about their trade and the items they will have to sell. It is consequently fair to say that the standard of service in German shops is higher than in Britain, though of course the bad-tempered shop assistant is a phenomenon found everywhere.

German shops open at eight or nine in the morning, and close at six in the evening. In the suburbs and in small towns, many shops close for lunch from 1 pm to 3 pm. The trouble with this arrangement is that the only way to find out if a given shop takes a lunch break is by trial and error; it is safest not to attempt to go shopping between one and three. On Saturdays, all shops close at 2 pm, except on the first Saturday in the month (and on other Saturdays near Christmas) when they stay open until six. The one Saturday a month on which the shops do not close until six is known as "long Saturday".

A table supplied by the Federal Statistical Office gives statistics for the expenditure of an "average household". Of a total of 926 Mark spent, 364 went on food, 105 on clothing, 98 on rent, 58 on education and entertainment, 80 on transport, 87 on household goods, 53 on drinks and tobacco, 30 on laundry and "body care" and 40 on heat and light. Comparing these figures with the Family Expenditure Survey by the British Ministry of Labour, we find that the German spends slightly less than the Englishman on alcohol, tobacco and transport, slightly more on clothing, considerably more on food, and almost exactly the same on housing. The remaining categories on the German list did not have exact equivalents in the British Survey results since the latter referred vaguely to "services".

The German housewife has to go shopping more often than her British counterpart, for the simple reason that fewer goods are delivered to the house. In some country areas, grocers will deliver to specially-treasured customers, but grocery delivery in town is almost unheard-of, except to a customer who is an invalid. Milk must be fetched from the "dairy shop", since for some reason Germans regard milk delivery as unhygienic. (I can imagine that the hotter weather in Summer would tend to make milk go sour more quickly than in Britain.) Most Germans use tinned milk for their coffee anyway, and no milk in tea.

There are more bookshops in Germany, despite the fact that books are more expensive. There are also more flower shops, and these are open on Sundays from 11 am to 1 pm. As described in the previous chapter, it is customary to take flowers to one's hostess if one is invited out, and because Sunday is the big day for visiting, flower shops often do a roaring trade in these two hours.

In butchers' and fish shops, the customer has a wider choice than in Britain. A butcher's shop is a wonderful sight on Friday and Saturday, for the weekend stock is in, and this includes a wide selection of sausages, some of them up to three feet in length. German shops seem to take more trouble over window displays than do British shops. This applies not only to fashion shops, but also to grocers, chemists and butchers.

Fig 17 Typical German butcher's shop. Photo: Glyn Hatherall

Fig 18 Grocer's shop with a good selection of wines. Photo: German Tourist Information Bureau.

Health food stores are known as "Reformhäuser" and are more numerous than in Britain. There is also a clear distinction between an "Apotheke", run by a qualified dispensing chemist, and a "Drogerie", which sells brand-name drugs, cosmetics and such things as toothpaste and films. A Drogerie is forbidden by law to sell any drug (e.g. aspirin) of which an overdose would be dangerous.

The German's lower expenditure on alcohol and tobacco, referred to above, is deceptive, for many alcoholic drinks are cheaper and the German customer gets more for his money. There seem to be more wine shops in Germany, though I may be mistaken in this impression. Moreover, grocers and supermarkets also sell wine and beer. A cheap bottle of wine costs less than 2 Mark.

One thing the British tourist may miss is the "sub-post office", where the post office is part of a shop which sells other goods. German post offices are nothing but post offices.

The foreign tourist who does not want to buy tin models of Cologne Cathedral but who prefers a more usable souvenir has a wide choice in Germany. Clocks, watches and electrical goods are cheaper in Germany than in Britain. But they are subject to high rates of customs duty when one returns, and may therefore not be so cheap in the long run. German leather goods are a better buy. These are excellent value for money, and there is a large range to choose from. It is inadvisable to make one's purchases in the big leather stores in city centres — prices are lower in the suburbs and in the leather departments of the department stores. West

Fig 19 A popular souvenir with tourists is a china figure from the "Hummel" series, based on the work of a German nun, Bertha von Hummel, who died in 1946. The figure pictured here is known as "Merry Wanderer". Hummel figurines are manufactured by W Goebel, 8633 Oeslau, Postfach 46/47, who supplied this photo.

German stainless steel is also of good quality, as is their porcelain, which shows much more adherence to "modern" slim styles than the produce of British manufacturers. For children expecting a gift from Germany when you return, you can buy a musical box or beer stein; though be prepared for contradictions like a "souvenir of Bavaria" musical box playing "Swedish Rhapsody". Some other items that make excellent souvenirs also figure among Germany's more interesting exports, and will be discussed in the chapter on "Imports and exports".

East Germany

Despite the rising standard of living, East German shops still have a poor selection

GOING SHOPPING 41

of goods. Much home-produced material is of a shoddy quality, and imported items are expensive. The comparative price table overleaf shows that the bare necessities of life are cheap, but luxuries are more expensive than in West Germany. Some shops specialise in imported goods; they are often called "Exquisit", but are known colloquially as "intelligentsia shops", since only those on high salaries can afford to shop there.

In 1966, 68·2% of retail trade turnover was handled by the cooperative societies and the state trading organisation (Handelsorganisation, known as the HO). These shops receive better delivery facilities than the private shopkeeper, and can often stock goods which he never handles. By various forms of pressure, mainly by reducing supplies, the state has persuaded more and more shopkeepers to turn their businesses into state or semi-state enterprises. The number of private shops has declined from 219,007 in 1950 to 73,585 in 1966. The state organisation and the cooperatives run a hiring service for all sorts of goods, particularly for camping goods in summer.

Fig 20   Camping with hired tents near Erfurt, East Germany. Photo: Lex Hornsby & Partners.

The tourist who wants a souvenir from East Germany has a problem. I have sometimes solved it myself by buying some item of kitchen equipment not found in Britain, such as an onion chopper (too complicated to explain here!). Dresden china makes good souvenirs, but is expensive — an ash-tray of "second quality" porcelain about four inches square cost me 15 Mark.

In the large towns and in the luxury class hotels there are "Intershops" at which various articles can be purchased at low prices in foreign currency. These shops sell foreign perfumes, cigarettes and spirits, besides radios, cameras and binoculars. Prices in the windows of an Intershop often look even cheaper than they really are, for they are marked up in dollars, not Mark! It is a common experience in Berlin for a foreign tourist to be accosted by a local resident who asks if the tourist could go to the nearest Intershop and buy him some "Western" cigarettes, for which he will pay in East German currency. Strictly speaking, this practice is illegal, but as the East German authorities need to lay their hands on all the foreign currency they can get, I doubt if they would treat an offender harshly.

Some East-West price comparisons 1967

	West Germany DM	East Germany MDN*
Potatoes, 5 kg	1,74	0,85
Sugar, 1 kg	1,25	1,64
Butter, 1 kg	7,81	9,60 - 10,00
Pork chops, 1 kg	8,35	8,00
Man's haircut	2,97	0,90 - 1,30
Tobacco, 50 grams	1,50	3,00
Coffee, 1 kg	17,06	60,00 - 80,00
Man's suit, part-wool	173,00	203,00 - 218,00
Man's shoes	35,60	42,00 - 48,00
Electricity, 1 kWh	0,15	0,08

* Mark der deutschen Notenbank, the old name for East Germany currency; changed on 1 January 1968 to Mark der DDR.
Sources: "Statistical Yearbook of the Federal Republic of Germany 1967" and "Democratic German Report" 19 May 1967.

Growing up

The aim of this chapter will not be to give answers to the questions "Are the young Germans sceptical?" or "Has Germany got a rebellious youth?" These questions are not sensible ones, for any generation in any country has a wide range of individual opinions, and national generalisations are almost always misleading. What I shall attempt here is a sketch of the way of life which German youngsters lead.

Many of the games they play are similar to those played in Britain, including Blind Man's Buff, chess, draughts, charades and forfeits. Apart from the language difference, a German game of "Telegrams", "Hangman" or "Kommando" ("O'Grady Says") is identical with the British game. Other games have some variations. When a German child plays "I-spy", he does not give the initial letter of the object to be guessed but an ambiguous description of it, such as "red with a black tail on its head" — a common clue for a candle! And there are, of course, German games not known in Britain, such as "Potato Duel", played by two at a time. Each player holds in his left hand a table-spoon with a potato on it, and in his right an empty spoon. The aim is to remove the opponent's potato while keeping your own.

Because German children go to school for the morning only, and are home by 2 pm, they have more free time than their British counterparts (even allowing for

Fig 21 Germany has more snow than Britain, so German youngsters have more opportunity for winter sports. Photo: Glyn Hatherall.

more homework). The EMNID survey in 1966 showed that half the schoolchildren questioned (minimum age 14) had over five and a half hours each week-day, over eight hours on Saturday and all day on Sunday as "free time". A further third had the same amount of time on their hands each weekday, but slightly less on Saturdays or Sundays.

How do they spend all this free time? Simply "being with friends" was the most frequent answer for the whole 14-21 age group, followed by "listening to pop and dance music", "learning in order to get on at school or in my job", and "resting from work". Hobbies took seventh place in the list, books and magazines eighth, and sport eleventh.

The schoolchildren were also asked how much pocket money they had. The most frequent figure, given by 32%, was 20-40 Mark per month. (Germans always think in terms of months when they are talking about money). 22% received between 10 and 20 Mark each month, 15% between 40 and 60, 11% between 5 and 10, and only 9% more than 60.

Nearly every German child passes through what is known as the "Karl May age". Karl May was a prolific writer who lived from 1842 to 1912. He specialised in Westerns, and his vivid imagination enabled him to describe countries he had never visited. His collected works comprise sixty-five volumes, mainly about America and North Africa. His two best-known characters are the Apache chief Winnetou and the master gunman Old Surehand. May's later years were clouded by the attempts of malevolent critics to dig up details of his early career (including prison sentences for fraud and theft) in order to blacken his name. Even today, his works sell in huge quantities; by 1954 it was estimated that over eleven million Karl May volumes had been sold.

Among the boys in Germany, adventure stories, Westerns and detective novels are particularly popular. The 1966 EMNID survey showed that these books were favourites with 60% of the boys in the 14-17 age range. They were followed by

---

How do you spend your free time?

Order of preference based on answers to EMNID survey 1966
1 Being with friends
2 Listening to pop and dance music
3 Studying in order to get on at school/work
4 Resting from work
5 Discovering something new
6 Cinema and dancing
7 Hobbies
8 Reading exciting books and magazines
9 Self-education (unconnected with school/work)
10 Motor-cycle or car
11 Sport (active participation)
12 Reading interesting or intelligent books
13 Joking (in German "albern und scherzen")
14 Sport (as spectator)
15 Getting to know the world through books and travel
16 Hiking, walks in the country
17 Fixing things, model-making
18 Music, painting, literature
19 Doing nothing at all
20 Chess, cards and games

text-books (24%), travelogues and books on animals (22%) and a rather mysterious category "youth stories" (16%). With the girls, love stories were the most popular (38%), followed by "youth stories" (29%) then Westerns, adventures and crime fiction (27%).

I asked a Cologne bookseller what authors children preferred. Among popular foreign authors, she mentioned Defoe, Twain, Blyton and Spyri. Apart from Karl May, German authors included the Brothers Grimm, Ursula Bruns (who writes girls' stories about ponies) and Erich Kästner (best-known in Germany for "The Flying Classroom", abroad for "Emil and the Detectives").

Television also plays a large role in the lives of German youngsters. In the 1966 EMNID survey, the 14-17 age range were asked how often they watched television. 6% watched once a week, 11% twice, 14% three times, 16% four times, 10% five times, 7% six times, and no less than 22% seven times a week. 13% either had no opportunity, or were not interested. Their preferences are given in the chapter on Radio and television, but worth pointing out here is the fact that they claim to be highly selective in what they watch. Of the whole 14-21 age range, exactly half said that they looked through the programmes in advance and decided what to watch. 17% were even more selective, and switched on only for a few specific programmes. 12% said that they mostly switched on a programme to see what it was going to be like, and stuck with it if they liked the start. Only 18% said that they had no influence on what was switched on.

After the Second World War, youth organisations in both parts of Germany had to start from scratch, for only the Hitler Youth had flourished during the Nazi era. There was, in the immediate post-war years, a general apprehension about all organisations and uniforms, and many people were reluctant to "get involved". Even in 1964, the EMNID researchers found that 54% of the 15-18 age group were not members of any organisation.

But for those who have overcome this prejudice — or apathy, call it what you will — there is a wide range of youth organisations. The German Sport Youth is the largest, with two and a half million members. The religious organisations (Federation of German Catholic Youth and Evangelical Youth Work-Group) each have over a million members. The Scouts and Guides flourish, though to a lesser extent than in Britain. The political parties and the trade and office-workers' unions also have their own youth organisations. A central body for coordinating the work of all the organisations is the German Youth Ring, which sees its job as representing the whole youth of the country. For this it receives a huge government grant — four and a half million Mark in 1963. Of particular interest to young people from abroad are the German Student Travel Service and Europe Student Travel, which arrange subsidised travel facilities at considerably reduced prices.

At the age of 15, most German boys and girls have a series of dancing lessons. If the school they are going to is a single-sex school, these lessons are arranged on a class-to-class basis with a nearby school for members of the opposite sex. The whole thing is taken seriously, and mid-way through the course there is a formal party dance, to which partners must be invited and fetched in true gentlemanly fashion (often with a bouquet). It is during the dancing course that many German youngsters start "dating". On the whole, young Germans tend to go around in groups, and pairing off is less frequent than in Britain or the USA. The 1964 EMNID survey found that, in the 15-18 age group, only 13% of the boys and 24% of the girls were "going steady". It is unthinkable for a young girl in Germany to go to a public dance alone, and a German couple told me that they would be horrified if their son (then aged 18) were to start dating a girl whose parents did

46   HOW THEY LIVE

Fig 22   Young people in a Jazz Club in Berlin. Photo: German Tourist Information Bureau.

not lay down strict rules as to what time she had to be home. What is known in Britain as "back-row behaviour" is unknown in German cinemas, and when walking together, a German couple will tend to walk arm-in-arm rather than hand-in-hand.

East Germany

East Germany has only one youth organisation: the Free German Youth. (The Society for Sport and Technics, referred to in the chapters on "Armed forces" and "On holiday", is not a youth organisation in the accepted sense, but more of a cadet corps.) The Free German Youth, together with its junior organisations the Young Pioneers (for the 6-10 age group) and Ernst Thälmann Pioneers (10-14), has over three million members. The maximum age for ordinary members is 25, but those who are already in leading positions (in party jargon, those who are "important functionaries") by that age can continue their membership. The senior

Fig 23 Members of the Free German Youth at a rally in Karl-Marx-Stadt. Photo: Zentralbild/Koard.

48 HOW THEY LIVE

Fig 24 In both parts of Germany, youngsters who cannot go away for their holidays can take part in day-time camps near their home. They return home each evening. This camp is in East Germany (near Apolda, in Thuringia) and the participants pay only one Mark each for a month's holiday. Photo: Lex Hornsby & Partners.

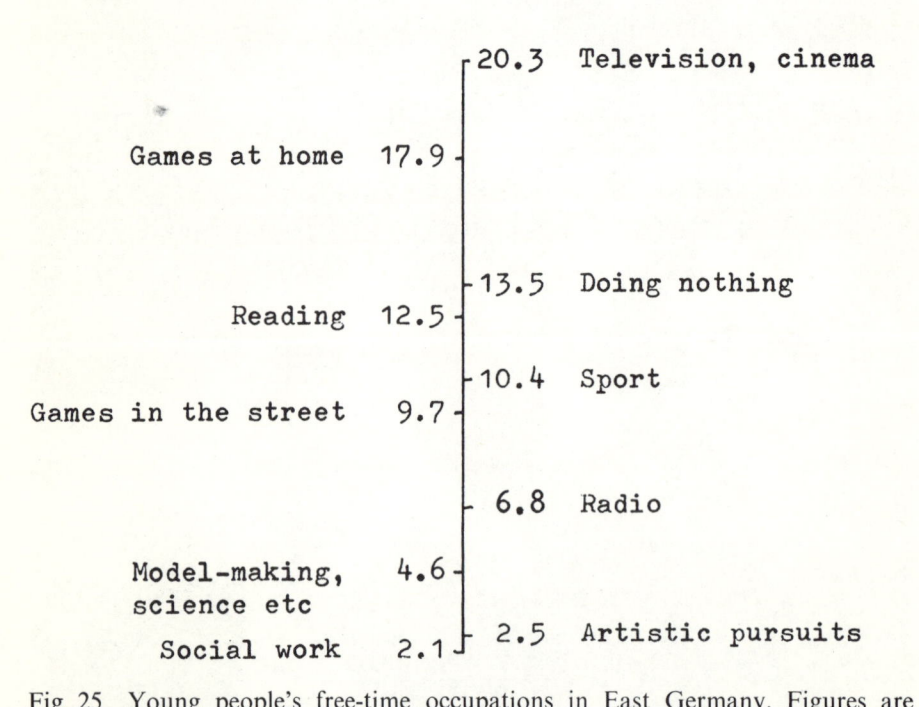

```
                                    20.3  Television, cinema
   Games at home      17.9

                                    13.5  Doing nothing
         Reading      12.5
                                    10.4  Sport
Games in the street    9.7

                                     6.8  Radio
     Model-making,     4.6
        science etc
       Social work     2.1           2.5  Artistic pursuits
```

Fig 25 Young people's free-time occupations in East Germany. Figures are percentages, based on survey results first published in the magazine "Pädagogik", East Berlin 1964.

branch, the Free German Youth proper, is party-controlled and is primarily a political organisation aiming to foster the ideals of Socialism among young people. But at the same time it organises many non-political events such as dances and film shows. In 1964 it was the Free German Youth that ran a large-scale German Youth Meeting in East Berlin. Its members wear distinctive bright blue uniforms. Membership is swollen by those who join in the knowledge that to be a member will be a big help when they apply for jobs or university places, but it is impossible to estimate just what proportion join for that reason. Each year, the Free German Youth runs a "Fair of the Master-craftsmen of Tomorrow", at which young inventors display their work; small exhibitions are run beforehand in different towns, and the whole thing culminates in a huge national exhibition, normally at Leipzig.

HOW THEY WORK

Men and machines

Just under a third of all employed persons in West Germany work in industrial firms with ten or more employees. Of every five workers in industry as a whole, four are working in firms which have over a hundred names on the pay-roll. Small firms with less than ten workers are responsible for just under 2% of the total industrial turnover.

Fig 26 Although large manufacturing organisations are now the order of the day, small firms still produce work of high quality. This violin-maker is in Münster. Photo: Glyn Hatherall.

Between 1950 and 1960, the gross national product in West Germany rose by an average of 7·5% per annum. This compares with 2·6% in Britain and 3·3% in the USA. In recent years, however, the rate of increase has fallen off. The 1965 figure was only 4·5%, compared with 2·3% in the United Kingdom and 5·9% in the USA.

For those who like figures: in 1966, West Germany produced 2,515,275 cars, 205,252 lorries, 1,378,864 electric refrigerators, 2,276,464 television sets, 4,134,995 radio sets and 115,953,000 electric light bulbs.

Why, it is often asked in Britain, does German industry thrive? Apart from the start given by American aid after 1945 and the success of planning from the top, one of the most important reasons has been the fact that Germany is not constantly losing foreign orders because of strikes. In 1966, West Germany lost 27,000 working days through strikes; this compares with an average of 2,500,000 days per year in Britain, and Britain's figure in turn compares favourably with those of many other countries.

But to say that West German workers do not strike is merely to beg a second question: why don't they strike? There are several reasons. Firstly, the workers are well off. Since 1950, wages have increased by 203% ("take-home" pay, not gross earnings!) and prices by 38%. According to the statisticians, the average industrial worker in West Germany earned 873 Mark per month in 1966.

However, there is more to it than that. An important difference between Germany and Britain is the structure of the trade unions. In the Confederation of German Trade Unions there are sixteen mammoth organisations, each concerned with a specific industry. This in itself reduces the possibility of demarcation disputes to a minimum. Moreover, the unions and management negotiate wage contracts for a set period, which then take on binding legal force. Unions who try to take unconstitutional action to change the contract within this period can be — and sometimes have been — sued for breach of contract. The unions are rich and respectable.

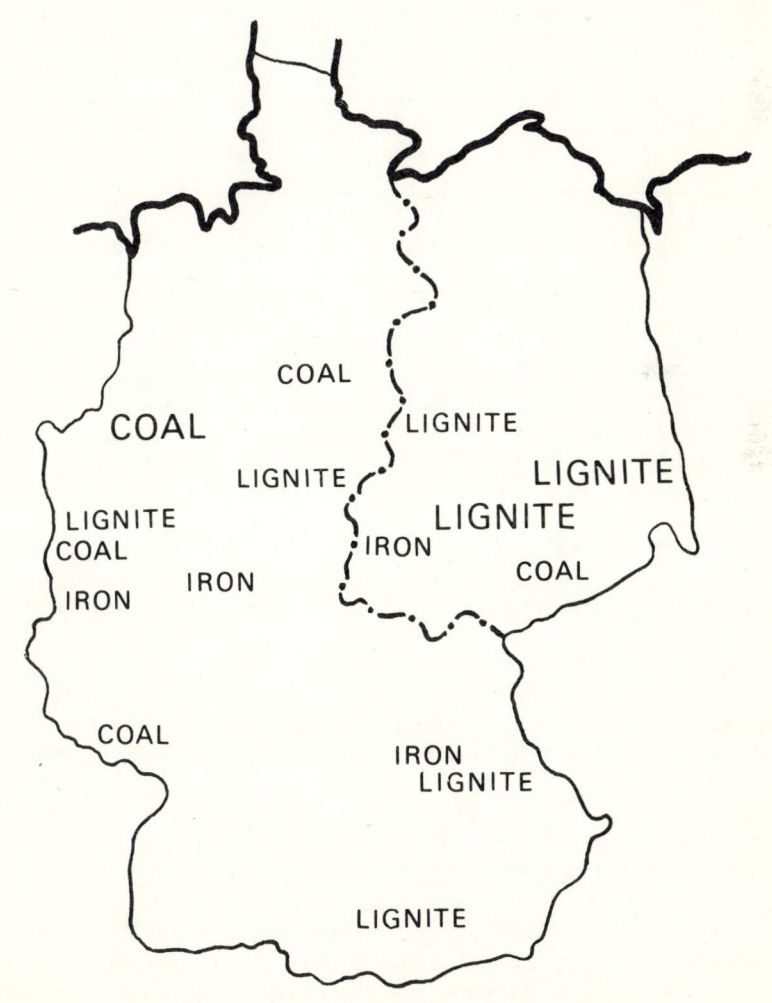

Fig 27   Raw materials for German industry

They run their own commercial bank and levy high subscriptions from their members (sometimes up to 3 Mark per week).

Another institution which helps maintain good industrial relations is the works council. This is obligatory for all non-state companies with more than five employees (more than ten in forestry), and its duties and rights are laid down by law. Elections to the works council are by secret ballot, and the members must be given time off with pay to attend meetings. The employer is bound to discuss with the council any proposed sacking, as well as matters such as hours of work, breaks and holiday arrangements. In public companies, workers' representatives also make up one-third of the supervisory council (originally intended to be a shareholders' watch-dog committee).

Agriculture

Just under 60% of the total area of West Germany is used for agricultural purposes. Every tenth West German works on a farm, and the country produces 80% of its own food requirements. For potatoes, sugar and milk, the figure is 100%. Only 5% of the butter has to be imported.

The average size of a farm in West Germany is 22 acres — compared with an average of 112 acres in Britain and 194 acres in the USA. There are over 100,000 small farms under five acres in Germany. Only 10% of the farms are over fifty acres. Since 1955, the Government has been obliged by law to submit an annual report on agriculture (known as the "Green Report") and details of the sum to be allocated in state subsidies to farmers. Recently, Germany has been spending some two and a half billion Mark each year on improving the agricultural situation. Partly as a result of this, the loss of agricultural workers (from five million in 1950 to under three million in 1966) has been compensated by a rise in mechanisation. The number of tractors on West German farms rose from 138,000 in 1950 to 1,236,544 in 1966.

East Germany

The growth of East German industrial production has been no less remarkable in recent years than that of West Germany. Admittedly, the all-time high of 1959 (12·8%) has not been repeated, and by 1967 it had dropped to a mere 6·8%. But even this "mere" 6·8% is much higher than the British rate of growth.

At present, around 44% of all workers in East Germany are employed in industry. The biggest employers are the chemical industry (282,038 workers), textiles (273,861), electrical engineering (236,875), general engineering (206,723) and foodstuffs (119,704).

Of a total of 13,451 industrial enterprises in 1966, 3,843 were state-owned, 5,512 were semi-state and 4,096 were private companies. But this picture is deceptive, for the state firms are by far the largest. They employ no less than 2,737,455 workers, compared with only 344,602 in semi-state organisations and 98,079 in private industry.

In the early post-war years, a decisive factor in the East German economy was the number of Soviet Companies, Russian-owned and employing half a million workers in 1952. These were returned to German control (and state ownership) in 1953.

There is only one trade union in East Germany: the Free German Trade Union. It is party-controlled, and can be said to be a government propaganda-machine rather than a trade union in the anti-management sense. It rejects all strike calls on principle, pointing out that in a state-owned industry the workers would be

Fig 28 The Wartburg (car) is one of East Germany's best-known products. This one is parked in the forecourt of the Wartburg Castle, from which it takes its name. Photo: Lex Hornsby & Partners.

striking against themselves. (State-owned industries are known as "people-owned" or "socialist" industries.)

Workers in East Germany are paid according to a complicated system by which hourly rate and piece-work rates are added to form the total sum paid out. Both can be increased by incentive bonuses for the individual's work or for the work done by his collective (team), and the piece-work rate is dependent upon his fulfilling or not fulfilling a predetermined "Norm". If he exceeds his Norm, he gets more money. It was a general raising of "Norms" which sparked off the mass protests of June 1953.

An unusual feature of the East German labour scene is the "National Reconstruction Scheme" (Nationales Aufbauwerk, usually abbreviated to NAW). This was begun in 1952 in Berlin, and later extended to the whole country. The idea is that workers are encouraged to volunteer to work a given number of unpaid hours each year to help build a hospital, a nursery school, or some such building, or to provide equipment needed for some social purpose. The whole scheme is run by a sub-committee of the National Front (the body which incorporates the political parties and mass organisations). In 1963 — the last year in which official statistics of the scheme were published — the total value of NAW work was 385,000,000 Mark.

Agricultural collectivisation was begun in 1952 but not intensified until 1960, when nearly all farmers in East Germany were persuaded to join cooperatives — all, that is, who did not emigrate to the West. By 1965, 93·9% of all farms in East Germany were collective farms. The official term is Agricultural Production Collective — in German, Landwirtschaftliche Produktionsgenossenschaft, or LPG for short. There are three types of LPG. Type I is the simplest form, in which only the land is collective property. In type II, the working animals and machines are also collective property, and in type III all livestock, machinery and land is common property. This latter type is the ultimate goal, though the other two types will probably last for many years.

The total area of arable land in East Germany is well over half that of West Germany, yet West Germany has ten times as many tractors. Partly for this reason, output per acre has not increased at the same rate as in West Germany; indeed, the production statistics are most unimpressive, and show no really steady increases.

Kilograms per hectare (2.47 acres)

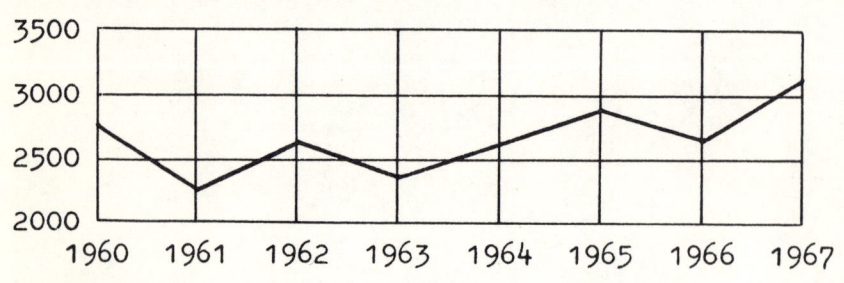

Fig 29   East German cereals production

This has been attributed also to the fact that farmers, once they join the collectives, suddenly discover that they are entitled to fixed working hours and holidays, which an independent farmer never adheres to. Every autumn, young students "volunteer" in true military fashion ("you, you and you") to help with the harvest. They help willingly, however, because for a holiday job the work is well paid.

Exports and imports

In 1887, earthenware jugs were on sale in Britain bearing the caption "A Present from Margate". There was a public outcry when it was discovered they were made in Germany. Consequently, a law was passed in Britain insisting that all goods which entered Britain should bear the name of their country of origin, if the customer would otherwise be misled into thinking that they were British made. Thus the phrase "Made in Germany" was born — a phrase which has in later years become linked with thoughts of "German efficiency" and the "economic miracle".

Not that the confusion has been completely resolved. A few years ago, some German friends of mine were visited by relatives who had been living in the Congo for some years. There were presents for all, including a leather wallet inscribed "Souvenir d'Elisabethville". Inside, however, was another inscription: "Made in Western Germany".

In the years following the Second World War, West German exports boomed. In 1950, West Germany's foreign trade involved 11,374 million Mark worth of imports and 8,362 million Mark worth of exports — a trade deficit of just over three billion Mark. Thanks largely to American aid and wise planning, this had changed by 1952 to a small surplus of 706 million Mark. Since then, things have never looked back. By 1966, total exports had reached 80·5 billion Mark, and imports 72·6 billion Mark. This was an increase of some 800% over 1950, and of over 100% in comparison with 1959.

One of the most important developments during the fifties and sixties has been the growth of the European Economic Community. The EEC countries bought no less than 36·3% of Germany's exports in 1966, and supplied 38·2% of her imports. The EFTA countries bought 25% of the exports and supplied 16·5% of the imports, while the North American continent was responsible for 13·9% of the imports and 10% of exports. The countries of Eastern Europe still play only a small role in West Germany's foreign trade — in 1966 they accounted for 4·3% of her imports and 4·1% of her exports. The latter figures do not include trade with East Germany, which for political reasons is not regarded by West German statisticians as "foreign trade". It is equivalent to just under 2% of her trade with "bona fide" foreign countries.

Germany's biggest single customer is France, followed by the Netherlands and the USA. In the list of leading exporters to Germany, the USA leads France and the Netherlands. Britain occupies sixth place in the list of Germany's suppliers, and ninth in the list of her customers.

The most important of Germany's imports is foodstuffs, which — including those taken for pleasure more than for nutrition — account for 8·9% of her imports. Non-ferrous metals and semi-manufactured metalware, taken together, amount to a further 7·2%, with textiles a close third at 7·0%. Non-ferrous metals also occupy second place in the list of imports from Britain; first place is taken by non-electric machinery, and third by textiles.

Engineering products are Germany's biggest earners, accounting for 20·9% of her total revenue from exports. In 1965, chemical products were beaten for second place by farm vehicles. Of the items Britain buys from Germany, non-electric machinery is by far the most important, followed a long way behind by transport equipment, electrical machinery and chemicals.

But revenue value is not necessarily a criterion for an item's interest, and a list of Germany's best-known and most interesting items might include the following:

Electrical goods including generators, compact power stations, telephone networks, radio and television sets. The best-known names are Telefunken, Grundig and Siemens. These and other German firms excel in the field of tape recorders, and many German language laboratories are used in Britain.

Motor vehicles especially cars. The huge Mercedes and the compact, ultra-conservative Volkswagen are the best-known. The latter firm is the biggest car producer in Europe, and it has been said that "to describe a Volkswagen is as superfluous as to describe an apple". (One suspects that this may have been first said in a Volkswagen advertising office.)

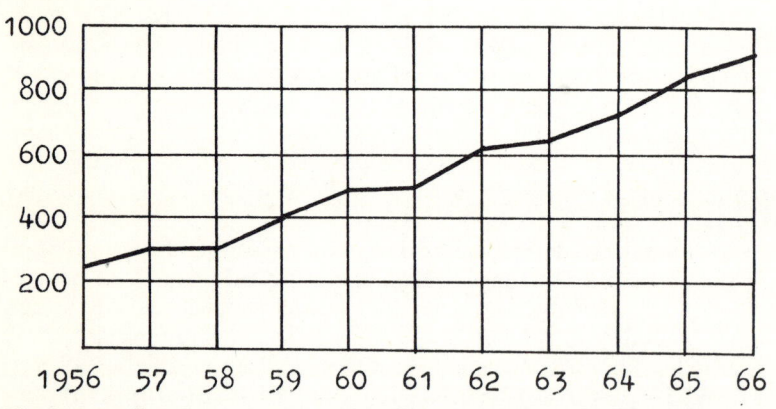

Fig 30 Volkswagen exports (excluding cars built outside Germany)

Precision mechanics and optics Every second German camera is sold abroad, and in 1966 seven million spectacle lenses were exported. Among the best-known German cameras are Leica, Agfa, Zeiss Ikon and Voigtländer — but even an apparently English camera, the Ilford Sportsman, bears the inscription "Made in Western Germany".

Chemical products including synthetic fibres and drugs. The leading name here is Bayer, famous for its aspirins.

Eau-de-Cologne which is not a perfume but a freshener. In recent years, "perfumed Cologne" has become popular. The best-known name is a number — 4711 — the number given to the factory in 1794 by the French, who occupied the city and gave each building its own number so as to avoid the complications presented by German street-names.

EXPORTS AND IMPORTS

Wood carving particularly from the Black Forest and Bavaria. In the Black Forest they specialise in cuckoo clocks, always elaborately carved and often painted. Oberammergau is a centre for religious wood-carving, and Mittenwald for violins.

Fig 31 Bavarian wood-carving from the works of Anton Cappius KG, 813 Starnberg, Postfach 120.

East Germany

East Germany's foreign trade has not shown the same rapid growth as that of West Germany, but if the important differences between the starting positions (American aid to the West, massive war reparations extracted from the East) are taken into consideration, the achievement is noteworthy. Since 1955, East Germany's foreign trade has increased by some 130%, and the turnover in 1966 was 27 billion Mark.

Three-quarters of East Germany's foreign trade is with the Socialist bloc; this includes 41% for trade with the Soviet Union. Only 22% of her trade is with "capitalist countries". She is the Soviet Union's main trade partner, and supplies about a quarter of Russian imports.

Of East Germany's non-Socialist trade partners, the Netherlands is the most important, taking 143,300,000 Mark worth of East German exports in 1966. Second place was occupied by Britain, with 114,700,000 Mark worth, and third India, followed closely by Austria. Only forty million Mark were received by East Germany for exports to the USA. West Germany was a much better partner, spending no less than 1,288 million Mark on purchases from East Germany.

More than half the revenue for exports is earned by the metal-working industry; exports from this branch have increased ten-fold since 1950. This includes the building abroad of textile works, power stations, cement factories and sugar refineries.

Again, revenue and interest-value of exports are two different things. Among East Germany's more interesting exports are:

Cameras from the original Carl Zeiss factory in Jena (now state-owned). The same factory is noted for its optical equipment.

China from Meissen, the oldest porcelain manufacturing centre in Europe. What the Germans call "Meissner Porzellan" is known in Britain as Dresden China.

Glass another Jena product, and an industry which arose directly from the needs of the optical and camera producers in the same town.

Wood carvings from the Erzgebirge (Ore Mountains), particularly elaborate Christmas roundabouts. Unfortunately, few of these are exported, and they are expensive.

Fig 32 Adding the fine detail to a piece of Dresden China. Photo: Lex Hornsby & Partners.

Fig 33 An Erzgebirge Christmas roundabout makes a good background when you are singing carols. The choirboys are from Dresden. Photo: Lex Hornsby & Partners.

In the office

German office-workers are at their desks long before many of their British counterparts have started their breakfast. Most German offices begin the day's work at 8 am, and finish at 5.30 in the afternoon. German businessmen make appointments early in the day; this can be an advantage to the foreign salesman who wants to fit in as many visits as possible during a short stay, but can be annoying to the tourist if the appointment at an "unearthly hour" is suggested by a German friend. Whatever the time of an appointment, Germans tend to be stricter on punctuality than the British. (Only in academic circles is unpunctuality a built-in feature of the system. Most lectures start fifteen minutes after the official time.)

It should not be imagined that because the Germans start earlier they work harder. Lunch-breaks are usually quite flexible, and top executives particularly take a long mid-day break. Friday afternoon is a bad time to call on a German businessman, because if he holds a senior position, there is a fair chance that he will not be in his office. At the office in which I myself worked in Germany, it was also the custom to stop work an hour and a half early on days when a colleague was celebrating a birthday. We all gathered in one room, and spent the rest of the afternoon drinking coffee, eating cream cakes and chatting.

„Wer hat schon wieder den Würfelzucker geklaut?"

Fig 34 "Who's taken the sugar?" — by Moese. Reproduced from "Junge Welt".

IN THE OFFICE

Many German officials have set hours each week during which they are available for visitors. These hours decrease with seniority. Offices which have much contact with the general public often stipulate that "customers" may only come during the mornings.

There is a distinction in Germany between the "Angestellter" and "Beamter". Beamten are public servants, employed either by the state or by a public body. They have many rights, including excellent pension terms and sick benefits, security and general "status". In return, they must swear an oath of allegiance to their job and of secrecy concerning all official matters, and they have no legal right to strike. All public servants who have not attained Beamte status, and all office workers employed by private companies, are Angestellten.

German bureaucracy dates back to the great days of Prussia, and has a mixed reputation. It is praised for its business-like attitude, but criticised for its impersonality. There is certainly more form-filling in Germany than in Britain, and German officials are less likely to fill in the form for a customer. If you take to a German office a form which is incorrectly completed, the chances are that they will simply send you away with a new one, and with a few choice remarks about their time being wasted. But this is a generalisation, and there are also officials who are more friendly and human.

Fig 35 No German office is complete without a battery of rubber stamps. Photo taken in Münster by Glyn Hatherall.

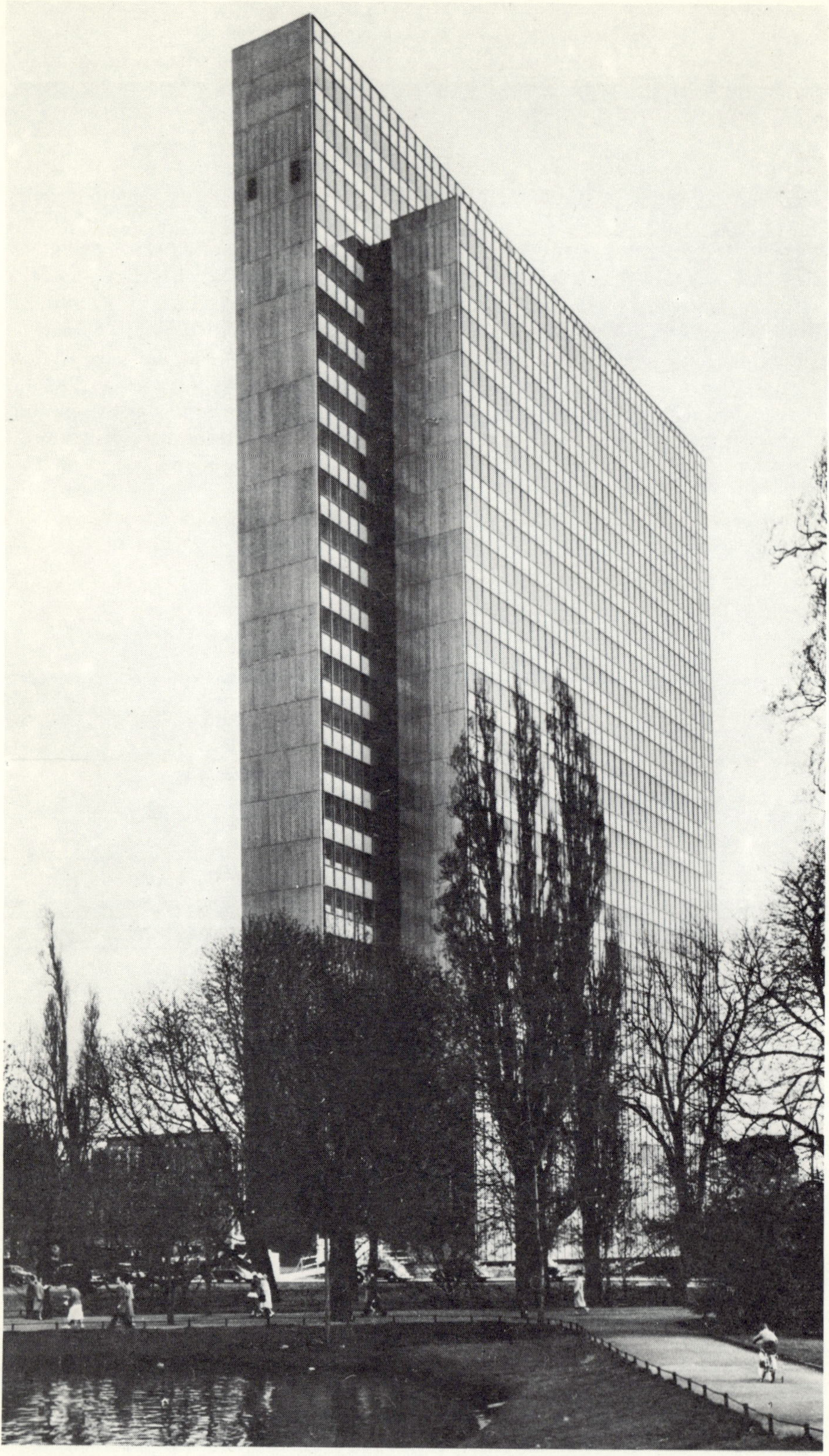

Doing business

There are various types of business company in Germany, all of which must be registered in the Commercial Register. A firm with individual proprietorship is known as an "Einzelfirma". An ordinary commercial partnership in which all partners have unlimited liability is called an Offene Handelsgesellschaft (OHG). In a Kommanditgesellschaft (KG), only one of the partners (the "Komplementar") need accept full liability, while the others (the "Kommanditisten") are liable only to the extent of their investments. A "Kommanditgesellschaft auf Aktien" is one in which the Kommanditisten are shareholders. More common types of company are the joint stock corporations, known in German as Aktiengesellschaften (AG), and limited liability companies (Gesellschaften mit beschänkter Haftung, or GmbH for short). In both of them, the partners' liability is limited to the extent of their investment; but while an AG issues shares which can be exchanged on the stock market, a GmbH partner must go through legal channels in order to alter the value of his investment. Every AG must have a supervisory council ("Aufsichtsrat"), and if there are more than 500 workers, they must supply one-third of the members of this body. The minimum capital for an AG is 100,000 Mark, for a GmbH 20,000. A share in an AG must have a minimum face value of 100 Mark; the minimum investment in a GmbH is 500 Mark.

Taxes Earned and unearned income, be it of individuals or of companies, is taxed in West Germany — either as income tax or as corporation tax. There is also a property tax, and death duties. What the Germans call "transaction taxes" are levied on land purchase, exchange transactions, insurance and gaming. Special duties are payable on tobacco, coffee, tea, sugar, beer, oil and sparkling wine as specific commodities. The state has a monopoly for the manufacture of brandy and matches, and receives licence duty from firms who have been granted permits to produce these items.

West Germany's new Turnover Tax Law (usually referred to as Added Value Tax) that came into force on 1 January 1968 was part of a general move to make the tax systems of all EEC countries conform to a common pattern. France brought a similar law into effect on the same date, and it is possible that a similar tax system will eventually be adopted in Britain. The new German law provides for two forms of the tax: Import Turnover Tax ("Einfuhrumsatzsteuer") and Added Value Tax ("Mehrwertsteuer"). For both forms, the rate of tax became 11% in July 1968, with a reduced rate of 5·5% for certain goods.

Exporters to Germany are mostly concerned with the Import Turnover Tax. This is levied by the German Customs when they assess Customs Duty, etc and is based on the value of the goods including transport charges to the first place of destination in Germany. Added Value Tax is payable on delivery to the purchaser, but because the law defines delivery as handing over to shipping agents, post, railways, etc, only Import Turnover Tax is payable if this handing over is done outside Germany. If the seller himself delivers the goods or is involved in a distributive or manufacturing chain inside Germany, he is also liable to Added Value Tax. Each time the goods change hands, e.g. manufacturer — wholesaler — retailer, this tax is levied only on the increase in the price charged, thus avoiding the cumulative effect of the old laws. The net result for the German shopper is that she pays 11% tax on most of her purchases except food and agricultural products which bear only 5·5% tax. The idea is simple, but the book-keeping

---

Fig 36 One of Germany's biggest office blocks — the Thyssen Building in Düsseldorf. Photo: German Tourist Information Bureau.

and tax returns required by the Federal Tax Office are complex. British exporters can obtain information on this subject from the Export Services Branch of the Board of Trade, and American exporters from the German-American Chamber of Commerce in New York.

Local authorities in Germany receive income from land tax, profits tax, entertainments tax and a supplementary tax on land purchase. They also receive licence dues from dog owners and publicans.

Correspondence Nearly all German firms now use the same standard-size notepaper, known in German as "DIN A4" and measuring 21 x 29·7 cm. The heading includes almost all conceivable information about the firm. As well as the address and PO box number, there are also full details of the bank account (number and branch) and post giro account. All telephone numbers are included, plus — if necessary — space for individual departments to give their own extension number. There are frequently printed headings for "Ihr Zeichen" (your reference) "Unser Zeichen" (our reference) "Ihr Schreiben von" or "Bezug" (your letter of) and "Betreff" or "Betrifft" (Re:). Sometimes, the details of account numbers, together with telephone and telex numbers and telegram addresses, are given at the foot of the page. Private individuals writing to a firm should also use the same A4 size notepaper, and print or type their names at top left and addresses top right.

Window-envelopes are now almost universal practice, though some firms still type the envelope separately. Apart from white, blue and green are the most frequent envelope colours. Many German firms use lined envelopes, a refinement not so often seen in Britain.

The opening, in business letters, is not "Lieber Herr Müller" (Dear Mr Müller), but "Sehr geehrter Herr Müller!" (Very respected Mr Müller). The exclamation mark after this greeting is still general practice, though it is now permissible to use a comma instead. Letters close with the phrase "mit vorzüglicher Hochachtung" (with the greatest respect) or "Hochachtungsvoll" (respectfully). Many businessmen use only their surname as a signature, and it is too often illegible.

The ad-men

With the economic miracle in West Germany, there was a phenomenal increase in the sums of money spent on advertising. In 1952 it was only 565 million Mark. Ten years later almost six times as much (3,295 million Mark). By 1966, it had reached 4,643 million. Moreover, these official statistics show only the sums spent through the advertising trade; it is estimated that if direct advertising were included, the figures would be almost twice as high.

Advertising law in Germany is much stricter than in Britain, and official sources strongly urge foreign manufacturers to seek legal advice before advertising in Germany. The main law is the Law Against Unfair Competition of 1909, a rather vague general clause of which must be interpreted in the light of decided cases. All statements contained in adverts must be true, including all information about quality, quantity, price and origin. Remarks about competitors and their products should be avoided, and personal attacks upon competitors are strictly forbidden. There are certain conditions under which "comparison of systems" is permitted, but I have failed completely to understand the technical jargon in which these are couched.

The advertising industry is organised by the Central Council of the Advertising Trade (Zentralausschuss der Werbewirtschaft, or ZAW for short). This consists of representatives from the advertising agencies, the designers, the industries which engage in advertising and the media owners. There are standing committees for the different methods of advertising.

German advertising statistics distinguish between various groups of products. The most heavily advertised group in 1966 was "foodstuffs and allied products", which included alcoholic and non-alcoholic drink, tobacco and baby foods. Second came "body-care and cleansing products", a group which comprised everything from cosmetics to washing powder. "Machinery and vehicles" took third place, closely followed by "household goods" (including furniture) and "textiles and clothing".

In 1965, Allensbach pollsters tried to ascertain what the German public thought of advertising as a whole. Of the 2,000 people questioned, 45% said they thought advertising was "a good thing", 38% found it annoying, and 17% were undecided.

Methods

In general, the methods used by advertisers in Germany are similar to those used in Britain. There are, however, some important restrictions placed on advertisers by law. If something is offered as a "free gift" with the product to be advertised, the value of the "gift" may not exceed 3% of the product sold. There are also restrictions on vouchers sent by post. It is illegal to use the "Xd off" technique to publicise a price reduction. Nor are shopkeepers allowed to sell at a lower price an article taken from a certain shelf, if the fixed price prevails for the main stock.

Press Advertising in newspapers and magazines accounts for over 80% of the total sum spent on advertising each year. There are over two thousand newspapers and periodicals to choose from, some of which will be mentioned in the chapter on "The printed word". Because the dailies have smaller circulations than their British counterparts, the bulk of advertising goes to the magazines. (The one exception in the dailies is "Bild", which has a circulation of four million and was charging 116,480 Mark for a whole-page advert in 1966.) Most magazines provide facilities for advertising in selected regions only. "Der Spiegel" and "Die Zeit" appeal above all to the more intelligent and more influential sections of society, and are read by more men than women. "Stern" and "Quick" are middle-brow journals read by almost equal proportions of both sexes. "Heim und Welt", "Das Neue Blatt" and "Constanze" are women's magazines. There are several specialist papers covering single interest-groups — including 135 for the building trade alone. The German equivalent of our consumer magazine "Which?" is "DM", but the German version is less sophisticated and does not enjoy the same reputation for scientific accuracy.

Loose inserts in newspapers and magazines are more widely used than in Britain. It is not unusual to receive a complete house magazine inside a daily paper.

Radio and television Radio advertising is possible in some of the regional broadcasting companies (which will be enumerated in the chapter "Radio and television"), but not in those covering the main consumer areas of Hamburg, North-Rhine-Westphalia, Lower Saxony and Schleswig-Holstein. Radio Luxembourg broadcasts a German programme throughout the day, and includes advertising similar to that of its English programme. The regional programmes of the "First Programme" on television include advertising in the early evening. The "Second German Television" includes networked advertising in five-minute

Fig 37 This hoardings pillar is being used temporarily for a political purpose — a call for reunification. Photo: Glyn Hatherall.

interludes on weekdays at 18,40, 18,55, 19,25, and 19,55. Costs vary considerably according to the time at which the advert is broadcast.

Cinemas Most cinemas show special publicity films, but there is a limit of six minutes in any one performance. There are several film-producing and -hiring firms throughout the country. Advertising rates vary from about 30 Mark per minute per week in small cinemas, to 300 Mark per minute per week in the larger cities.

Posters Apart from hoardings similar to those in Britain, most towns in Germany have several poster columns in the middle of the pavement. These can hold several different adverts at the same time. The Federal Railways offer poster and display sites in stations and on their trains. Placard space is also available in trams and buses — and an advertiser with a large budget can even hire a tram or bus and convert it into an advertising float.

Magazine libraries There are in Germany nearly two hundred thousand "Lesezirkel", or magazine libraries. These lend magazines to cafes, hotels, doctors' waiting-rooms etc. Each magazine is protected by a thick folder which circulates for eight to ten weeks. The folders provide an excellent medium for local and national advertising.

Circulars and direct mail Owing to the labour shortage, canvassing and hand-delivery of circulars is somewhat restricted in Germany. More popular is the distribution of literature by post. There is a special system organised by the Post Office whereby literature can be sent to specific groups of individuals, or specific professions. There is also advertising space in telephone directories, and in post offices and telephone call-boxes.

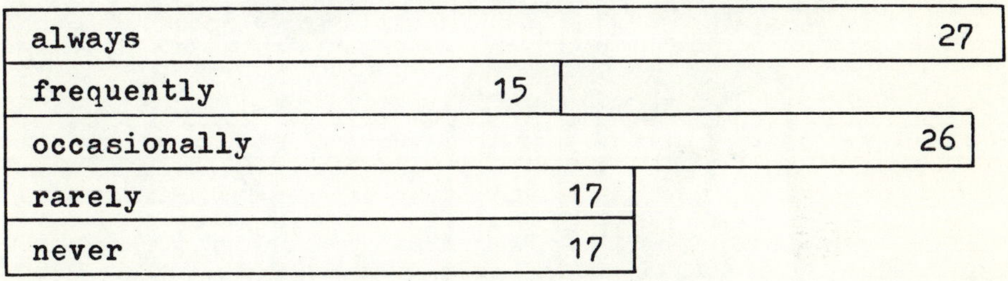

always	27
frequently	15
occasionally	26
rarely	17
never	17

Fig 38 "Do you read printed advertising matter sent to you by direct mail?" German statistics quoted in "Advertiser's Weekly", December 1967.

Shop displays Advertisers can either arrange exclusive window displays in shop-windows or cooperate with other firms to organise combined displays of a given type of article. Inside the shops, newcomers to the market can arrange for their own counters, which they stock themselves — thus testing the market without the store having to buy the goods.

Gifts Germans make more use of advertising gifts than their British counterparts. Gifts come in all shapes and sizes, but the most popular are items of office equipment, such as ballpoint pens and calendars.

Lectures and film shows A particularly popular form of advertising is the lecture or special film show at a local cinema, invitations for which are distributed beforehand. I remember receiving one such invitation which was combined with a "lucky number" scheme. My ticket, I discovered from the list of winning numbers on the back, was one of the lucky ones, and if I attended the lecture, I would receive a "24-piece breakfast set". I went along, feeling rather pleased at the prospect of a free prize. To my amusement, I discovered that nearly everyone else in the cinema had also won the same prize — six plastic egg-cups, six plastic spoons and twelve paper serviettes.

Trade fairs For foreign firms wishing to bring their goods to the attention of German retailers and wholesalers, the trade fairs are the most important means of advertising. There are nearly fifty trade fairs in Germany every year, the most important being the Hanover Fair each spring, which attracts nearly six thousand exhibitors. This is a fair for the experts and for retailers, while the Spring Fair and Autumn Fair in Frankfurt are more concerned with the consumer. There are specialist fairs for many types of goods, including books, electronic components, boats, furniture and food. In conjunction with British trade associations, the British Board of Trade organises collective exhibits for UK firms wishing to use

Fig 39 East German manufacturers of transport and loading equipment demonstrate their products at the Leipzig Spring Fair. Photo: Lex Hornsby & Partners.

the facilities offered by German trade fairs. Full information about Germany's trade fairs can be obtained from the Ausstellungs- und Messe-Ausschuss der Deutschen Wirtschaft, 5 Köln, Engelbertstrasse 31a.

The complex situation described above clearly indicates the need for foreign firms wishing to advertise in Germany to call in expert advice. The German advertising advisers have their own association, the Bund Deutscher Werbeberater und Werbeleiter eV (43 Essen, Brunnenstrasse 29). The advertising agents are represented by the ADW Verband Deutscher Werbeagenturen und Werbungsmittel eV (6 Frankfurt, Friedrich-Ebert-Anlage 18).

East Germany

As a country in which profit-making is of comparatively little importance, East Germany has much fewer adverts than the countries of Western Europe. There is a central advertising agency known as "DEWAG" (short for Deutsche Werbeanzeige-Gesellschaft) in Berlin. The International Press Institute survey in 1959 found that of six East German newspapers studied, only three had over 15% advertising; the central Party organ "Neues Deutschland" gave up only 4% of its space to adverts.

Foreign firms wishing to advertise in East Germany must do so through the "Interwerbung" organisation (104 Berlin, Tucholskystrasse 40), which is run jointly by the Chamber of Foreign Trade and DEWAG. The easiest way of reaching many East German firms is at the Leipzig Fair in March and September each year. The spring fair is the larger of the two, and attracts more than nine thousand exhibitors from seventy countries. The address of the Leipzig Fair Office is 701 Leipzig, Markt 11-15.

HOW THEY PLAY

A night out

"In every true man is a child who wants to play." This statement by Nietzsche has become a German proverb. And our picture of the German would be incomplete if, having looked at his home and work, we were to omit all reference to his leisure time.

The German who wants a night out has a wider choice than his British counterpart. In particular he has a better range of restaurants with musical accompaniment, where you can sit and sip your wine while listening to a Bavarian band, or a Rhineland trio, or a cabaret. If you live near a river, you can go on an evening boat tour. The boats are floating restaurants, with music — and sometimes even dancing — while you eat and drink. While the Britisher will only join in pub sing-songs when he is with a crowd of friends, the German is quite willing to join strangers in hearty renderings of traditional melodies. (It was to enable foreign tourists to join in German songs that I offered to compile an "Anglo-German Songbook", published by Pond Press in 1968.) In Bavaria, many of the hotels put on an evening's entertainment with a regional flavour, including traditional dances and a brass band, besides good, clean jokes in broad dialect. Then there are the "Tanzcafes", serving only a small selection of meals and more expensive wines, but making up for the lack of variety by having a dance floor. There is no German equivalent for the British type of dance-hall.

The biggest claims on the Germans' evening leisure hours, however, are made by the theatre and the cinema.

Theatre

For the German, the theatre is more than a place of entertainment. He goes in search of what Kenneth Tynan has described as "cultural nourishment", and the resulting atmosphere is one of "appreciative calm" (Tynan's phrase again). There is little rustling of paper, and coughing is stifled.

When going to the theatre, the men wear dark suits, the ladies cocktail dresses. This is more than a mere tradition — many Germans believe that dressing up puts you in the right mood for appreciating a good feast of culture. Germans never take their overcoats into the theatre, not even into the "gods". The cloakroom is free (although a tip is sometimes expected) and there is a peg allocated for every seat in the theatre, so cloakroom tickets are unnecessary.

The printed programme contains more information than a British theatre programme. Many German theatre programmes contain pictures, together with learned articles on the play or on some connected theme.

At the end of each act, and particularly at the end of the play, the audience will call for more curtain calls than one is used to in Britain. But if the audience is young, it will not hesitate to show disapproval with boos and whistles.

During the interval the foyer has an atmosphere resembling that of a large-scale official reception. Drinks and light refreshments are on sale, but at exorbitant

Fig 40 Gala night at Düsseldorf Opera House. Photo: German Tourist Information Bureau.

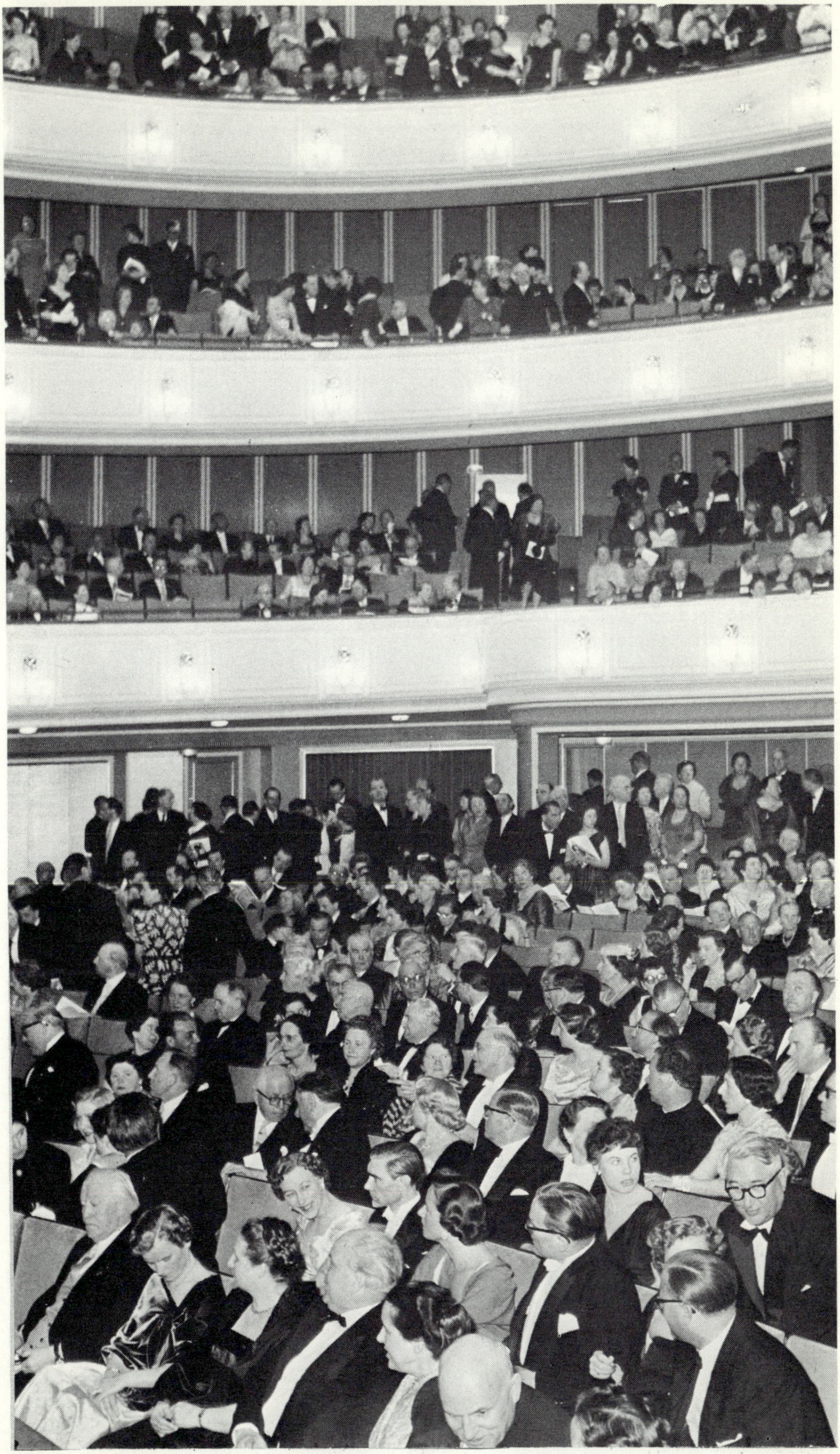

Fig 41   Typical German theatre ticket

prices. The "traditional" interval drink is champagne mixed with orange juice, but this is a tradition few can afford to maintain at current price levels.

Most German theatres produce several plays a year in repertory. The theatres are often subsidised, and the "Intendant" or artistic director has considerably more freedom than the manager of a theatre which has to make a profit from each play. Of the 190 theatres in West Germany, 135 are subsidised by the state or by the municipal authorities. Subsidies total 500 million Mark a year, about £50 million — a figure which dwarfs the total grant of £6 million for all Arts Council work in Britain. An "Intendant" in Germany will frequently take an unknown writer's play and include it in his programme merely to test audience reaction to it. This has drawbacks from the audience's point of view. In Britain, when you decide to see a play in a professional theatre, you know somebody must think it is worth investing money in; in Germany, this is not necessarily the case.

Fig 42   The new theatre at Münster. Photo: Glyn Hatherall.

Most big towns in Germany have their own theatre, and the "provinces" are much better catered for than in Britain. Many of the theatres pride themselves particularly on the work of their producers and set designers. After 1945, German theatres had to make do with the minimum of equipment, and developed a style of presentation which has left its mark today in simple scenery.

An analysis by Kenneth Tynan of the programmes of sixteen leading West German theatres in 1962-3 showed that 33% of the plays were by Classical authors, 15% by writers of the Ibsen-Hauptmann period, 12% were modern light comedy and 40% were other contemporary plays.

Apart from Berlin, which has twenty theatres, the main centres are Hamburg, Bremen, Bochum, Düsseldorf, Cologne, Mannheim and Munich.

A few words must be said about the German cabarets. These are mostly of a political nature, and include some sharp criticism of contemporary affairs. They flourish in both parts of Berlin, and also in Cologne, Düsseldorf and Munich. One drawback, from a tourist's point of view, is that the sketches are mostly in top-speed German, and are difficult to follow even if one knows the language well.

Cinema

With the exception of the news cinemas, German cinemas show separate performances for all films. The cinema is cleared at the end of each performance, and there is little interruption from late-comers. Seats are bookable in advance.

Fig 43 "Excuse me, but you're sitting on my seat." Cartoon by Förster, reproduced from "Junge Welt".

Smoking is prohibited in nearly all German cinemas, though in some of the larger ones people who wish to smoke may sit upstairs behind a glass screen.

Under the "Youth Protection Laws", children under six years of age are refused admittance to cinemas. Films carry a certificate which gives the age above which children may be admitted; this can be 6, 12, 16, or 18. The "Film Evaluation Office" at Wiesbaden gives films a mark for quality, and those which are judged to be of particularly high quality carry a reduction of entertainment tax for cinemas which show them.

Germans sometimes complain that there is a lack of good German films, yet their country has made many valuable contributions to the screen. Emil Jannings' portrayal of the Judge in "The Broken Pitcher" is a notable performance, as is the same actor's interpretation of the Professor in "The Blue Angel", a film better known as one of Marlene Dietrich's biggest hits. "The Cabinet of Dr Caligari" was a film with Expressionist art in its scenery, and "M" was the intriguing title of one of the first great sound pictures. More recently, the film versions of "The Captain of Köpenick" and "Faust" have been acclaimed all over the world, while in Germany itself "We Wonder-Children" poked fun at those who had misused the opportunities given by the post-war economic miracle. But the West German film industry has also produced a disproportionate number of sentimental films which show idyllic countryside but precious little of value, and in recent years they have produced several Westerns.

Most of the imported films come from the USA. According to the most recent edition of "Germany Reports", there are some 200 American films now circulating in Germany, compared with 60-70 French, 50 British and 30-40 Italian.

East Germany

In a total of 93 East German theatres, the annual audience is around twelve million. The theatre is an instrument of policy, designed to help educate the populace in the ideals and theory of Socialism. Programme notes help by indicating the necessary interpretations — such as the link between William Tell's fight for freedom and the struggle of workers in West Germany against "monopoly capitalism". At the 1964 Shakespeare Festival in Weimar, the final scene of "Hamlet" was altered beyond recognition because, the programme explained, we now know that men like Fortinbras do not bring happiness to their subjects.

There are five Children's Theatres run by the Free German Youth and the Young Pioneers. In 150 "Workers' and Farmers' Theatres", nearly five thousand amateurs help build up a socialist culture for the working class.

The two most famous theatres in East Germany are both in East Berlin. They

Fig 44   Scene from the film "Divided Heaven". Photo: Lex Hornsby & Partners.

are the "Comic Opera" and the "Berlin Ensemble"; the latter is run by Helene Weigel, widow of the playwright Bertold Brecht.

In the East German political cabarets, the jokes are not limited to those in tune with the party line. Indeed, when I first saw one of these performances, I was pleasantly surprised at the amount of freedom allowed the satirists. One of the sketches poked fun at the whole concept of "transition stage" which is fundamental to Marxist philosophy and denotes the Socialist state midway between capitalism and communism.

There is only one film producing company, known by its initials as DEFA. As in other countries, the number of cinemas and the attendances are continually falling as the television-viewing audience increases. Many of the East German films are polemical in nature, but there have been some artistic successes, particularly among filmed novels. These include the film version of Bruno Apitz' "Naked among Wolves" (a story about Buchenwald) and Christa Wolf's "Divided Heaven".

Sport

Many young Germans are not content with the passive enjoyment of theatre or cinema during their leisure hours, but want to put this time to some more practical purpose — such as improving their physical fitness. In an earlier chapter, the word "sporting" was used with regard to smart fashions. Indeed, the word "sport" seems, to a German, to conjure up ideals of physical fitness and excellence rather than concepts of fair play. This is not, of course, to accuse the Germans of disregarding the "spirit of the game", but it seems to me that they pay less attention to it than the British. The German language has no equivalent for our phrase "it isn't cricket".

The emphasis on individual fitness rather than on team spirit and fair play is reflected in the Germans' choice of sports. With the exception of football, the top five sports are individual as opposed to team games. The EMNID survey in 1966 asked young people between the ages of 18 and 21 to name the sports in which they took part. Swimming headed the list, being named by 61%, followed by football (33%), gymnastics (25%), table tennis (22%) and athletics (21%). Skiing and badminton were each mentioned by 19%, hiking and cycling by 15% and skating (including roller skating and ice hockey) by 11%. All other sports were listed by less than 10% of those questioned.

Sport is organised mainly by the sports associations, of which by far the largest is the football association, with over two million members. The total membership of the 34,500 sports associations and clubs is 6·8 million.

The father of West Germany's sports facilities was Carl Diem, who died in 1962. He was concerned with the provision of better facilities since 1906, when he

Fig 45 Cartoon by Gabbert, reproduced from "Junge Welt".

Fig 46 Six-day cycle race in Berlin, an annual event that draws large crowds. Photo: German Tourist Information Bureau.

first joined the newly-formed German Olympic Committee. In 1920, a law was passed calling for 3 square metres of playing field per inhabitant. (The original demand was for 5 square metres, but this was turned down.)

After the Second World War, a Sport University was founded at Cologne, to investigate and carry out research into all aspects of sport. Four years later, in 1951, the German Olympic Committee was reconstituted. There were many recommendations for the provision of more sports facilities, culminating in the ambitious "Golden Plan" of 1959. The statistics for the demands made in this plan are impressive: the planners called for 31,000 children's playgrounds (average size 800 square metres); 14,700 communal and school sports grounds (average 8,500 sq.m); 10,400 gymnasia and sports halls (average 265 sq.m); 5,500 gymnastic halls and rooms (average 120 sq.m); 2,625 learner swimming pools (indoor, sizes from 6 x 12·5 to 8 x 16·6m); 2,420 open-air swimming pools (various sizes) and 435 indoor swimming pools.

The principle on which the plan was based was simple: 5 square metres of playing facilities per inhabitant. Equally important was the siting of the facilities. Children in the 3-6 age group should find their facilities within 100m of their home, those in the 7-12 age group within 500m, and those in the 13-17 age group should have theirs in conjunction with the school grounds, or not more than ten minutes' walk away. (All these figures, however, apply only to urban areas with over 5,000 inhabitants. Provision of facilities in other areas was also regulated, but could not be as efficient.)

An English friend once told me of a swimming pool which he had used in Berlin. It included ladies' and gentlemen's hairdressing salons, a public telephone, a Sauna bath, a Turkish bath, and a cafeteria-bar where one could purchase anything from a light meal and cakes to beer or coffee. The changing-room facilities were faultless, and adjustable showers compulsory.

By 1964, about a quarter of the "Golden Plan" had been realised. The plan remains, however, the goal for the future. According to official statistics, the Federal Government spends 30 million Mark each year on sports facilities, the Länder 40 million and the local authorities 150 million. Sport is obligatory in all schools; two hours a week is the average in primary schools, three in secondary schools.

Besides those taking part actively in sport, there are of course many who watch as spectators. West Germany has forty-nine stadia capable of holding over thirty thousand spectators. Five million people watch the football matches each Sunday. (Yes, football is a Sunday sport in Germany.) There are over seventy thousand teams to choose from, but the most popular are the teams in the Federal League; here football is a tough business, and some observers feel that there is not much sportsmanship left when players earn salaries as high as those paid by the top clubs. The interest in sport is shown by the fact that when Cologne won the German championship in 1962, special editions of the Cologne newspapers were on sale in the suburbs within twenty minutes of the final whistle. (There are probably better examples than this on record, but this is one of which I was an eye-witness.)

Fig 47 "What, is the game over?" Cartoon by Moese, reproduced from "Junge Welt".

SPORT

East Germany

Until 1964, the German representatives at Olympic Games meetings entered as a single team. From 1968 onwards, however, separate teams were entered by East and West. This is, as the West maintains, a submission on the part of the International Olympic Committee to East Germany's claim to recognition as a separate state, but I had the feeling at the time of the 1964 games that the joint team was already something of a farce. East German newspapers reported the successes individually as "West German" or "GDR" successes.

In 1966, East Germany had a total of 14,000 sports grounds of varying sizes. Sport is organised by the German Gymnastics and Sports Federation (DTSB) which has 1·7 million members in seven thousand clubs. Children between the ages of six and fourteen can take part either in school sports clubs or in special children's groups of the DTSB. In addition, many sports events are run by the Free German Youth, and by the Society for Sport and Technics (GST), the latter body specialising in military sports and pre-military training.

East German sportsmen have been highly successful in recent years, but have lost much sympathy in the West because of the way they are treated by their own authorities. They are often given nominal jobs in factories but paid high salaries

Fig 48 Basketball in the open air at the National Youth Sports Festival in East Berlin. Photo: Lex Hornsby & Partners.

in order that they should have enough time off for training. When they win, the authorities use the successes as a means of showing the greatness of their country; in short, sport is used for political ends. Similarly, sportsmen's congresses are used as platforms for political speeches. The big congress in July 1966 was used as an excuse for a forum, the main topic of which was the exchange of letters between the East German government and the West German Social Democratic Party.

On holiday

That mythical figure, the average West German, takes 28 days' holiday each year — so the statisticians tell us. This is less than the Italians (39 days) and the French (35), but considerably more than the British (only 18).

In July 1967, the Allensbach Institute asked 2,000 West Germans if they had taken a holiday away from home the previous year. Three in every five said they had. Of these, half had been abroad. Going abroad is particularly popular among those who live in the South: 63% of the Bavarians had been outside Germany, but only 46% of the North Germans.

The reason for this is not hard to find. The most beautiful scenery in Germany is in the south, and thus many North Germans want to visit this part of the country, while the Bavarians are less eager to visit the north. Moreover, "going abroad" for a German usually means going south to Italy, Spain and Yugoslavia, and the Bavarians have a much shorter journey to reach these countries.

What are the Germans looking for when they go on holiday? A clue to this may be found in another Allensbach poll, in which those questioned were asked to forget reality and say where they would like to go if they had an unlimited holiday budget. The winning centres were Capri, Paris, Rome, India, New York, Jerusalem, Egypt, Greece and — in ninth place — Britain. Although those who named Capri were clearly thinking of the sun and the sands, the other resorts and countries named seem to suggest that "places of interest" were equally important in the choice of a holiday venue.

I must confess, however, that this does not tally with the impression I have obtained from talking to German friends. Quite the reverse. The families I know best are quite clear that what they want on holiday is not a cultural feast, but a really good rest. Though not necessarily with hot sun and sandy beaches.

Holidays in Germany

While many Germans are leaving the country for their holidays, many foreigners are coming in. In post-war years, the West German tourist trade has boomed. The number of overnight stays by foreign tourists rose from two million in 1950 to nearly fourteen million in 1966. The German tourist trade's best customers are the Americans, the Dutch, the British and the French.

As the West German tourist trade works on a supply and demand basis, the amount of hotel accommodation in different regions is a guide to their popularity. Every fourth hotel bed in West Germany is in Bavaria. Second in importance for the tourist trade is Baden-Württemberg, the administrative region containing the Black Forest, though this is relegated to third place if the Rhineland (i.e. North Rhine-Westphalia and Rhineland-Palatinate) is regarded as a single region.

Ignoring the administrative boundaries, there are five main tourist attractions:

— Upper Bavaria, with its Alpine scenery, waterfalls, quaint houses and fairy-tale castles;
— the Black Forest, in the South-West, an area of lower, wooded hills and fashionable spas;
— the Rhineland and Moselle Valley, with vineyards either side of the rivers and villages full of half-timbered houses;

— the Harz Mountains, still popular despite the fact that the most famous summit, the Brocken, is now in East Germany;
— and finally the North Sea Coast, more popular with the Germans themselves than with foreigners. This area includes the holiday island, Sylt, a favourite of all the "top people" in North Germany.

Three of these areas (Bavaria, Black Forest and Harz) are also popular in winter with winter sports enthusiasts. Foreigners, however, tend to prefer the higher slopes of Switzerland and Austria — though Garmisch-Partenkirchen, in Bavaria, is quite fashionable with foreign skiers.

Fig 49   Favourite holiday areas

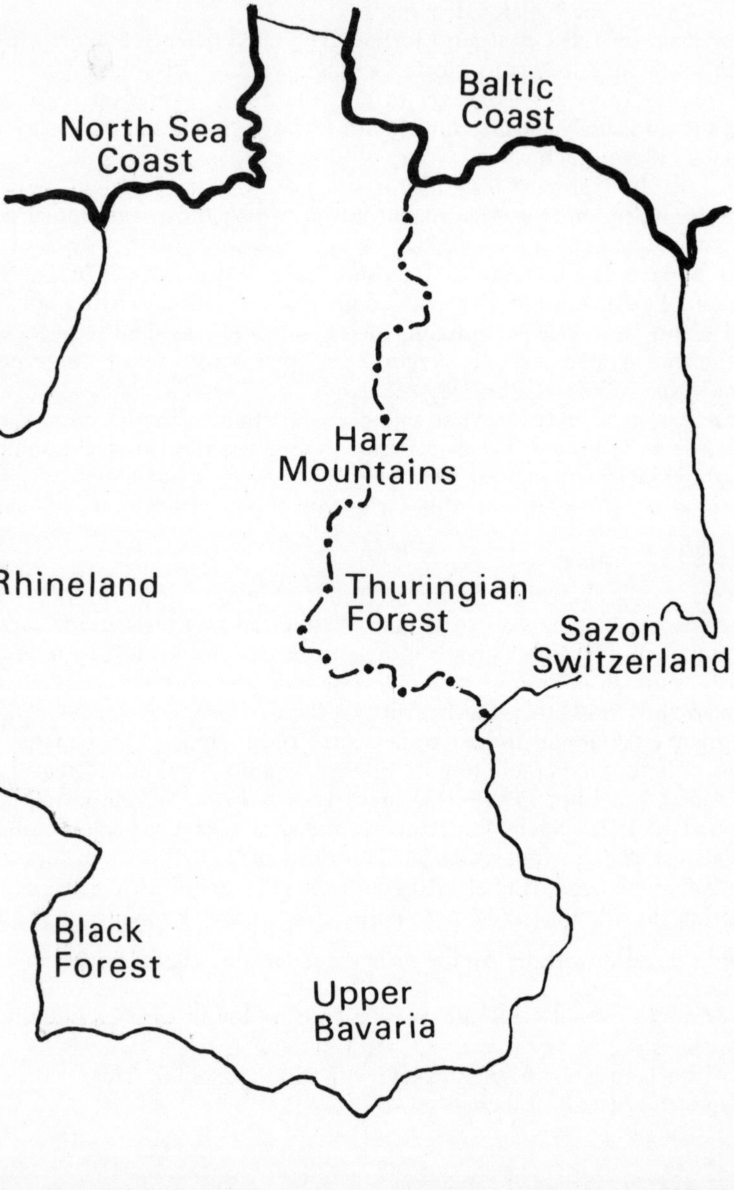

Fig 50 The Rhineland. This photo (from the German Tourist Information Bureau) shows the Lorelei Rock, where an enchantress is said to have lured sailors to their doom.

Foreign tourists also insist, of course, on visiting the main German cities. Munich, Hamburg and Berlin are particularly popular. Berlin alone has over three hundred hotels, private hotels and pensions.

By British and American standards, German hotels are cheap. Charges per night are around 16 to 18 Mark in first class hotels, 10 to 16 Mark in private hotels and pensions. To these, one must add 2,50 to 3 Mark for breakfast — continental style with rolls and coffee. It is, of course, possible to pay as little as 8 Mark for a room in a small pension, or 60 Mark for a luxury suite in the Berlin Hilton. For a meal, one can expect to pay between 4 and 10 Mark. The more courageous tourist, willing to try local dishes and stews (and the German national speciality, sausages) will find he spends far less than his more cautious compatriots who decide to "play safe" and order Wiener Schnitzel at every meal.

I do not claim to be an expert on German hotels, as I normally stay with friends, but the hotels which I know from personal experience have all been of high standards of cleanliness and service, though service at meals can often be slow. This is apparently due to a lack of hotel and restaurant staff. A German waiter or waitress works particularly long hours and can often be "on the go" from six in the morning until midnight. They have one advantage, however, over their British counterparts: a 10% to 15% service charge is universal practice. Voluntary tipping is limited to "rounding off" the bill to the nearest round figure. This is

84 HOW THEY PLAY

„Das Gepäck des Herrn auf Zimmer 507"

Fig 51 "Take the gentleman's luggage to room 507." Cartoon by Schubert, reproduced from "Junge Welt".

done, incidentally, when the bill is paid, and no tips are left under saucers or plates.

Holidays organised by companies are as popular in Germany as in Britain. According to a 1967 Allensbach poll, of those who went on holiday in 1966, every fifth went on a holiday organised by some such undertaking. The most famous is the Touropa-Scharnow group; it uses its own trains for some of its tours. The best-known travel agents in Germany are Harpag-Lloyd and the DER (Deutsches Reisebüro). Foreign tourists are also helped by a non-profit-making organisation, the Deutsche Zentrale für Fremdenverkehr, which runs the German Tourist Information Bureau in London and the German Tourist Information Office in New York. It should be stressed that these offices do not supply tickets or make reservations.

East Germany

In East Germany, the organised holiday is even more popular than in the West. Holidays are organised by the youth organisations and the trade unions at spectacularly low cost to the participants. A 13-day trade union holiday costs between thirty and a hundred Mark. Young people are attracted by the holiday camps run under the auspices of the GST (Society for Sport and Technics) and are prepared to put up with a small amount of military training that is part of any GST holiday. Both young and old appear to find cruises enjoyable; the two East German holiday ships "Fritz Heckert" and "Völkerfreundschaft" are very popular.

It is, however, easy to lose perspective when reading about these holidays. Although over a million East Germans spend a holiday in a trade union group each year, this still represents only a seventeenth of the population. A further 200,000 East Germans take holidays run by the state travel agency, "Reisebüro der DDR", and 600,000 go abroad to the other "socialist countries". Czechoslovakia is by far the most popular, with Poland in second place. Many old-age pensioners visit relatives in West Germany.

Official statistics state that 659,268 foreign tourists visited East Germany in 1966; of these, however, 223,848 were seeing the country only by means of a short city tour (presumably in Berlin) or in transfers. Most of the visitors (369,781) came from the other "socialist countries". Western countries from which the GDR attracts tourists include, in order of importance, Sweden, Denmark, France and Britain. The average length of stay by foreign tourists (excluding those on city tours) is three days.

What does the foreign tourist go to see in East Germany? Many go to the

Fig 52 The beach at Warnemünde. Beach-baskets like these are found at many continental resorts, often with their backs to the sea and the wind. Photo: Lex Hornsby & Partners.

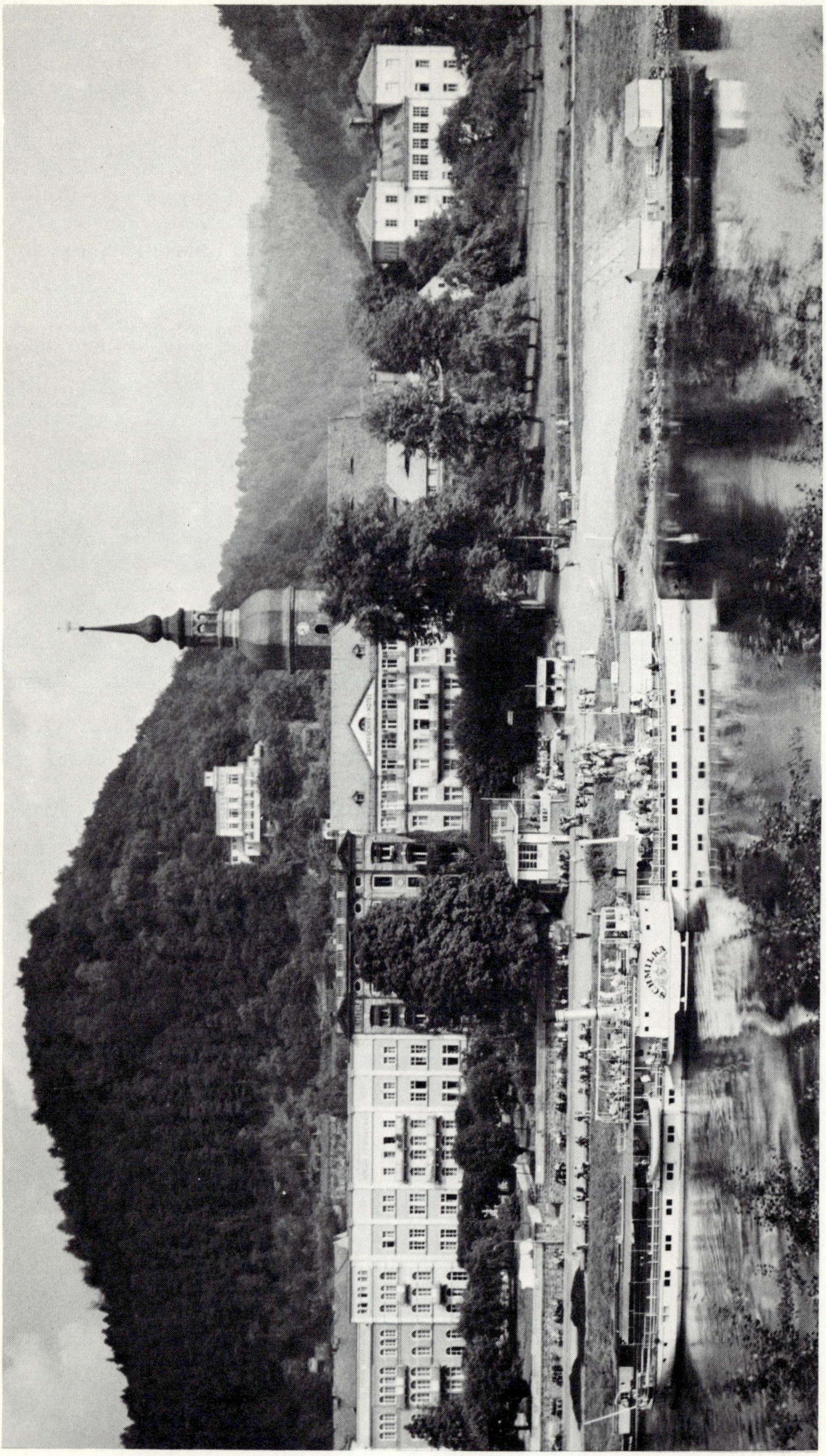
SCHMILKA

Fig 53   Saxon Switzerland — the Elbe at Bad Schandau. Photo: Lex Hornsby & Partners.

Leipzig Trade Fair, and many more to East Berlin with its famous museums and theatres. Apart from these towns, the best-known regions are:
— the Baltic Coast, with the seaside resorts Warnemünde, Kühlungsborn and Zinnowitz. The sea is tideless, and bathing is possible at all times;
— the remainder of the Harz Mountains, with legendary rocks and caverns;
— the Thuringian Forest, with wooded mountains and fast-flowing rivers;
— "Saxon Switzerland" and the Erzgebirge (Ore Mountains) in the South-East, with table mountains and fortresses.

Few people in Britain realise how easy it is to get a tourist visa for East Germany. Hotel accommodation is scarce, and one therefore has to book all hotels in advance. But apart from this, there is no more form-filling until one reaches the border. Hotel prices are fixed by law according to the category of the hotel, and foreign tourists have to pay for full board in advance (in foreign currency, which East Germany badly needs). As soon as you reach the border, however, money for all meals is refunded, so that you may buy meals either in your own hotel or elsewhere. Such refunds must be spent while in the country, and the money will not be changed back into foreign currency.

In some towns, third-class hotels are available at £1 13s 4d (US $ 4,00) per day, but mostly tourists must take second class at £2 9s 6d (US $ 6,00) or first class at £2 17s 9d (US $ 7,00). In many of the major centres, there are also luxury hotels at £4 10s 9d (US $ 11) per day. These prices sound high until one realises that the refunds for meals are £1 4s 0d for third class, £1 12s 0d for second, £1 16s 0d for first and £2 10s 0d for luxury class hotels.

Fig 54   A luxury hotel in Leipzig. Photo: Lex Hornsby & Partners.

Service in the southern part of East Germany is even slower than in the West, because of the even more acute shortage of staff. Prices are worked out to the nearest Pfennig, so that "rounding off" the bill is a convenience for the customer as well as pleasing the waiter.

The Reisebüro der DDR is keen to help foreign tourists plan their holidays in East Germany, though some of its branch offices in East Germany are less helpful than one would wish. Their London branch (known as Berolina Travel Ltd) is much more conscious of the need for customer service.

Attracting foreign tourists to East Germany is, however, no easy job. In 1963, a joke circulated in Eastern Europe about a lottery said to have been organised by a Polish radio station. First prize: one week's holiday in East Germany. Second prize: two weeks' holiday in East Germany.

Excuses for a celebration

Those foreigners who describe the Germans as a dour, humourless nation have not seen them celebrate. They have a peculiar talent for changing their whole nature and "letting themselves go" to join in the spirit of whatever they are celebrating. German visitors to Britain often despair of the stolid British party that consists of standing in groups, sipping cocktails and trying to make conversation. The Germans, on the other hand, regard parties primarily as an occasion for dancing and for feasting and drinking.

The calendar year opens in Germany with a two-month Carnival season. This does not mean that the whole country is involved in Carnival throughout this period; only a small proportion of the population attend the earlier Carnival dances and the festivities of the various Carnival societies. But when the season reaches its climax on the weekend before Shrove Tuesday, nearly everyone becomes involved (at least in Southern Germany and the Rhineland). The Thursday is known as Women's Carnival, and on this day the women go out celebrating together. On the Saturday and Sunday evenings, private parties are held that frequently last all night. Others attend the fancy-dress Carnival balls organised by the societies. There are also "Carnival Sessions", at which humorous speeches are made and special Carnival songs are sung. On the Monday there is a huge

Fig 55 "May I have the pleasure?" Carnival cartoon by Schubert, reproduced from "Junge Welt".

„Darf ich bitten?"

fancy-dress parade, and many of the onlookers dress up too. In all the pubs, the Monday and Tuesday are days of general celebration, as the guests link arms and sway from side to side singing the Carnival songs. Then, on Ash Wednesday, the season is suddenly over, and it is tradition that a fish meal should be eaten. In Munich, it is the custom to go to a fountain and wash out your empty purse! In this city, incidentally, the season is not called Carnival but "Fasching"; in Swabia it is known as "Fasnet" and includes the Fools' Dance, a procession of members of the Fools' Guilds (which date back to the days of court jesters) wearing enormous masks.

Fig 56   Carnival in Münster. Photo: Glyn Hatherall.

Good Friday is kept more strictly in Germany than in Britain; no shops are open. On Easter Morning, the Easter Eggs are not put on the breakfast table, but are hidden in the garden where the children have to search for them; they are often brightly coloured and may even have pictures painted on them. Traditionally, it is the Easter Hare who has hidden them. Chocolate eggs are on sale in Germany as in Britain; one can also buy chocolate Easter hares.

May Day is the workers' festival, and there are processions in the towns and

EXCUSES FOR A CELEBRATION

Fig 57 Many German customs involve beer-drinking, and beer-mugs of all shapes and sizes are required. This page from a manufacturer's catalogue (Ambert KG, 5410 Höhr-Grenzhausen, Postfach 210) shows four of the sizes available and lists others. "Hohlboden" means "Hollow base".

villages. In Bochum the apprentices have a special procession which dates back to 1398.

Ascension Day is also Father's Day. The men go out together to the pubs, and often come home the worse for drink. I can clearly remember lying awake in bed in Germany one Father's Day and hearing the revellers come home singing long after midnight. Mother's Day is the second Sunday in May, and is celebrated with present-giving.

Whitsun is the main time for "Schützenfeste", marksmen's contests accompanied by a fun-fair. In the middle of the fair-ground there is always a large marquee; this is a temporary pub, and there is nearly always a band playing songs for the drinkers to "join in and sing".

Corpus Christi is a religious festival observed in most Catholic areas with a procession; children who have recently been confirmed join in the procession in their navy blue suits and white dresses.

At any time during the summer, but particularly on or near the third Sunday in October, churches celebrate "Kirmes". Traditionally, this is the church anniversary, but it is often combined with a harvest festival. It is an occasion for gay decorations and for dancing in the streets, and the participants are by no means limited to the members of the congregation.

St Martin's Day, 3 November, is celebrated with lantern processions by the children, who sing special songs for the occasion.

Advent is celebrated by lighting candles indoors, one on each of the four Sundays in Advent. They are normally made into an Advent wreath, which is either put on a table or hung from the ceiling.

On St Nicholas' Day (the night of 5/6 December), the Saint is said to leave small presents, particularly fruit and nuts, in the children's shoes for them to find next morning.

Christmas For a German, Christmas means Christmas Eve. At six or seven in the evening, the housewife will call the members of the family into the living-room, which she has kept locked all day. They find the room decorated and lit with candles, and on the table are a number of plates, one for each member of the family. The plates are piled high with sweets, chocolates, nuts, biscuits and fruit. Either by the plates or under the Christmas Tree are the gifts for all members of the family. In the south, it is traditionally the Christ-child who has brought the gifts, whereas in the north it is Father Christmas. The Christmas Tree — a German custom introduced to Britain by Prince Albert — is nearly always decorated with real candles rather than artificial lights. After the members of the family have joined in the best-known of all German carols, "Silent night, holy night", they wish each other a happy Christmas and open their presents. The celebrations are normally kept within the family circle in the narrowest sense of the word — even grandparents are not always welcome if they do not live in the same house. Many families go together to the special Christmas services in Church. There is no Christmas pudding in Germany, but there is a kind of Christmas cake known as Stollen. In the north, goose is a traditional Christmas dish.

New Year's Eve rounds the year off with a grand party, and the new year is welcomed with fireworks. This is also the time for fortune-telling; one popular method is to pour molten lead into a saucer of water and interpret the shape the lead takes as it sets.

Fig 58 Germans everywhere insist on celebrating Christmas Eve. Cartoon by Werner Brähne, reproduced from the Desch Collection.

Fig 59 Real candles on the Christmas Tree. Photo: Press & Information Office, Bonn.

Local customs

Apart from the customs described above, which apply in many parts of the country, Germany is rich in local customs.

In Münster, the children dance round a pyramid of lanterns on St Lambertus' Day (17 September). The lanterns are made from hollowed-out beetroots. While they are dancing, the children sing songs associated with St Lambertus.

In Heidelberg, the fourth Sunday in Lent (Lätare) is celebrated by a procession of children carrying hazel wands sprigged with violets and hung with eggs, apples and "Brezeln" (cakes or buns twisted into a double ring).

At the end of the summer the Rhineland villagers celebrate their wine festivals, to which visitors come from miles around. The largest, such as Königswinter and Braubach, attract trainloads of people from Cologne and the Ruhr. Wine is sold by the glass in the streets, and there are vintners' processions.

Dürkheim, in the Palatinate, has a famous Sausage Market every September. Apart from the sale of sausages, this is also a huge fair-ground and boasts the largest barrel in the world, with a capacity of 1,700,000 litres (453,000 US gallons or 374,000 British gallons). The barrel is used as a restaurant, where excellent wine is served.

On 24 August every year, the village of Markgrönningen in Baden-Württemberg celebrates its famous "Shepherds' Race"; the shepherd lads and girls run barefoot, the latter carrying pots of water on their heads.

Another custom in the Baden area is connected with harvest. A glass of water is placed on the edge of planks above the dancing harvesters. If a girl wants to compete for a live cockerel, she must lift up her partner at the right time for him to knock over the glass.

Fig 60 Local customs

Dinkelsbühl, in Bavaria, celebrates a "Children's Tribute" every year in July. Dances and a historical play commemorate a deputation of children who saved the town from destruction by the Swedes during the Thirty Years' War.

The little town of Furth near the Czech border is the scene of an annual "Dragon's Fight" at Corpus Christi. A realistic dragon is done to death in the middle of the town.

Two Munich festivals are worthy of mention, and both are connected with beer. In March, Munich marks the start of the Salvator (beer) season; the guests of honour taste the first barrel in the morning, and in the afternoon everyone goes to the Salvator premises. Munich is better known for its October Festival, which takes place — ironically enough — at the end of September. This is held on the St Theresa Meadows, and attracts several million visitors. In theory it is an agricultural exhibition, but most of the visitors go for the beer, which flows freely in the beer-halls erected by the Munich breweries. Bavarian brass bands supply a musical background.

Fig 61   Munich's October Festival. Photo: James G Maguire, Dublin.

There are many more local customs, and they are described in books devoted entirely to this subject. Before leaving this topic, I will mention one rural custom, in the Alps. The cattle that have been grazing on the upper pastures all summer are led down to the valley in the autumn adorned with ribbons, artificial flowers and huge bells. The cows lead the way, followed by the calves, then the oxen, with the herdsman and his wife bringing up the rear.

East Germany

The political division of the country is still too recent an event to have made much effect on national customs, and most of what was said in the early part of this chapter applies to East Germany also. A festival of which more is made in East Germany is, of course, May Day. Every village celebrates, and in farming areas there is a custom of decorating the tractors. East Berlin has a large parade on the Moscow pattern.

In some areas of East Germany, the girls go to a stream on Easter morning and collect water in a jar. Provided they have not spoken while doing so, if they wash in this water it is supposed to keep them beautiful all year.

In the Harz Mountains, there is a "Grass Procession", in which young girls parade with sheaves of grass and garlands.

The Sorb minority, numbering about a hundred thousand, have their own customs. On the Thursday before Easter they celebrate the "Birds' Wedding"; young people go singing from house to house with garlands adorned with eggs and ribbons. The householders reward them with light refreshments and sweets.

Public holidays

Businessmen may wish to note the following summary of public holidays, for there is little point arranging to visit a German town if one's business associates will not be at work. National public holidays in West Germany are New Year's Day, Good Friday, Easter Monday, May Day, Ascension Day, Whit Monday, the Day of German Unity (17 June), the Day of Repentance and Prayer (a Wednesday towards the end of November), Christmas Day and Boxing Day. In Baden-Württemberg and Bavaria, 6 January is also a public holiday, and 8 August in Augsburg. Many Catholic areas keep Corpus Christi and All Saints' Day (1 November) as public holidays; the same applies in the Saarland and parts of Bavaria to the feast of the Assumption of Our Lady (15 August).

Although there are no official public holidays for Carnival, many offices — particularly in the Rhineland — are in a rather chaotic state on Shrove Tuesday and the day preceding it.

In East Germany the public holidays are New Year's Day, Good Friday, May Day, Whit Monday, Republic Day (7 October), Christmas Day and Boxing Day.

THEIR GOVERNMENT AND INSTITUTIONS

Government and politics

From the habits of the individual German, our attention now turns to Germany as a country, to the state structure and its institutions.

West Germany is a federal state consisting of ten regions or "Länder". The characteristics of each "Land" will be discussed in a chapter entitled "Looking at a map". What concerns us here is the collection of regions together, the country as a whole and its central administration.

The Head of State in West Germany is the Federal President. He is independent of all political parties and may not hold any other paid post during his term of office. He has far less power than the President of the USA. His duties include representing his country abroad, meeting foreign dignitaries and signing laws. He also appoints the Federal Judges.

There are two chambers in the parliament, the Bundestag (lower house) being the more important because it is elected by direct mandate. The upper house (Bundesrat) consists of representatives of the different Länder.

The lower house consists of 496 individually-elected members from the Federal Republic and 22 from West Berlin. Because of Berlin's four-power status, the West Berlin members have no voting power. The members from West Germany are elected by a complicated process devised by a Belgian called d'Hondt. What it amounts to is that half the members are elected by constituencies, while the other half are elected on a party list basis. Each voter thus has two votes: one for a person to represent his constituency and one for a party list.

In most cases, the lower house can pass what laws it likes, and the upper house can only delay matters while the bill is discussed by a joint committee formed of members of both houses. Only if it is proposed to change the constitution, or if the finances or powers of individual Länder are affected, can the upper house stop a bill completely.

The leader of the government is the Federal Chancellor. This is the man in whom real power is vested. He appoints his cabinet of ministers, and with them he determines Government policy. Each minister has more power than his British counterpart, for any new German law must be signed, not only by the President, but also by the Chancellor and by the Minister concerned.

Political parties have long names, and are consequently known by their initials.

CDU (Christlich-Demokratische Union) The Christian Democratic Union has held the political reins since 1945. It emerged as a party based on the old Catholic Centre Party of the Weimar Republic. After the war, it was clear that a Catholic party could not obtain a majority, and thus an alliance with the Protestants was formed. By 1968 Catholic members were in a 3:2 majority. Until 1963, the reins were held by Konrad Adenauer, who with the help of his economics minister Ludwig Erhard brought the country from devastation to prosperity. He also led West Germany further and further away from the East. Erhard's rule as Chancellor lasted less than four years (1963-6) before he was forced to hand over to the Swabian Kurt Georg Kiesinger. In Bavaria, the party goes under a slightly different name, the Christian Socialist Union (CSU) and is led by a fiery orator, Franz-Josef Strauss. He was involved in the arrest of the "Spiegel" editors in

Fig 62 Franz-Josef Strauss (right) congratulates Kurt-Georg Kiesinger on the latter's nomination as CDU candidate for the Chancellorship in 1966. Many observers felt that Kiesinger owed his nomination to Strauss' influence. Photo: Associated Press.

1962 (see chapter on "The printed word"), and was forced by public opinion to resign as Defence Minister. He rejoined the cabinet in 1966.

SPD (Sozialdemokratische Partei Deutschlands) The Social Democrats, after many years in opposition, joined the coalition government in December 1966. They claim roots in the last century, but the most important date in their history is 1959. At that year's conference (in Bad Godesberg) they ditched all remnants of socialism and there is now little to distinguish CDU from SPD policy. The present SPD position is a shade to the right of the British Labour Party. (It was thus rather ironic that Chancellor Kiesinger, on a visit to London in October 1967 should accuse the Labour Party of conservatism.) At first, the SPD opposed West Germany's rearmament, but later agreed to the CDU proposals for full integration with NATO. The party headquarters in Bonn are in temporary accommodation; this, the party explains, is because they still regard Berlin as the true capital. This gimmick is now getting a bit worn.

FDP (Freie Demokratische Partei) The Free Democrats became the main opposition party in 1966 when the CDU-SPD coalition was formed. They call themselves liberals, but differ from the British Liberal Party in their dependence upon big business for support and in the absence of co-ownership from their programme. They advocate massive state support for various sections of the community, but nevertheless their electoral performance in recent years has shown a steady decline.

DFU (Deutsche Friedens-Union) Because the West German constitution requires a party to obtain 5% of the total votes in the country before it can be represented in parliament, the German Peace Union has not been represented in recent parliaments. It is a rather odd mixture. It undoubtedly contains many Communists, and in the eyes of some it took over the role of the Communist Party when the latter was banned by the Federal Constitutional Court in 1956. However, the DFU also contains non-communist intellectuals who see it as the only anti-militarist party. In the 1961 elections, the DFU used Albert Schweitzer's picture on its posters.

NPD (Nationaldemokratische Partei Deutschlands) The only party whose star has really been in the ascendancy in recent years has been the National Democrats, formed in 1964. There had been right-wing extremist parties before, but the NPD has so far been more successful than they ever were. They are often called the neo-Nazis, but one should in all fairness point to the absence of anti-Semitism from their programme. Many people fear that a continued rise in the strength of the NPD could be very dangerous. In 1968, their strength in the country as a whole was around 6%.

Election day in Germany is very different from its British counterpart. The system of sending cars for voters is unknown — indeed, so is the whole canvassing process. The Germans seem to have a feeling that asking somebody how he is going to vote is a serious threat to democracy. As a result, the amount of work done at election time by unpaid volunteers is much less than in Britain; most of the work is done by paid assistants. I once went to a German local party office, and offered my assistance for a forthcoming campaign. Instead of giving me a few hundred envelopes to address (as a British election agent certainly would have done) they told me that they had enough paid help laid on. Most of the money goes on elaborate multi-colour posters, which are stuck on hoardings and lamp-posts, not in supporters' windows. There is no restriction on putting more than one poster on any lamp-post, and I can remember being most amused on one occasion at a row of lamp-posts on a bridge in Cologne; each lamp-post had no less than four posters, and each poster was for a different party. The posters were thus destroying each other's effect, and were a complete waste of money.

In answer to the question, "Generally speaking, are you interested in politics?", Allensbach pollsters in 1965 received 39% affirmative answers, 43% "not particularly" and 18% "not at all". But the number of those who are interested is steadily increasing; in 1952 it was only 27%, and in 1960 only 30%. Nevertheless, in 1964 only 19% of the participants in another Allensbach poll said that they frequently discussed politics. When asked in 1965 if they would like their own son to become a politician (imagining, if necessary, that they had a son), 51% replied definitely not, 35% that they were undecided, and only 14% that they would welcome such a decision on their offspring's part.

When asked in 1965 what they considered the most important political question, 47% said "reunification", 27% "economic problems, wages, prices, currency" and 10% "East-West detente". Most Germans seem to be reasonably optimistic about the long-term prospects for reunification; in 1965, 53% said they believed it would come about by peaceful means one day, but that it would probably take many years. Only 5% believed it would come about within five years, and 37% did not believe it would ever come about by peaceful means. Meanwhile, the majority (69% in 1964) are opposed to recognising East Germany.

Support for recognition of the East comes mainly from the left-wing intellectuals who are opposed to all major parties. Indeed, it has often been said that the true opposition in West Germany today is outside the party political set-up. It is the intellectuals, the writers and the students who come out most fiercely against the sacred cows of West German official attitudes. But their role is far more that of the professional dissenter than that of the politician making concrete alternative proposals. Their mouthpieces have been the magazines, notably "Der Spiegel" and satirical organs like "Pardon". Sometimes, they are allowed to run television programmes for a number of months or years; among the most renowned recently have been "Panorama" and "Hello, Neighbour". Such programmes frequently hit the headlines, often because the producers have presented an over-biased case for one or other of the anti-government intellectual viewpoints.

By the beginning of 1968, however, student opinion was swinging noticeably towards the left and adopting more sensationalist tactics — thus forfeiting the support of the middle-of-the-road intellectuals and the "Spiegel". Only time will tell whether the student movement holds the seeds of a rebirth of true Socialism in West Germany.

East Germany

In theory, the central power in East Germany is in the hands of the parliament, known as the People's Chamber. This body is elected on the basis of a party list system, but a single list is drawn up for all the parties by a body known as the National Front, to which all parties belong.

The party with effective control is the Socialist Unity Party (SED) which was formed as a result of a merger in 1946 between the Communists and the Social Democrats. Its First Secretary is Walter Ulbricht.

All other parties are designed to appeal to specific sections of the community while supporting the same policies as the SED. These are the Liberal Democrats (LDPD), the remnants of the old liberals, the Christian Democrats (CDU) for Christians who support the regime, the Farmers' Party (DBD) and the National Democrats (NDPD) who are mostly former Hitler officers and soldiers, or former Nazis who in the words of an official booklet "have broken with their past".

Fig 63 "Praise for the Working Class and its party — the Socialist Unity Party of Germany." Such slogans are a common sight in East Germany; this one I saw on a factory wall in Rostock. "We just ignore them", a rather cynical East German friend once told me. Photo: author.

In addition to these parties, the mass organisations are also represented in the parliament. These are the youth organisation (FDJ), women's organisation (DFB), trade unions (FDGB) and cultural organisation (DKB).

The number of seats which each party or organisation receives is determined, not by the voter, but by the National Front. This body presents a list to the voter who has the power to affirm it as a whole or to strike out names he does not like. He is encouraged to do the former, and to do so by open affirmation of his support. Incredible as it might seem, the members elected are not those with the most votes, but those placed highest on the list, which is compiled in advance. This often amazes the outsider, but is laid down by law. A candidate can lose his seat only if he is struck off the list by over half the electorate — and as strong pressure is exerted to accept the list as it stands, this is officially admitted to be virtually impossible in practice. Polling day in East Germany, therefore, decides nothing. East German authorities make much of the democratic way in which candidates must address public meetings and gain support there before being nominated. Never having witnessed such a meeting, I am unable to judge; but if British adoption meetings are anything to go by, the chances of a candidate losing his nomination must be remote.

This section opened with the words "in theory", and a point should be made here that there are two other important organs in the state apparatus. These are the State Council and the Council of Ministers. The State Council replaced the Presidency on the death of the first President, Wilhelm Pieck; it has wide powers of policy making, and often the People's Chamber merely rubber-stamps decisions made by the State Council. The Council of Ministers is an executive organ, carrying out the instructions of the parliament and State Council. Many decisions seem to be taken by the Chairman of the State Council — the SED party boss Walter Ulbricht.

Fig 64 Walter Ulbricht (left) takes the oath of office after his re-election as Chairman of the State Council in 1967. Photo: Lex Hornsby & Partners.

Schools and colleges

Few government institutions have as much influence on a national way of life as an education system. In West Germany, educational administration is in the hands of the regional ("Länder") Ministries of Culture, though policy is co-ordinated by a Standing Conference with permanent offices in Bonn.

German children start school at the age of six. Official handbooks do not give the number of nursery schools; I have the impression that they are more common in Germany than in Britain. But in the German primary schools ("Volksschulen") there is no gradual transition from play to work as there is in Britain. German teachers seem uninterested in the play-school ideas of Montessori or Froebel. True, on the first morning, the German child is given a paper cone filled with sweets, and the whole day is one of celebration — but then work starts in earnest.

The school a German child will attend after his primary education is completed depends to a certain extent on where he lives. The individual "Länder" have more autonomy than British education authorities, and there is no national policy on comprehensives. Most areas have a tripartite system, one of the constituent parts being the Volksschule itself. The least able children stay at the Volksschule until the end of their school career. Thus the upper classes of the Volksschule are in some ways similar to the British Secondary Moderns.

At the age of ten, however, the German child can transfer to one of two other types of school. One is the "Realschule" (or "Mittelschule" as some Länder call it), which is rather along the lines of the technical schools envisaged in Britain's 1944 Act but seldom realised. The other type is the grammar school (called either "Oberschule" or "Gymnasium") which takes pupils up to the age of 18 or 19.

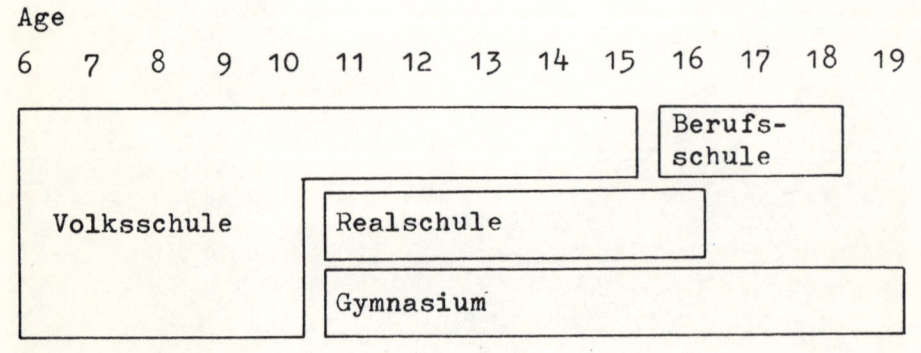

Fig 65 West German schools: the basic pattern

At either of these schools, the 16 year olds may take an examination known as the "Mittlere Reife". This is sometimes compared to Britain's "O level", but the comparison is misleading. The German qualification is based either on work done throughout the year or on an internal examination. There is no external examining board. Like the "O level", however, it is an assessment of work in a large number of subjects, but it is not possible to pass in merely one or two. You have to be an all-rounder to get your "Mittlere Reife".

The pupil at the "Gymnasium" aims at completing his education with the "Abitur" exam. Again, the comparison with the British equivalent (the "A level") is misleading. The Abitur requires attainment of a certain standard in written and oral examination in several subjects. The exam is conducted by the schools, but under the general control of the education authorities. Whoever has passed his Abitur exam has the right to sign on at any German university he likes. Maintaining this principle in an age of mass education has led to serious overcrowding problems at many universities, and a few medical and scientific faculties have had to introduce a limit to the number of students they will take on each year. Though such limits are common practice in other countries, many German professors feel that introducing them in Germany is a negation of a centuries-old academic freedom.

At all types of school, the pupils must be on their toes the whole time if they want to succeed. Instead of termly or annual examinations, there are frequent "Klassenarbeiten" (class tests which may take up as many as five consecutive school periods). Students whose work in these is not up to standard — even if only in two or three subjects — will have to remain in the same form the following year. A warning that the work is unsatisfactory is sent to parents some months in advance. Such letters are sent in official envelopes, traditionally blue in colour, and are known as blue letters. There must be few Germans who have completed their school career without their parents having received one of these communications.

German pupils do not have such freedom of subject choices as their British counterparts. There is no system of "subject sets"; the class remains together as a unit for the whole timetable. In the Gymnasium, only a minimum of specialisation is allowed. A whole school or stream is either Classical (concentrating on Latin and Greek), Modern Language (concentrating on English and French) or Mathematical-Scientific. This has the disadvantage of giving less choice than the British system. On the other hand, it makes for a stronger form spirit; a German's "Klassenkamarad" can be a friend for life.

School hours are normally from 8 am to 1 pm. There is no school meals service, for the children go home to lunch. They work a six-day week, Monday to Saturday.

There is little social life at a German school. They have no prefect system, but the school elects its Head Boy ("Schulsprecher") and each form has a form captain ("Klassensprecher"). Some schools have a committee representing all the forms. Frequently, a class will go with its form teacher for a day's hiking outing. Class holidays take place during term time; these may be at a hostel owned by the school or even abroad.

With few exceptions, West German education authorities tend to be more conservative than those in other countries. The result is a system which, to the outsider, seems backward and full of faults. The percentage of working-class children who reach university is ludicrously small. Since the Abitur is the only formally recognised examination, those who fail to complete a Gymnasium course or who attend Volksschulen or Mittelschulen for their secondary education leave with no real "paper qualifications" — and in some areas only one child in twenty gets his Abitur! Many of the teachers seem aloof, and German visitors to Britain are often surprised at our friendly pupil-teacher relationships. The classical languages have retained too much of their snob value in many schools, and in their history lessons many young Germans learn so much about ancient Egypt and the Greeks that not enough time is left for adequate treatment of post-1930

German history. In country areas the establishment of viable school units has been hindered considerably at primary school level by a conservative adherence to the principle of denominational schooling. Germans themselves agree with many of these criticisms — but the wheels of change grind slowly.

Technical, higher and adult education

Apprentices spend three years on part-time education at a technical school ("Berufsschule"). They normally attend nine hours a week, and at the end of the course they take an examination. Some decide to study at a specialist technical school ("Berufsfachschule") before they start their apprenticeship.

Many apprentices want to take things a little further, and attend part-time at a more advanced "Berufsaufbauschule", from which they may proceed to a specialist college known as a "Fachschule". There are fifty different varieties of Fachschule, including those for agriculture, forestry, building, mining, engineering and welfare work.

For those who wish to go to universities but have not obtained their Abitur, there are special Evening Gymnasia and "Institutes for Obtaining University Entrance Level". Those who wish to learn more without taking examinations can go to any of over a thousand People's Universities ("Volkshochshulen") offering a wide range of adult education courses. Germany is also well endowed with language schools of every size and description.

In 1966, German universities and other institutions of university status had a total of 266,870 German and 23,406 foreign students. 76·2% of these were at the nineteen universities, 21·5% at the nine technical universities, 1·3% at single-faculty colleges with university status, and 1% in theological colleges.

The German university student has greater freedom than his British counterpart. In most faculties he can study for as long as he wishes before taking his final exam, and he has almost complete freedom in putting together his own course from the many lectures and seminars available. This poses a problem to many freshmen, who do not know where to start — and many universities give surprisingly little guidance in this respect.

Nearly half the students (48%) are in the faculties of Arts or Social Sciences. The remainder are divided almost equally between the technical faculties (15%), natural science (16%) and medicine (16%).

Financially, German students get a raw deal by British standards. The British student can claim at least a minimum grant almost as if it were his birthright, but the German student is lucky if he gets a grant at all — unless his parents are living on a very low income. Mostly, the parents are the source of a student's basic income, which is supplemented by holiday jobs and, for many students, by term-time jobs as well.

The student societies at German universities are different from those in Britain. Whereas the British "clubs" are mostly concerned with specific interests (such as the Radio Society, the Motor Club or the Wine and Food Club) the German students prefer general organisations. During my own stay at Bonn (1964-5) that university had, apart from the students' union and the faculty societies, a total of 101 student organisations, of which 34 were religious, 11 political, 20 international organisations, 17 miscellaneous and 19 duelling societies. It is this latter group which has earned German students a bad name abroad, since with their pride in their fraternity colours they are distinctly nationalistic in outlook. The aim of the "duelling" is not to defeat your opponent, but to show courage by standing still while he hits you with his sword. This is supposed to be character-developing — but to my mind, the type of "character" developed is not wholly desirable. For-

SCHOOLS AND COLLEGES

tunately, despite the number of fraternities to choose from, this type of activity attracts only a minority of the students.

Most students complete their course with a State Examination, but many go on to take a Doctorate. In future the Master's Degree will become more common, in the attempt to encourage students to study for shorter periods and follow more closely defined courses. Germans with a doctorate like the title to be used by all and sundry. In the early years of the century, the wife of a doctor used to insist on being called "Frau Doktor" although she herself might not have such a degree. Even today, it is easier to call your lawyer and medical practitioner "Herr Doktor" — you need not bother to remember his name. If you don't know whether a German acquaintance has a doctorate or not, call him "Herr Doktor" anyway; if you are wrong, he will correct you — but feel flattered!

East Germany

The basic school in East Germany is the Polytechnic High School, which takes pupils from 6 to 16 and gives them all a comprehensive education. Those who want to study further may do so at an Extended High School for a further two

Fig 66 First day in school for an East German boy. An older pupil explains the textbooks. Photo: Lex Hornsby & Partners.

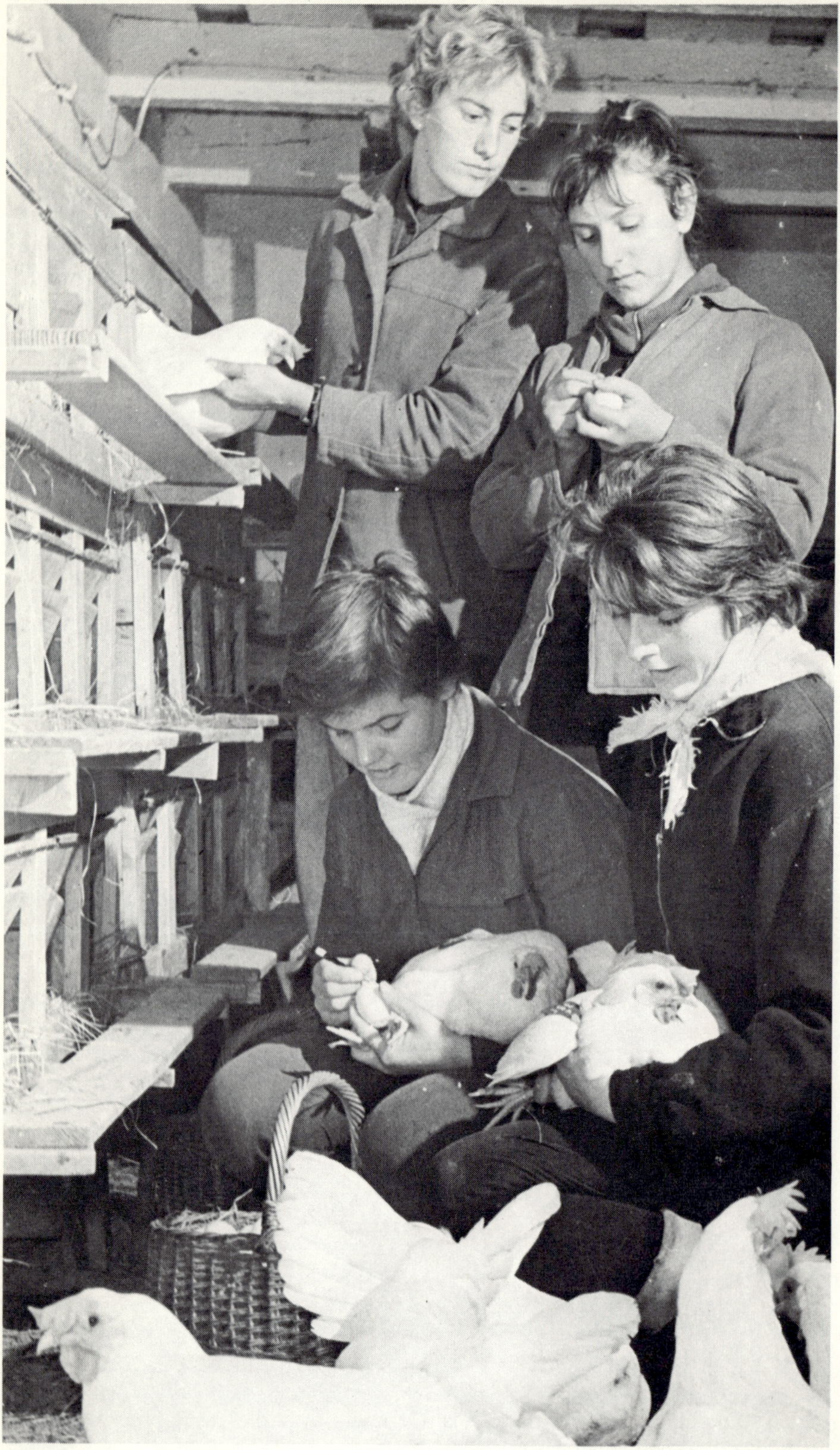

SCHOOLS AND COLLEGES 107

Fig 67 Practical education on a farm. Relating education to life is a strong point in East Germany. Photo: Lex Hornsby & Partners.

years. There are a few special schools for pupils gifted in languages, maths, sport and music.

From the seventh year onwards, one day a week is set aside for practical work in a factory or on a farm (known as the Instruction Day in Socialist Production — the initials in German are UTP). In the final two years, there is also instruction in the theory and practice of one's chosen career. From the ninth school-year on, pupils are paid for the work they do during the UTP. They start at 40 Mark a month, which is increased by 10 Mark per month each year.

There are 49 universities and colleges in East Germany, and in 1966 the total number of students was 106,422. Admission to a university is determined by a selection committee, which has specific instructions to take into account a student's political attitude. All students must include the principles of Marxism-Leninism in their studies.

The ideals of Socialism permeate the education system. For example, schoolchildren are asked during their German lessons to punctuate sentences which reiterate party slogans. Every class has a parents' committee, whose job is to ensure maximum cooperation between home and school. And throughout the system, the children of workers, farmers and Party members are given priority.

Fig 68 This school near Karl-Marx-Stadt is one of many which offer parents a special course to enable them to help their children with their homework. Here they are learning Russian. Photo: Lex Hornsby & Partners.

The church past and present

Of all German institutions, the Church is by far the oldest, and it is the only one which has managed to survive unaltered the upheavals of the present century.

German theologians have a mixed reputation in other countries. On the one hand they are known for brilliant academic probing into the meaning of the Gospels and into the whole concept of the deity; on the other they are accused of boring their congregations with interminable sermons.

Some of the earliest German theologians were also the literary figures and thinkers of their day, and have consequently been omitted from this chapter as they will be mentioned in those on "The literary heritage" and "A nation of thinkers". The most prominent mediaeval theologian was Meister Eckhart (1260-1329); he saw God as the sole reality, outside of Whom every phenomenon is illusory, and into complete union with Whom every believer must try to arrive by means of intensive contemplation. This belief was open to criticism on the grounds that it reflected Oriental mysticism rather than orthodox Pauline and Augustinian Christianity, but Eckhart and his followers were able to name a few "Church Fathers" with whom they had points of contact. One of Eckhart's disciples was Suso, who carried asceticism to a degree that might be described as self-torture. But most of the like-minded thinkers who became known as the Friends of God or Brethren of the Common Life struck a healthier balance between this asceticism and the soft extreme. The anonymous "Theologia Germanica", said to have been written about 1350, stressed contemplation and humility rather than drastic penance. Martin Luther praised it as the most formative book in his life apart from the Scriptures and the works of Augustine.

Luther's career is outlined in a later chapter ("A little history"). He was welcomed as a national champion against the intellectual and financial claims of the Italian clergy, but lost much popular support by dissociating himself from the social demands of the poor. He also lost the friendship of some of his fellow-reformers, who went beyond him in matters of doctrine, particularly where the Eucharist was concerned. The Swiss Zwingli and the Frenchman Calvin won a fair number of supporters in Germany, who laid claim to the specific title "Reformed" for their congregations and formulae, whereas "Evangelical" and "Protestant" came to be terms reserved for the Lutherans. One of Luther's colleagues, Andreas Bodenstein (known as Carlstadt) left him to follow the Anabaptists, whom Luther persistently confused with the Zwinglian church although it had harshly suppressed them. The Anabaptists embraced all manner of dissidents, who today would probably be scattered among the Pentecostalists, the Quakers, Jehovah's Witnesses and the Communist Party. The Peace of Augsburg (1555) gave rulers the right to determine the religion of their states, but left little freedom of choice to their subjects. Militant reformers of the Anabaptist type were suppressed everywhere, and free thought flowed into harmless mystical channels, under teachers like the visionary cobbler, Jakob Boehme.

The horrors of the Thirty Years' War revealed among members of the Lutheran Church new depths of personal devotion. A pastor named Spener founded groups known as "Colleges of Piety", which gave a name to the movement, and some

THE CHURCH PAST AND PRESENT 109

of his followers wrote fervent hymns which have taken firm root in England, partly in Wesley translations.

The celebrated German modernism known as "Higher Criticism" dates from the early 18th century, although French and English sceptics contributed to it throughout. Attacks on the authenticity of the Bible grew in boldness from the moderate Wolff and Semler through Bahrdt, Lessing, Reimarus, Eichhorn, Paulus and de Wette to the unbridled erosion of Graf and Wellhausen in the eighteen-seventies. But conservative Biblical scholarship was never suppressed; the height of the 19th century modernism still permitted the work of Delitzsch on the Psalms, Keim on the New Testament and Hengstenberg on the Prophets. Meanwhile, a more subtle encroachment on orthodoxy took place in the subjective, individualistic devotion promoted by Ritschl and Schleiermacher. This

Fig 69 Wayside crucifixes are a common sight in Bavaria and the Black Forest. One of the excuses for their erection is that they mark spots where road accidents have occurred. Photo: German Tourist Information Bureau.

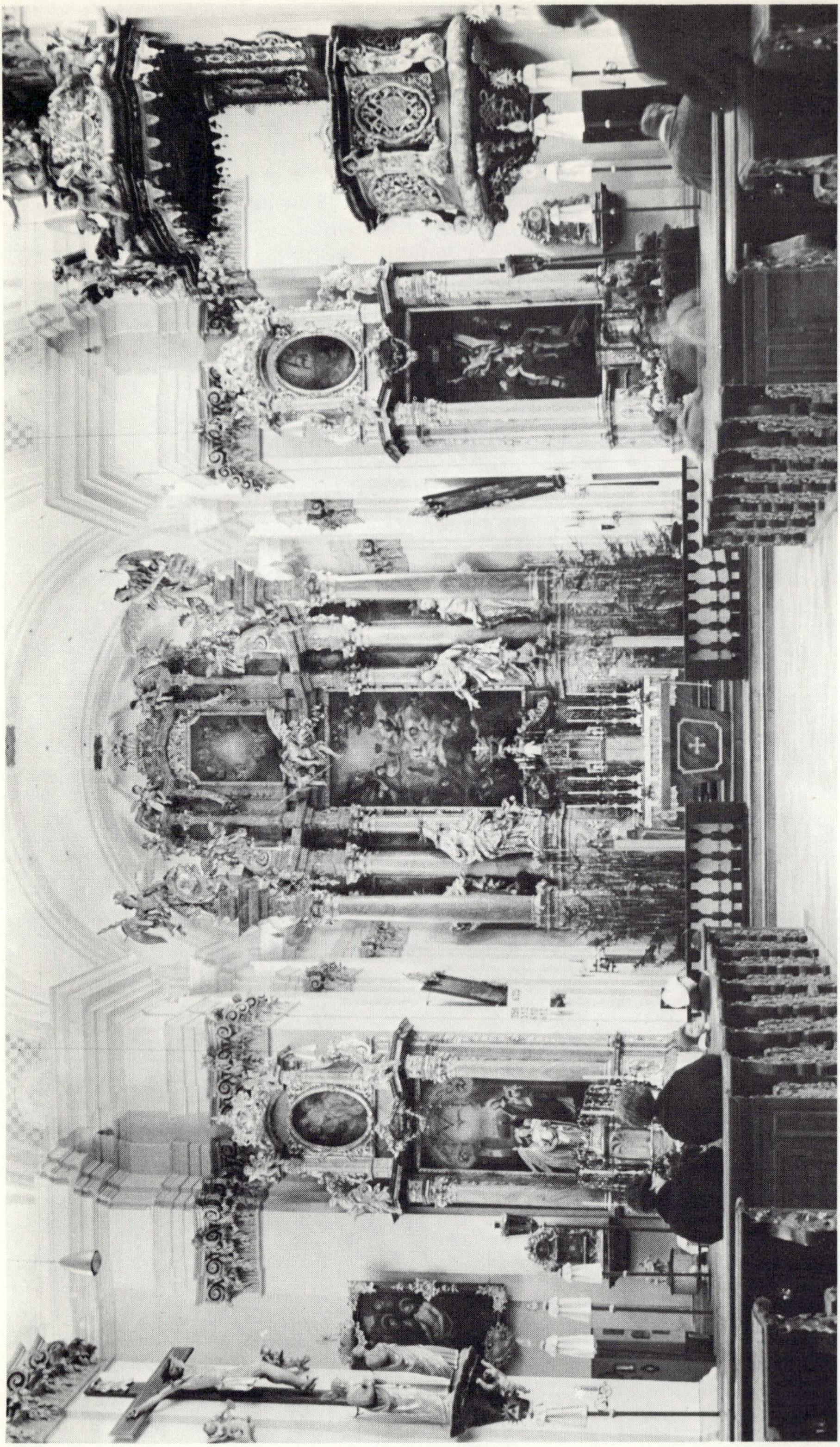

Fig 70 Baroque church in Bavaria. Photo: Glyn Hatherall.

was the nearest equivalent to the Pietism of an earlier age, but further divorced from any dogmatic confession of faith. In our present century, the debate has been led by the Swiss theologians Barth and Brunner, the American Niebuhr and the German-American Tillich, who is best known for his attempts to unite philosophy and theology in his "systematic theology".

The contemporary situation

An Allensbach poll in 1949 asked the simple question, "Do you believe in God?" This was answered in the affirmative by 78% of the people questioned. Only 6% gave a straight "No". 10% replied "Yes, according to my own conception, not according to dogmatic church teaching", and 6% gave no reply.

Ever since the 16th century, Germany has been split in two by the division between Protestants and Catholics. According to official statistics, 50% of the West German population is Protestant, 45% Catholic and 3% members of other religious communities. But these figures take no account of those whose link with their Church is purely nominal, and they ignore regional divergences. Bavaria and the Rhineland are largely Catholic areas; Hesse and the northern areas predominantly Protestant. Allensbach polls in 1953, 1954 and 1964 are consistent in showing that total churchgoing is around 35% of the population — considerably higher than in Britain, but still making nonsense of the quoted membership of the Churches.

Confirmation (for Protestants) and First Communion (for Catholics) are the two main religious ceremonies affecting young people in Germany. For both, the boys wear dark blue suits and the girls snow-white or black dresses, according to regional variation. The girls wear a myrtle garland, and the boys a sprig of myrtle

Fig 71 Modern church interior, Münster. Photo: Glyn Hatherall.

in their button-holes. After the ceremony the whole family gathers for a party. Friends and relatives give presents, often books of a religious nature or autograph albums. Girls may also receive jewellery, money or even something for the "bottom drawer". Cards and flowers are sent by all friends and relations and are often so numerous that parents put a "thank you" advert in the local press. In villages, the front door of a house where a child is celebrating First Communion is decorated with white flowers. In short, the festivities are so elaborate that the social occasion tends to swamp the religious significance — a criticism frequently made of British Christmas.

Sunday in Germany is the "Continental Sunday", a day of pleasure and recreation. Church services start early in the day, and many attend the earlier ones. The afternoon is traditionally taken up with a Sunday afternoon stroll. Cinemas and theatres are open; for restaurants and pubs it is often the busiest day of the week. There is also plenty of professional sport, including football.

The West German churches are less dependent upon voluntary contributions than are their British counterparts. Instead, there is a church tax, payable through the income tax authorities. This has legal force, and amounts to 10% of income tax. Those who do not belong to any church may declare themselves to be agnostic or atheist and pay no tax — but this deprives them of the right to Christian burial. Few are prepared to renounce religion so unequivocally.

East Germany

The East German state demands from its subjects their complete loyalty to the ideals of Socialism; it cannot tolerate any other body which claims their unlimited allegiance. But people are not prevented by force from attending Church. The old are left to worship as they wish, while the young are subjected to a steady flow of anti-Christian propaganda in the schools. Church attendance is seen by East German clergy as encouraging, though it is nothing like the theoretical membership figures (80% Protestant, 11% Catholic).

A Youth Dedication Ceremony has been introduced to take the place of Confirmation. At the ceremony, the youngsters pledge themselves to their country and to Socialism, and they receive a book called "Space, Earth and Man", which interprets world history from a materialist standpoint. The Dedication Ceremony is held on the Sundays which used to be kept for Confirmation, and the churches have had to change the date of their own ceremony.

Financially, the East German church is in a bad way, since church tax has lost its legal force, and the large Church estates which used to provide a considerable revenue were mostly confiscated during the land reform in the late 'fifties. In order to survive, the East German church has to rely on gifts from West Germany.

The unity of the Protestant Church in East and West has long been a bone of contention between Church and State. The Socialist Unity Party insists on a separate-state doctrine, and any organisation which seeks to maintain unity with the West is suspect. However, the Church itself is determined to maintain its unity.

Large sums of money have come from state funds to restore old churches destroyed in the war, and for the Church's social work. But on the whole, the state authorities resent the Church's opposition to their doctrines. At Jena, the university has a chair of Scientific Atheism, and all East German students must study Marxism-Leninism.

An East German pastor explained to me that there is a positive side to all their difficulties. "Our situation here is far more genuine. Being a Christian means something, and there is a demand on one's loyalties which makes decision and commitment essential."

Law and lawbreakers

Whereas British law is based largely on precedent, German law is far more precise. It is based on two books, the Criminal Law Book and the Civil Law Book, originally written at the end of the last century but continually brought up to date (now separately in East and West). These books lay down the minimum and maximum penalties for all offences, and judges' sentences must fall within these limits. Moreover, as a German friend explained, "If you are thinking of committing a crime, you can look it up in the Criminal Law Book first and see how long you'll get for it". The final decision of the judges is based on mitigating circumstances or on circumstances which make the crime more serious.

The accused in a German trial is cross-questioned by the court, not as a witness in his own defence. His relatives do not need to give evidence unless they wish to do so, and even if they do, they will not be under oath. All other witnesses are asked before the trial if they are related to the accused.

Police summonses need not be obeyed; the only body entitled to issue a summons is a court. The police (whether in civvies or in uniform) can enter a house only if they have a warrant or if they have reason to suspect that the criminal will try to escape or to cover up his crime. The police are armed and can use their pistols if a call to stop has been disobeyed and if there is any danger of flight or of the crime being obscured.

All Germans over the age of 16 must have a personal identity card, and the police may demand to see this at any time. It is also useful to banks, etc when they need to have a proof of identity for money transactions. In each town, there is an "Einwohnermeldeamt" (inhabitants' registration office) which must be notified within a week of any change of address.

All limited companies must have a "supervisory council", and the chairman of this council may not be the same person as the managing director. The latter, however, retains control over the firm until such time as he is dismissed by the supervisory council.

All debts expire if the creditor fails to demand repayment within two years. If the creditor sends a warning by registered letter, and the debtor does not reply within a given period stated in the letter, the creditor can ask for a court order of payment. If this, too, is unheeded, the bailiffs automatically move in with powers of confiscation.

In literature put out by German firms, you will sometimes find the words "auf Wunsch". This means literally "on request". It does not mean "you can have it for the asking", but "at extra cost"!

Partners to an agreement frequently fix an "Erfüllungsort", or place at which any disagreement should be taken to court. A German firm can also include in a contract with an employee or agent the clause that he should not go over to a competing firm within three years of leaving their employment. Some British agents of German firms are wary of agreeing to this — but they can do so without hesitation, since German law is not enforceable abroad.

Some German industrial standards have legal backing. Thus it is illegal to use an electric plug which does not bear the sign VDE ("Union of German Electricians"). And the German post office has the right to refuse any mail which does not conform to standard sizes.

Courts

If two parties have a private dispute, their easiest course of action is to go to an arbitrator, a private judge known in German as a "Schiedsrichter". (This can cause confusion to foreign visitors, who often only know the word "Schiedsrichter" in its use to mean a referee in a football match!)

The lowest form of public court is the "Amtsgericht" (district court). There are 889 of these, and they can try minor criminal offences (giving up to two years' imprisonment) and civil disputes up to a value of 1500 Mark. Next come the 93 "Landgerichte" (regional courts), which try major criminal and civil cases, and can act as courts of appeal for cases tried by the district courts. They also deal with cases referred to them by the district courts.

Cases of treason, etc are dealt with by the "Oberlandsgerichte" (superior regional courts, of which there are 19) or by the "Bundesgerichtshof" (Federal Court) in Karlsruhe. These also deal with cases referred to them by lower courts, and can act as courts of appeal on judgements passed by lower courts.

The most important court is the "Bundesverfassungsgericht" (Federal Constitutional Court) which deals with all matters affecting or offending against the Constitution. The Basic Law (or constitution, passed in 1949) also envisaged the setting up of a Supreme Federal Court, but this has not yet taken place.

In addition to the full-time professional judges, the German system also makes use of "Schöffen", who are lay judges comparable with British Justices of the Peace. They may, however, never act alone, but only in conjunction with a full-time judge. They can be used in the district and regional courts if the nature of the case warrants their employment. In cases of particularly severe crimes coming before the regional courts, jurors are also called in.

There is also a wide range of special courts at all levels for specific types of offender and dispute. These range from the one-man juvenile courts at district level, to the Federal Financial Court in Munich.

Punishment

German courts impose two main types of punishment: imprisonment and fines. Imprisonment can take a number of forms, ranging from simple arrest ("Haft") for up to six weeks, to jail ("Zuchthaus") for life (or up to fifteen years). "Zuchthaus" includes work on the part of the convict — either in the prison or outside — and whoever has been sentenced to any period of Zuchthaus is disqualified for life from holding any public office.

In West Germany the death penalty has been abolished, although in 1967 Allensbach interviewers found that 50% of the population were in favour of such a penalty (as against 31% against and 19% undecided). This result contrasts sharply with the findings of Gallup surveys in the USA, where support for the death penalty dropped from 68% in 1953 to 42% in 1966.

Number of crimes

In 1966, 680,407 people were found guilty by West German courts. Of these, 98,081 were under 18 years of age. Of all crimes, 51·5% took place in large towns; 53% were solved. Of crimes excluding traffic offences, 62·2% were theft or misappropriation, and 3·0% were sexual offences.

East Germany

The number of crimes per 100,000 inhabitants in East Germany is only a third of the West German figure. But the extent of this difference appears less striking if traffic offences (which make up only 11% of the total in East Germany) are excluded.

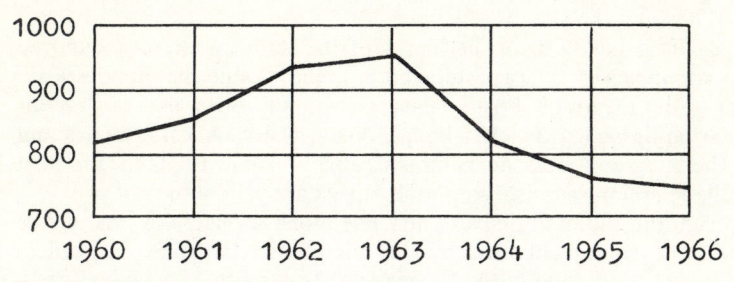

Fig 72   Crimes per 100,000 population in East Germany

Justice is seen, not as an abstract ideal, but as the will of the working class. Judges and Schöffen are elected for periods of four years at a time, and must show their support for the ideals of the socialist movement.

In factories, works disputes are settled by means of "Konfliktkommissionen". These consist of eight or twelve members elected at the nomination of the party organs. They cannot impose fines or prison sentences, but can order the accused to make a public apology.

In farms, villages and towns, a similar system operates under the name of "Schiedskommission". These have special instructions to deal with those members of the community who do not do an adequate job of work.

Every "Kreis", i.e. every town, has its own court, consisting of many "Kammern", or sub-departments. Each Kammer consists of one judge and two Schöffen. Similarly each administrative region has its own regional court; these are responsible for appeals against sentences passed by the local courts, and for more serious crimes and offences against the state.

The highest court is the Supreme Court ("Oberstes Gericht") which has "Kollegien" for separate fields, such as criminal law and family law.

Since 1957, it has been a crime in East Germany for citizens to leave or attempt to leave the country without permission; this is punishable by prison sentences of up to three years. Similarly, it is a crime to help others to leave. However, the first part of this law does not apply to those who left before the building of the Berlin Wall. The law is defended by the party bosses on the grounds that the labour force must be preserved and protected from West Germans who would abduct East Germans if they had half a chance. However, this official line cuts little ice with many East Germans who complain at being "shut in".

Post and telephone

The German Post Office has been in the hands of the state for the last hundred years; it is now administered by two state bodies, the "Deutsche Bundespost" (West Germany) and "Deutsche Post" (East Germany). Both use the colour yellow for all their equipment; for letter-boxes, post-office vans, cars, lorries and buses, and even the telegraph messengers' crash helmets! As in England, the Post Office also runs the telephone service, so phone kiosks are yellow too.

In addition to running the mail delivery and telephone service, the Post Office owns and controls the equipment used by the television companies. It licences television and radio sets and collects the licence fees. It runs its own savings bank and giro cheque service (described in the chapter on "Money and banking"); it sees to the paying of pensions, accepts subscriptions for newspapers and magazines, and runs its own country bus service. Many of these activities — particularly the banking service — are so profitable that the normal mail service is able to run at a loss.

The word "run" kept creeping into the last paragraph as I wrote it, and when applied to the Post Office, it is appropriate; for there can be few organisations so concerned with speed and efficiency. The Post Office is currently being so successful with its rationalisation and streamlining, that in recent years an annual increase of 5% in volume of work has been met by a 1% increase in staff.

Germany is more ambitious than Britain when it comes to pictorial and commemorative stamps. All West German stamps carry the caption "Deutsche Bundespost" — though in West Berlin special stamps are sold with the caption "Deutsche Bundespost Berlin". Letters inside Germany cost 30 Pfennigs, postcards 20; letters to destinations abroad cost 50 Pfennigs, postcards 30. Surprising as it sometimes is to foreign visitors, mail to other countries within the European Economic Community goes at inland rates. German stamp machines have little handles, which must be turned after the money has been inserted. The American practice of a surcharge on stamps bought from a machine is unknown in Germany.

Minimum postal rates 1968

(All these charges increase with weight — rapidly in the case of air mail)

	Inland	Britain	USA (surface)	USA (air)
Postcard	20	30	30	50
Letter	30	50	50	70
Printed paper	10	20	20	40
Registered letter	1,10	1,30	1,30	1,50

The Bundespost deals with thirty million letters a day, over nine billion a year. This means 159 letters per inhabitant per year.

The first fully automatic sorting office was opened in Darmstadt in 1961, and

---

Fig 73   A selection of German stamps taken from normal business mail addressed to the publishers of this book. Photo: Pond Press.

PHILHARMONIE
20
DEUTSCHE BUNDESPOST BERLIN
Deutsche Bundespost
TDM
DEUTSCHE BUNDESPOST
EUROPA
CEPT
30
DEUTSCHE BUNDESPOST
50
Deutsche Bundespost
40
DEUTSCHE BUNDESPOST
DEUTSCHE BUNDESPOST
15
DEUTSCHE BUNDESPOST
20
75 Jahre Drehstromübertragung
DEUTSCHE BUNDESPOST
20
DEUTSCHE BUNDESPOST
30
FRIEDRICH VON BODELSCHWINGH
DEUTSCHE BUNDESPOST
30
Deutsche Bundespost
10
DRESDEN/SACHSEN
DEUTSCHE BUNDESPOST
50
Deutsche Bundespost
30
DEUTSCHE BUNDES
25
ERNST-REUTER-PLA
50
DEUTSCHE BUNDESPOST BERLIN
WOHLFAHRTSMARKE
10+5
DEUTSCHE BUNDESPOST
30
EUROPA
CEPT
20
20
LORSCH/H
DEUTSCHE BUNDESPOST
DEUTSCHE BUNDESPOST
DEUTSCHE BUNDESPOST
70
WESTFALEN
WOHLFAHRTSMARKE
50
+25
BUNDESPOST
Deutsche Bundes
30
DEUTSCHE BUNDESPOST
WEISSENBURG/BAYERN
DEUTSCHE BUNDESPOST

118   THEIR GOVERNMENT AND INSTITUTIONS

similar equipment is being installed throughout the country. Automatic sorting calls for fluorescent stamps and for postal guide numbers for all towns and villages (like the American ZIP codes and the recently-introduced postal codes in Britain). These are based on regions; Cologne is 5000, Siegburg (near Cologne) is thus 5200 and the village Siegburg-Mülldorf is 5201. (The final "noughts" can be omitted; thus 5000 and 5200 can be written as 5 and 52.) For tourists and business-

Fig 74   Postal guide numbers: the main centres

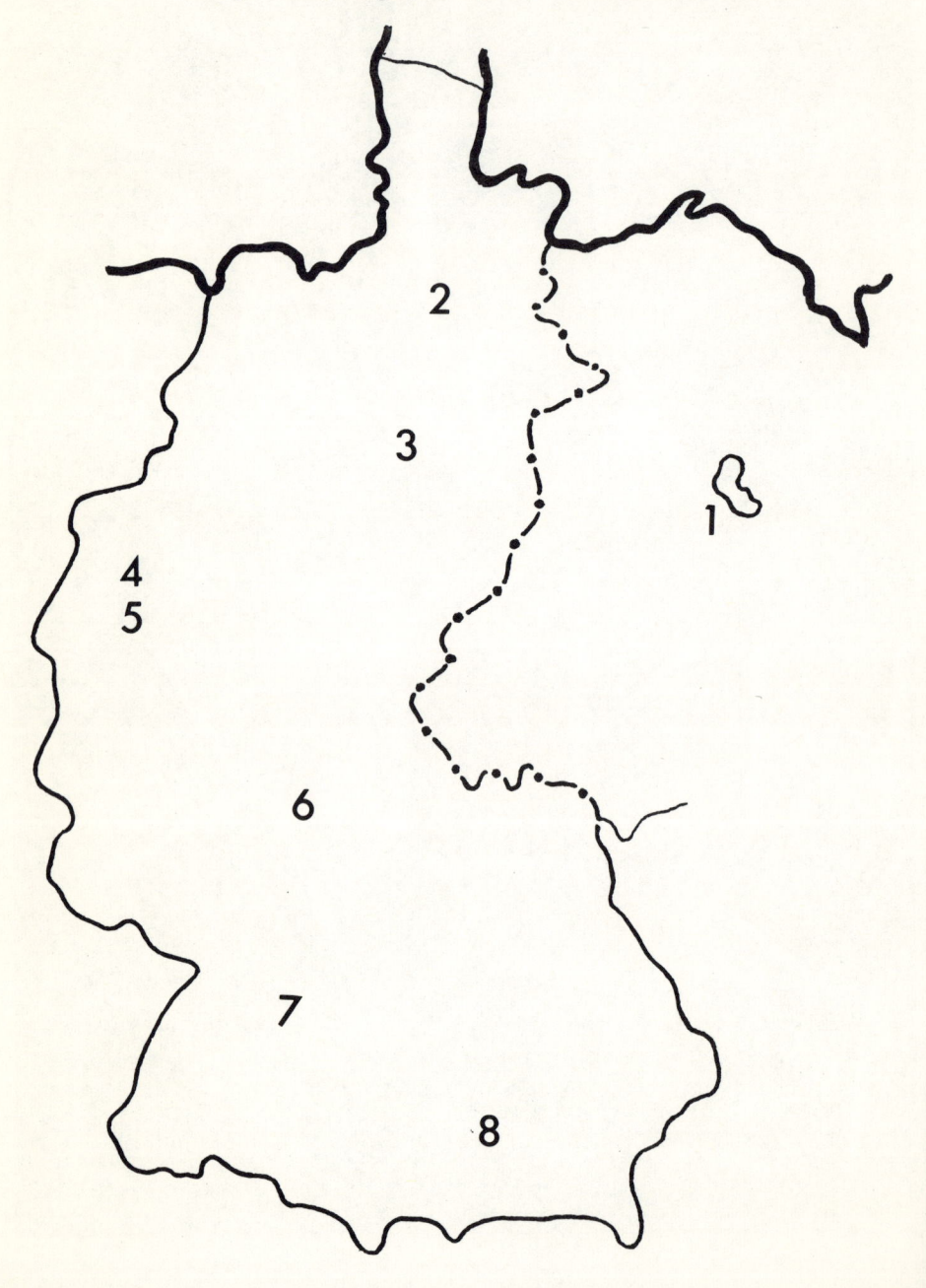

POST AND TELEPHONE

men, the postal guide number in an address can be a good indication of its location. The main areas are:

1 West Berlin
2 Hamburg
3 Hanover (Hannover)
4 Düsseldorf
5 Cologne (Köln)
6 Frankfurt
7 Stuttgart
8 Munich (München)

From the guide number, it is also possible to judge the size of the place concerned; the simpler the number, the larger the town. Thus 28 will indicate a larger town than 8021, the two numbers referring to Bremen and Höllriegskreuth respectively. (Never heard of Höllriegskreuth? Precisely!)

There are two categories of parcels in Germany, namely "Pakete" and "Päckchen". Pakete are large parcels travelling as 2nd class mail, while Päckchen are small parcels that count as 1st class mail.

Money can be sent by money order. The sum to be paid is sent into any post office, and its equivalent delivered the other end by a special "money postman". (This does not apply if the money is to be paid into a bank or a giro account.) "Money postmen" also handle wireless and television licence dues, newspaper subscriptions and goods sent on a "cash on delivery" basis. It is customary to give such a postman a small tip if he brings you money.

The proper way to write an address in Germany is to write first the guide

Fig 75 Even post offices celebrate Christmas. Photo: Glyn Hatherall.

number, then the town, thirdly the street and finally the house number, e.g.

        Frau   Herrn
        Marie Silcher   Hans Müller
53   Bonn   5   Köln
        Kleinstrasse 123   Veledastrasse 69

Telephone

In 1966, the Bundespost handled nearly five billion local calls and over two billion long-distance calls. Every seventh German has a telephone; a smaller proportion than in Britain. Germany is ahead of Britain in subscriber trunk dialling, and most long-distance calls in Germany are dialled by the customer.

Many German coin-box telephones can be used for local calls only, and in Germany a local call means a call within a single exchange (with the exception that calls between Bonn and Bad Godesberg have recently been made local calls). Long-distance calls can be made only from coin boxes marked "Ferngespräche". Coins inserted can be seen in a small window, and drop through automatically when more money is needed; if the caller has inserted more money than is necessary, surplus coins are returned. If there is no reserve, but the time paid for is about to expire, a light signal indicates "Bitte zahlen" ("Please pay"); this is, to my mind, far more civilised than the British pay-tone pips. Long-distance calls can also be made from a private phone and from a post office, but in both cases no warning indication is given of the passage of time. There is no time-limit on local calls.

Many foreign calls can also be dialled by the caller (though, contrary to the practice gradually being introduced in Britain, this is not possible from coin-boxes). The number to be dialled for a foreign call can be formidable. Thus when I telephone my publisher from Germany, I have to dial 004419977425! Dialling codes for towns within Germany are also all-figure codes, and German phones have no letters on the dial. The codes dialled from coin-boxes differ slightly from those used when phoning from a private telephone or from a post office. Cheap

Fig 76   How to remember complicated telephone numbers — a suggestion by Karl Weissmann. Reproduced from the Desch collection.

rates operate from 6 pm to 7 am on weekdays, and from 2 pm on Saturday to 7 am on Monday.

In a German telephone directory, the names are arranged under exchanges. Thus in the Cologne area directory, all Godesberg numbers are listed together. This can be complicated if the name of the exchange and the name of the town or village are not identical. To find a telephone number of a subscriber living on the Island of Sylt, one has to look under the Westerland exchange.

German telephone alphabet

A = Anton	I = Ida	S = Samuel
Ä = Ärger	J = Julius	Sch = Schule
B = Berta	K = Kaufmann	T = Theodor
C = Cäsar	L = Ludwig	U = Ulrich
Ch = Charlotte	M = Martha	Ü = Übermut
D = Dora	N = Nordpol	V = Viktor
E = Emil	O = Otto	W = Wilhelm
F = Friedrich	Ö = Ökonom	X = Xanthippe
G = Gustav	P = Paula	Y = Ypsilon
H = Heinrich	Q = Quelle	Z = Zacharias
	R = Richard	

Telegrams and teleprint

Apart from ordinary telegrams and congratulatory telegrams, there are also urgent telegrams (at double the normal rate), radio telegrams for ships at sea, and pictorial telegrams for photographs and drawings. Pressmen and members of the public can send special press telegrams to any newspaper at a reduced rate. Letter telegrams are also sent at a reduced rate, but the service is slower. The number of telegrams sent in Germany is slowly decreasing. This is probably due in part to the use of teleprint facilities; by 1966, Germany had 66,200 teleprint connections, as many as the rest of Europe put together. German teleprint users can dial Austria, Belgium, Britain, Denmark, Finland, France, Holland, Hungary, Luxemburg, Norway, Sweden and Switzerland direct.

East Germany

The pattern in postal and telephone services is basically the same as in West Germany. The difference is in the amount of automation. East Germany lags far behind in this. Most internal long-distance phone calls and all foreign calls are still hand-operated.

Postal guide numbers were introduced in 1964. The fact that West Germany had left certain series free for East German guide numbers was deliberately ignored, on the grounds that the two are now separate states. Since many East and West German guide numbers now overlap, East Germans are asked to write an O before West German and foreign guide numbers.

According to the generally reliable West German publication "Die SBZ von A bis Z", East Germany has over fifty control points for post censorship, checking mostly post coming from or going to the West.

East Germany is a prolific producer of commemorative postage stamps, many of them beautifully designed.

Telephone calls between East and West can be booked only from the West and there is a long waiting time (some people claim to have waited twelve hours). This time can be reduced by making the call "urgent" and paying double, but even then you may have to wait a few hours.

The printed word

Despite the increasing popularity of television, statistics show that the written media are suffering no decline in Germany. On the contrary, publication sales are on the increase.

Newspapers
The total number of copies sold each day in West Germany is lower than in USA and Britain. Germany sells only 315 papers per 1,000 population, as against 350 in America and 573 in Britain. But Germany has a large number of local papers. Whereas the British press is mainly concentrated on Fleet Street, there is no such concentration in Germany. True, one particular firm in Hamburg (the Springer concern) controls some 38% of all daily papers; but many of these are printed outside Hamburg. The Germans are fond of their local paper, even if it is only a local edition of a paper. Consequently, no fewer than 1,200 daily papers appear in cities, large and small towns all over the country. With a single exception (to which reference will be made later) these papers have a daily edition of less than half a million copies. They are financed largely by local "small ads" which fill page after page, particularly on Saturdays. Local papers contain international and national news, as well as what one would expect in a weekly "local rag" in Britain.

German papers are, for foreign students of the language, difficult to read. They seem to have developed a style of their own. At an international holiday course in Bonn University, one of the students taking part complained, "I can read a book or short story in German with some ease, but when I try to read a paper I can't understand a word". This was greeted with applause, because many others present had shared his experience. The difficulty lies partly in formalistic vocabulary, partly in verbose syntax.

The one really big newspaper in Germany is a tabloid called "Bild-Zeitung". This is one of the Springer papers, and sells over four million copies every day. It is read mainly by manual workers, but also many students and members of other social groups; 10% of the readers are self-employed or are owners or managers of firms. The word "Bild" means "picture", and the photograph is just as important to this paper as the printed word. The editors believe in huge banner headlines and in short, snappy representation of news stories, most of them sensational. The political attitude of the paper is ultra-conservative.

"Bild" also produces a Sunday edition, and is the only West German paper to do so. As was mentioned above, the Saturday editions contain many pages of "small ads"; many of them also contain cultural supplements similar to those of the British "serious" Sunday papers. Among the advertisements, the most striking to foreign readers are the many from readers who are looking for prospective husbands or wives. They have developed a language of their own, in which a phrase like "bitterly disappointed" is more or less synonymous with "having a fatherless child".

The most important newspapers from a prestige and influence standpoint are "Die Welt", the "Frankfurter Allgemeine" and "Süddeutsche Zeitung". "Die Welt" is another Springer paper, and cynics have observed that the only difference between the two is that "Die Welt" contains some subordinate clauses! It follows the Springer conservative line, particularly with regard to East Germany. "Frankfurter Allgemeine" is another conservative paper, but has a high standard of literary style and is often recommended to foreign students. The "Süddeutsche", appearing in Munich, is a more liberal paper. All three have circulations between two and three hundred thousand.

Fig 77 A selection of West German national and local papers. Photo: Glyn Hatherall.

Fig 78   Reading the local paper. Photo: Glyn Hatherall.

Magazines

On the border-line between newspaper and magazines are two weekly journals "Die Zeit" and "Christ und Welt". The former appears in Hamburg and is in some ways similar to the "Observer"; it retains the "review of the week" which its British counterpart also ran for some time but has now discontinued. "Christ und Welt" appears in Stuttgart, and has a religious and conservative editorial policy.

Germany also has a weekly "news magazine", called "Der Spiegel". It is published in Hamburg, and the editor's independent views have caused much controversy ever since the paper began. In 1962 he was arrested on a charge of treason after having disclosed details of a NATO exercise; the charge was never proven, but the editor failed on a technicality when he tried to sue the authorities for unlawful arrest. The judges divided evenly, thus giving the defendant — in this case the government — a technical victory.

Of a multiplicity of weekly illustrateds, five have circulations over a million. These are "Stern", "Quick", "Bunte Illustrierte", "Neue Illustrierte" and "Revue". The first named has the highest circulation, and is by far the best from a quality point of view. It is produced by the same publishers as "Die Zeit" and frequently contains first-rate political articles.

In addition, there is a flood of brightly-coloured weekly tabloids, which concentrate on the love-lives of the film stars and of all the crowned heads of Europe. No whisper of scandal seems to escape them. Mostly, their stories come from outside Germany; the big exception was the non-romance of ice skaters Marika Kilius and Hans-Jürgen Bäumler.

THE PRINTED WORD   125

English-language magazines and newspapers about Germany

Published in West Germany:
 Scala International — monthly illustrated magazine
   (Frankfurter Societätsdrückerei GmbH, Frankfurt)
 The German Tribune — weekly extract of the German press
   (Reinecke Verlag GmbH, 2 Hamburg 22, Schöne Aussicht 23)
 The Bulletin — weekly survey of German affairs
   (Press and Information office of the Federal Government.
   Distributed in Britain by the German Embassy, in the USA
   by the German Information Center, New York).

Published in East Germany:
 GDR Review — monthly illustrated magazine
   (Verlag Zeit im Bild, Dresden)
 Democratic German Report — fortnightly news-sheet
   (108 Berlin, Krausenstrasse 9)

Published in Britain:
 The German View — monthly, a cross between a paper and a magazine
   (Curzon Publicity Ltd, 31 St James's Place, London SW1)
 Bulletin on German Questions — monthly digest of the German press
   (Gamma Publications, 15 Craven Street, London WC2)

Books

West Germany has two thousand publishing firms and four thousand bookshops. In 1965, Germany published 24,216 books, compared with Britain's 26,023 and the USA's 25,784.

Of the books produced, fiction accounts for 22·1%. Of these, 11% are crime fiction. Translations account for 12% of all new titles, and of these, 28% are by British, 23% by American, 20% by French and 3% by Russian authors.

Fig 79 In the lending library — cartoon by Fritz Czyk, reproduced from the Desch collection.

Like other countries, Germany has experienced a paperback boom in recent years. In 1965, every seventeenth title produced in Germany was a paperback — but this figure is deceptive, since paperbacks sell far more copies. Between 1950 and 1967, one paperback publisher alone sold eighty million books. Of particular interest to foreign students are the "Reclam" paperbacks, which cost only 80 Pfennigs.

Fig 80 The changes in "Reclam" covers during the past century. Reproduced from "The Bulletin".

Shakespeare-Dramenreihe 1865–1867   *Das Gesicht der UB 1867–1917*   *Die erste Modernisierung durch F. H. Ehmcke 1917*

Typographische Wandlungen des Umschlags 1865–1936

F. Häder 1936   *A. Finsterer 1947*   *A. Finsterer 1957*

Typographische Wandlungen des Umschlags seit 1936

Details of a few of the most important German writers are given in a later chapter under the heading "The literary heritage".

East Germany

The system of licensing newspapers and publishing houses, introduced in all four occupation zones after Germany's defeat in 1945, has been maintained in East

Germany, although the Western zones ended it in 1949. Licensing ensures a practical censorship over all newspapers. An editor who offends the government knows he will lose his licence. This does not mean, however, that papers are censored before issue, or that they appear with blank spaces. It simply means that, in order to keep their jobs, all editors follow the party line.

With two exceptions, all papers are published by the government party or the parties affiliated to the government "National Front" or the mass organisations such as the Free German Youth. The exceptions are the "Berliner Zeitung" and its evening edition "BZ am Abend"; and even these are run by a party member. 70% of the total circulation of daily papers is accounted for by those produced by the government party itself (which, in addition to its national organ "Neues Deutschland", also produces many local papers).

East German papers are, by Western standards, dull and stodgy. Even when they get away from politics, they tend to give the reader what they feel is good for his soul (without, of course, believing in the soul). They contain a lot of anti-Western propaganda, and believe that news is "agitation through facts". There is no such thing, for a communist journalist, as objective news. News is only worth printing if it serves the interests of the Party (and that, in East Germany, includes the spreading of the gospel that the West German government is evil).

Most of the papers contain very little advertising, and they presumably do not pay their way. I did notice, however, that a local paper in Weimar contained a surprisingly high number of adverts of the "husband/wife wanted" variety.

There are fewer magazines in East Germany than in the West, and those that do exist are printed on inferior paper. Two of the best known are "Zeit im Bild", which appears in Dresden, and the capital's "Neue Berliner Illustrierte". There

Fig 81 A new bookshop, opened in 1966, for the Freiberg Academy in East Germany. It cost half a million Mark to build. Photo: Lex Hornsby & Partners.

are, however, many specialist magazines for off-beat interests. The satirical and humorous weekly, "Eulenspiegel", contains some excellent cartoons.

Most of the publishing houses are state-owned; private firms account for only about 5% of the books produced. All bookshops seem to have the same books, and this would support the official statistic that the average edition of a book in East Germany is 19,800 copies. In 1965, 105 million copies of 5,310 titles were published. None of the books attacks Socialism or the government; many are translated from Russian. The number of titles produced rose continuously up to 1958, but then declined.

Radio and television

Radio

The German radio stations are, with two exceptions, regionally organised, and run on a "Land" basis. The West German Radio has its headquarters in Cologne, the North German Radio in Hamburg, the Bavarian Radio in Munich, the Hessian

Fig 82   West Germany's main radio stations

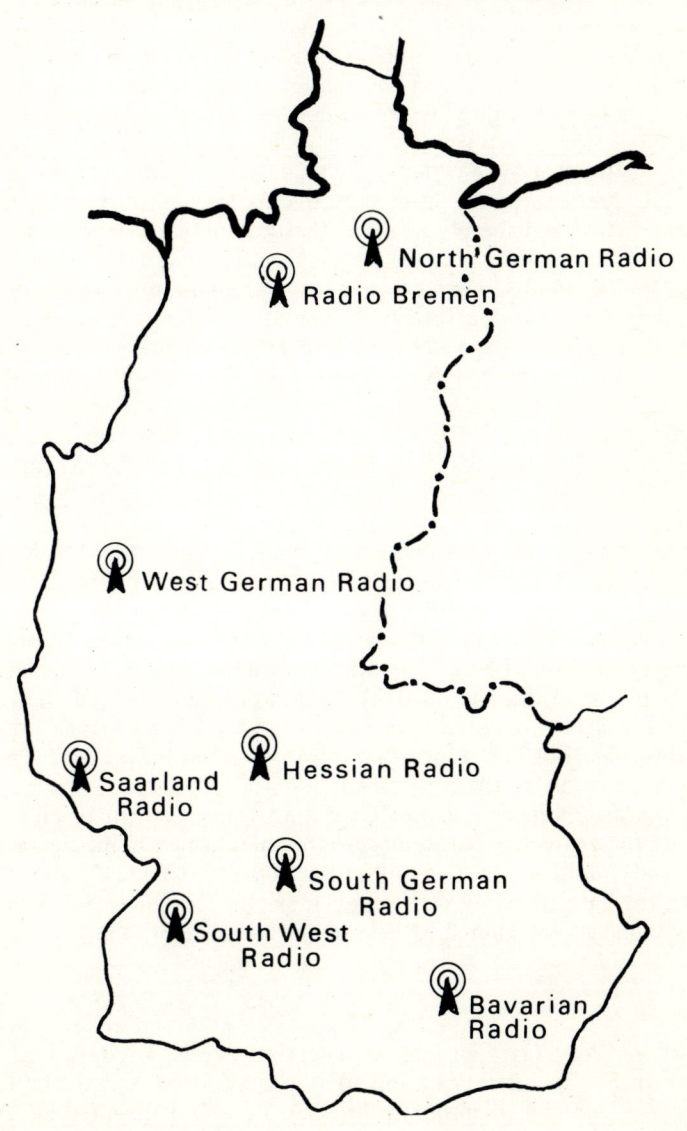

Radio in Frankfurt, the South-Western Radio in Baden-Baden, the South German Radio in Stuttgart and the Saarland Radio in Saarbrücken. The homes of Radio Bremen and Free Berlin Radio are obvious from the names.

These stations are independent of each other, but controlled indirectly by the Land governments in each case. Details differ, but the West German Radio may serve as an example. The Land parliament elects a 21-member Radio Council, which in turn elects a seven-man Administrative Committee. This body elects an "Intendant", who is responsible for the day-to-day running of the programmes.

In many of the Länder, party politics play a large part in the elections of these bodies. The Administrative Committees mirror the political constitution of the Land parliaments, and the Intendant often owes his appointment and reappointment to one or other of the political parties. However, in some of the authorities, a two-thirds majority is necessary for the election of an Intendant; this places the latter under a greater obligation to keep on the right side of both parties.

In general, the effect of such political influence on the programmes themselves is less than might be feared. A notable exception, however, was the case of Gert von Paczensky in 1963. Paczensky was editor of a television programme called "Panorama", and had been highly critical of the CDU government. ("Panorama" should not be compared with its far more sedate British namesake; it was often full of sharp criticism.) When Paczensky's contract expired, it was largely as a result of CDU pressure in the Administrative Committee of the North German Radio (which networked the programme) that a renewed contract was refused.

The two programmes not organised on a regional basis are the Voice of Germany ("Deutsche Welle") and German Radio ("Deutschlandfunk"). The former is a multi-lingual programme for foreign listeners; the latter is designed "to give listeners in both parts of Germany a comprehensive picture of Germany".

In Munich there are three stations financed by America; these are Radio Free Europe, Voice of America and Radio Liberty. A similar station is RIAS (Radio in the American Sector) in Berlin. The American Forces Network (AFN) and British Forces Broadcasting Services (BFBS) serve the needs of the foreign troops stationed in Germany.

Comparisons between the output of the West German Radio and the BBC (unfortunately prior to the introduction of Radio 1) show that the music output was 62·6% of the total output in the case of the German programme, and 56% for the BBC. Nevertheless, the BBC had by far the greater output of serious music (25% compared with 13·1%). Of the programmes put out by the German station, 12·3% were concerned with politics and economics, 13·1% with literature and education, 0·6% were drama and 0·7% sports programmes. (Of these, the only statistic which can be compared with BBC output is drama, which takes up 7% of BBC radio time. Further comparisons are prevented by the fact that different sub-divisions are made in BBC statistics.)

Some of the programmes are of a type almost unknown in Britain. The most important of these are the magazine programmes which combine records with interviews and oddities — a sort of cross between "Today" and "Breakfast Special". In the case of many of the pop music programmes, full details of the records to be played are published beforehand in the programme magazines.

Television

The titles of the West German television services are most confusing. The main service (known as the First Programme) is produced by a body known as the "Arbeitsgemeinschaft der öffentlich-rechtlichen Rundfunkanstalten Deutschlands"

(ARD), a combined authority representing the regional broadcasting companies. The main programmes are produced by one or other of the regions and networked by all the others; but from 6 pm to 8 pm individual regional programmes are shown. Commercials are allowed during the regional programmes, but no advertising is permitted during the main networked programmes.

In 1963, an organisation operating from Mainz began to produce a second service under the title "Second German Television" (Zweites Deutsches Fernsehen, or ZDF). It is sometimes called the "Mainz Programme". Now the ARD also produces a second service, officially called the "Second Programme of German Television", but popularly known as the "Third Programme" as it was the third to appear. Thus, as a German once explained, "the third programme is really the second programme of the first programme".

The content of the different services is roughly similar. Consequently, the following analysis of the First Programme for 1966 can be taken as typical (unfortunately not all the sub-heads coincide with those used in BBC statistics). The analysis of the German programme showed 34% current affairs, 12·6% drama (BBC 11·5%), music 0·8% (BBC 2·4%), entertainment 15·1% (BBC 6·9%), children's, young people's and women's programmes 12·8%, sport 10·9%, films 4·8%, news 8·8% (BBC 5·5%) and Eurovision programmes 4%.

Contrary to the impression made by the above statistics, I personally find German television programmes to be of a generally higher cultural level than those in Britain, though often at the expense of liveliness.

There is a tendency in Germany towards longer, less frequent programmes rather than weekly repetition. Most quiz programmes come only once a month, though they often last up to 90 minutes. Durbridge serials are very popular, but are shown in three 90-minute instalments, all in the same week! After the second instalment, many popular papers have their phone lines jammed with calls from readers asking if the paper knows who the culprit is.

The 1966 EMNID survey asked young people what their favourite programmes were. Films topped the list, being regularly watched by 73%; then came entertainment programmes with 51%, sport (36%) and current affairs (23%).

West Germany introduced regular colour programmes in the Summer of 1967, and was the first Western European country to do so (beating the BBC by a few months). A total of eight hours per week was produced from the start, half by the ARD and half by the ZDF. The programmes covered all fields except news broadcasts, and could be received in black-and-white by viewers without colour sets; the ARD colour broadcasts were shown in black-and-white on the First Programme.

East Germany

Radio services in East Germany are run by a central authority: the State Radio Committee. There are three major programmes (German Radio, Berlin Radio and Radio GDR I) and two less important programmes (Berlin Wave and Radio GDR II).

The general tone of East German radio reflects that of the newspapers. It is full of praise for its own government and full of criticism directed against West Germany. (The station known as German Radio, in particular, is aimed at an audience in the West as well as in the East.) But there are also some good programmes of serious and popular music. On Saturday evenings, German Radio has a long programme of slightly old-fashioned pop tunes.

East German television is run by a department of the radio committee, known as German Television ("Deutscher Fernsehfunk"). The programmes start early in the day and include many films. Of the total 1966 output, 20% was educational, 8% devoted to art and culture and 12% light entertainment.

Many East Germans watch West German television, which can be received in large areas of East Germany. This has been curtailed to some extent by encouraging young people to promise not to watch West German television, and also by building communal aerials capable of receiving East German programmes only.

Together with Poland, Czechoslovakia, Hungary and the USSR, East Germany is a member of the Intervision network, the Eastern equivalent of Eurovision.

„Die Fortsetzung dieses Rezepts bringen wir in vierzehn Tagen."

Fig 83 "We shall be giving you the rest of the recipe in our next programme, a fortnight today." Cartoon by Moese, reproduced from "Junge Welt".

Money and banking

During the nineteen-twenties, during the Nazi era and during the Second World War, the German economy suffered from chronic inflation. The Mark became almost worthless, and barter was the standard form of transaction. This was ended overnight by the Currency Reform of 1948. All West Germans were allowed sixty new "Deutsche Mark" (DM) in exchange for sixty old marks. All additional sums of old marks were exchanged at a rate of one DM to ten old marks.

Fig 84   West German coins and notes. Photo: Glyn Hatherall.

  The DM (referred to throughout this book as the Mark) is divided into 100 Pfennigs. For official purposes, these are the only two denominations used, but in conversation the Germans use the old term "Groschen" to refer to a 10 Pfennig piece.

A full stop or comma is placed between the number of Mark and the number of Pfennigs. Thus DM 14.35 (or DM 14,35 or 14,35 DM) means fourteen Mark and thirty-five Pfennigs. In a shop window this would appear as 14.³⁵ or 14,35.

For exchange purposes, the Mark is equivalent to about 2s 1d, and to 25 US cents (November 1967). No official comparisons for purchasing power are available, but before the 1967 devaluation of sterling, UN authorities calculating salaries for their officials took the cost of living in Bonn as being identical with that of London, but 18% lower than that of New York. This basis gives the Mark a purchasing power of 1s 10d or 30 US cents.

Banking

As the amount saved in Germany is increasing rapidly, any figures given for national investment soon become inaccurate. Suffice to say that until the early 1960's the Germans saved much less than the British, but that recent trends show a reversal of this. An EMNID survey in February 1967 showed that 38% of the participants saved on a non-contracting basis (i.e. at home, in a bank or savings bank) and 43% on a contracting basis (in the form of insurance or house-building policies etc). These two groups overlapped. The most common reason for saving on a non-contracting basis was "to have a reserve in case of emergency", an answer given by every fourth participant who saved in this way. Every sixth was saving for house-building or renovation, every ninth for holidays.

The only bank in Germany permitted to produce bank notes is the Deutsche Bundesbank (Federal Bank) in Frankfurt. This bank also controls the bank rate. The three other important banks are the Dresdner Bank, the Commerzbank and the Deutsche Bank.

German banks are closed on Saturdays. Most of them are open on Mondays to Fridays from 8.30 am to noon, and 2 pm to 3.30 pm. Some, however, work through the lunch-hour and close for the day at 2 pm. On Fridays, many banks stay open till 6 pm. For foreign exchange transactions, many railway stations have banks open for long hours every day (including Sunday).

Railways stations with foreign-exchange banks

Aachen	Essen	Karlsruhe	Mannheim
Bebra	Flensburg	Kassel	Munich
Berlin	Frankfurt	Kehl	Nuremberg
Bochum	Freiburg	Kiel	Passau
Bonn	Friedrichshafen	Koblenz	Puttgarden
Bremen	Hamburg	Konstanz	Saarbrücken
Brunswick	Hanover	Lindau	Stuttgart
Cologne	Heidelberg	Ludwigshafen	Trier
Düsseldorf	Kaiserslauten	Lubeck	Wiesbaden
			Wolfsburg

The use of cheques is less popular in Germany than in Britain, and a customer with a small account may be refused a cheque book. Most transactions are done by credit transfer; the customer sends a transfer note to his own bank, and the bank then arranges payment to the recipient's account, or — if necessary — by post. All customers have account numbers, and these must be given in all transactions; the personal "Good morning, Mr Smith" is not often heard at German bank counters.

To the impersonal atmosphere of a German bank one may attribute partly the popularity of the savings banks (which hold 60% of savings deposits) and post office accounts. The savings banks and post office both run two forms of account: savings accounts with high rates of interest, and giro accounts for efficient credit transfer services. Giro accounts pay low rates of interest, if any; several of them feel that the customer is getting a cheap and efficient service, and cannot expect interest as well.

The post office is at an advantage in the savings business because of its wide network. The holder of a post office savings book can pay money into or draw money from his account at any of 38,000 post offices in Germany or at any of the 2,000 post offices in Austria. He can draw up to 1,000 Mark on demand. Over a hundred towns have station post offices with a day and night savings account service. Similarly, the post office giro system is extremely efficient. Customers send the giro form in a post-free envelope to their giro office, and the office guarantee to handle it on the same or following day. The form has three sections: one is kept by the giro office, one is sent to the recipient, and one is returned to the customer as a certificate that the payment has been made. The post-office will pre-print the forms with the customer's account number, name and address. They will also issue him with ready-printed paying-in forms which others can use at any post office to pay money into his account. Germany has enjoyed a giro system since 1908, beating Britain to it by sixty years.

East Germany

At the same time as the West German currency reform, a new currency was introduced in East Germany. It is now (since January 1968) known officially as the "Mark der Deutschen Demokratischen Republik", but in the West it is frequently referred to as "DM-Ost". It, too, is divided into 100 Pfennigs.

I am often asked, "What is an East German Mark worth?" This apparently simple question has an incredibly complicated answer. On the international exchange market, 1 Mark der DDR is worth 0.30 DM (West). But if money is exchanged in East Germany at the official rate, one must pay 1 DM (West) for 1 Mark der DDR. (Foreigners get a slightly more favourable rate for their own currency: a dollar is exchanged for 4,20 Mark der DDR, a pound sterling for 10 Mark der DDR.) In terms of purchasing power, the Mark der DDR is worth around 0.75 DM (West). But because wages in the East are lower, the East German worker must put in as much work for 1 Mark der DDR as the West German worker for 1.25 DM (West). (These figures are based on the assumption that official statistics on both sides are honest — an assumption which might be questioned by some.)

Import and export of Mark der DDR is illegal, and there are severe penalties (including imprisonment) for this offence. Nevertheless, many visitors to East Germany feel it worth the risk, because of the more favourable exchange rate in the West. However, all visitors must fill in a declaration when they enter East Germany, saying how much currency they have with them, and there is in theory the danger that one may be searched on entering or on leaving the country.

As in West Germany, the savings banks have the lion's share of private savings: over two-thirds of the total. The state bank is the Staatsbank der DDR; all day-to-day business is handled by the Industrie- und Handelsbank der DDR. There are also special "Trade Banks" that deal with small investments and credits.

Road users

Many Western governments are now facing problems with regard to road transport, but Germany has its own particular headache. There are roughly as many cars per 1,000 population in West Germany as there are in Britain, but the number of accidents is much higher. The German total for road deaths (16,868 in 1966) is double the British figure. 45% of all German court cases are concerned with traffic offences.

Fig 85 The Autobahn network

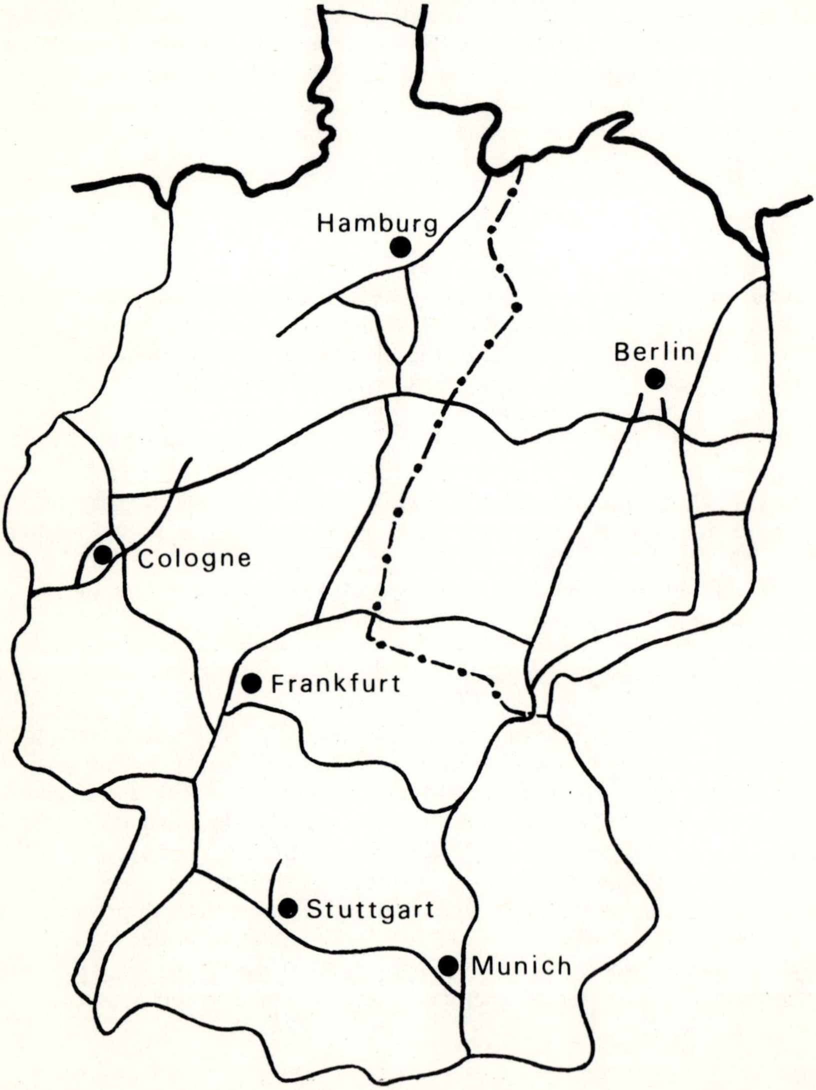

ROAD USERS 137

The tone of this opening paragraph may be taken to indicate that I am not impressed with German driving habits. German drivers can hardly blame bad roads for these figures. West Germany has some 90,000 miles of classified road, including some 2,000 miles of motorway — the world-famous "Autobahn". These motorways were planned before the war by the Nazis, mainly for prestige and military purposes; now, in peace time, they serve as an excellent network for the private motorist. One of the most important missing links (between the Ruhr and Hessen) is now being built.

Other major roads are known as Federal Roads ("Bundesstrassen") and are numbered. Minor roads are not numbered. Road signs showing directions are yellow in the case of Federal and minor roads, blue for motorways.

On all German roads, there is extensive road building all the year round, and this can mean long hold-ups, particularly when the traffic reaches its peak in Summer. On a Summer week-end, drivers will often avoid the motorway even on long journeys, because road works and accidents can cause mile-long queues.

Car registration plates usually give a good clue to the origin of the car. Thus B stands for Berlin, M for Munich and K for Köln (Cologne). The old trading towns who were members of the Hanseatic League carry the initial H for "Hansastadt" before the registration initial; thus HH means Hamburg, HL Lüback. Such letters are, in fact a more accurate guide to the car's "stable" than British plates, because a German driver moving from, say, Hamburg to Munich has to get a new Munich number-plate.

The German Highway Code has full legal force, so that many things which are merely frowned on in Britain are offences in Germany. It is an offence to turn right or left without signalling, to overtake when the road is not clear or to jump on or off a moving bus or tram; one can be punished for these offences even without having caused an accident.

In Germany one drives on the right and overtakes on the left, and there is a clear system of right of way. Unless signposted to the contrary, a vehicle coming from the right has an automatic right of way. Right of way is signposted in two ways; either by a yellow sign with a black number indicating that the road is a Federal Road, or by a red diamond. For "Give Way" an inverted triangle is used as in Britain, but without any writing on it.

This strictly controlled right of way makes most German drivers rather inflexible. If they know they are in the right they tend to drive on regardless, knowing that

„Den Witz kenn ich schon: Wir hatten die Vorfahrt!"   Zeichnung: Willy Moese

Fig 86 "I know what you're going to say: it was our road!" Cartoon by Moese, reproduced from "Junge Welt".

anyone who drives into them will have to foot the bill for damages. Consequently, town traffic in Germany drives at a higher speed than in Britain, and the effect on the British visitor is at first a bit frightening. There is, however, a speed limit of 30 miles per hour on all roads in built-up areas (but none on the open road).

The German "Sunday motorist" has an easier time than his British counterpart, because all heavy lorries over $7\frac{1}{2}$ tons and all lorries with trailers are banned from the roads on Sundays and public holidays between midnight and 10 pm. Any vehicle towing a trailer or caravan is restricted to 50 mph at all times and on all roads (including motorways).

Fig 87 The sign says "No parking", but the motorist is desperate. Cartoon by Klaus Pause, reproduced from the Desch collection.

Traffic lights control not only vehicles but also pedestrians. For the latter there are special lights showing a little red or green man. These lights must be obeyed, and it is a common sight to see a crowd of Germans waiting for the lights to change although there is not a car for miles. But when the lights do change, the pedestrians cross at once, often without looking to see if there is anything coming round the corner. Many traffic lights for motorists show the right speed to drive at if you want to catch the next set of lights while they are green.

Police signals to motorists differ from British practice. A German policeman stops traffic by holding out both arms and speeds it up by beckoning with a rapid movement. The method of indicating "get ready" is to raise the right arm. To allow traffic which has stopped to proceed again, the policeman simply turns sideways.

German policemen seem to be treated with less respect than their English counterparts. It is no uncommon sight to see a heated argument between a driver and a policeman! The police are empowered to impose spot fines and enforce blood tests for alcohol. Breath tests are not obligatory and cannot be used as sole evidence. In 1968, Germany is to follow the example of other Western European countries (including Britain) by making 80 milligrammes per 100 millilitres of blood the maximum permissible alcohol content. Blood tests — with higher

Fig 88 Cartoon by Lothar Ursinus, reproduced from the Desch collection.

safety limits — were introduced ten years earlier, but have had little effect on accident rates. In 1965, when the penalties were made much more severe, there was for a short period a mood of gloom over the whole country, and everyone became alcohol-conscious. A teacher in Bonn let me wait two hours for a train rather than drive me the twenty miles home after a Carnival party. But after a few months, German drivers realised that their chances of getting home without being caught were quite good, and the effects of the stiff penalties wore off.

Germany has only one major motoring organisation, the Allgemeiner Deutscher Automobil-Club (ADAC).

On the motorways, there is an excellent network of restaurants. A recent British Government survey of the British service stations found them to be inferior to their German counterparts. Many German motorway restaurants serve only full meals, however, and the tourist who wants egg and chips may be disappointed. .

Public transport Many German cities still use trams as a major means of transport; they are normally long, articulated vehicles. The method of payment varies, as most towns are now introducing automatic ticket-stamping machines. There is normally a standard fare, regardless of the distance travelled; this may be as high as 90 Pfennigs, which is a lot to pay for a journey of less than a mile.

There are more than 38,000 buses in West Germany. Services inside cities are usually run by the city authorities in conjunction with the tram services. Country bus services are run by the post office and the railways. In conjunction with other European railways, the German railways also operate a network of long-distance coaches: the Europabus service. These have hostesses on board who give a commentary on places of interest, and also sell Coca-cola.

140 THEIR GOVERNMENT AND INSTITUTIONS

Americans visiting Germany are frequently impressed by the cleanliness and dependability of the public transport services. What first strikes the British visitor, on the other hand, is the passengers' habit of pushing when getting on a bus or tram. Germans have not learnt to queue for their public transport, and during peak hours the crush at a bus stop can be appalling.

East Germany

There are far fewer cars on the roads in East Germany than in the West. According to official statistics, in 1966 there were 720,000 cars, just over a million motor-cycles and scooters, and about the same number of mopeds. Cars make up a smaller percentage of the total number of private vehicles than they do in the West. There are far fewer accidents, and less than two thousand fatal accidents each year.

„Da wir mit dem Motorrad verreisen, habe ich diesmal nur einen einzigen Koffer für mich gepackt"

Fig 89 "As we're going by motor-bike, I've only packed one case." Cartoon by Schubert, reproduced from "Junge Welt".

Speed limits are in force on all roads. In towns, it is 50 kilometres per hour (about 30 mph) for all traffic; on the Autobahn 100 km/h for cars and motor-cycles and 80 km/h for others; and on all other roads 90 km/h for cars and motor-cycles and 60 km/h for other vehicles.

Traffic going from West Germany to Berlin has to use the Autobahn and pay a road toll. There are quite rigorous checks at both ends.

The East German motoring organisation is the Allgeimener Deutscher Motorsport-Verband; it is better known by its initials ADMV.

Public transport in towns is heavily subsidised and cheap. Trams and buses are used, and the normal fare is only 20 Pfennigs.

Quicker by rail

Since 1949, West Germany has spent eighty-eight thousand million Mark on road building, and only thirteen thousand million on the railways. Nevertheless, while road traffic conditions verge on chaos, the railways are fast, punctual and clean — in short, a joy to the traveller, particularly if he is used to some British Rail services.

The cleanliness, it should be admitted, is achieved partly by the extensive use of plastic seat covers in second class compartments. The visitor from Britain may miss the comfort of British Rail upholstery.

The money spent on the railways has not been without results. In July 1962, Allensbach pollsters asked the question, "If you had to go on a journey of 1000 kilometres, which do you think would be the most pleasant way to travel?" No less than 46% of the participants voted for the railways, as against 29% for air travel and a mere 18% for travel by car.

Some comparative statistics (for 1966) may be of interest. The West German railways had 30,229 km of routes, the British 21,954. German railways carried 978,982,000 passengers, British Rail 834,957,000. As to goods, the German railways handled 300,289,000 tons, their British equivalent 213,536,000. And net takings were £936,000,000 in Germany, £483,800,000 in Britain. Despite these figures favourable to Germany, the German railways receive an annual subsidy of nearly £100 million.

There are various types of train in Germany. Ordinary slow trains are called "Personenzüge", while those that stop at some stations only are known as "Eilzüge". For a surcharge of 2 Mark you can travel by express ("D-Zug" or "Schnellzug"), and for 6 Mark by long-distance express ("F-Zug" or "Fernschnellzug"). Trans-Europe-Express trains are restricted to 1st class only, and within Germany there is an additional surcharge of 8 Mark; this is not paid by passengers travelling to or from destinations outside Germany. The latter two categories are extremely comfortable, and frequently have telephone and secretarial services on board. Telephone calls cost about 1 Mark more than the same call from a normal phone, and trains with telephones can be phoned from anywhere in Germany.

The fares in Germany are slightly lower than those in Britain, but this is hardly noticeable by travellers who think rail fares expensive anyway. As fares have a tendency to go up, it is not practicable to give a full price guide here, but a few examples of 1967 fares will give a general idea. They do not include surcharges:
Berlin-Bonn DM 50,20; Berlin-Frankfurt DM 43,60; Berlin-Munich DM 54,60; Bonn-Hamburg DM 40,-; Frankfurt-Köln DM 18,80; Hamburg-Kiel DM 9,60; Hamburg-Munich DM 62,-.

The 24-hour clock is used on all timetables. On station timetables, trains for which surcharges are payable are shown in red. Departure boards always show what time each train is due to arrive at its main destinations.

German platforms are lower than those in Britain, and some small stations have no platform at all. This means that the passengers must climb up into the carriages. If you have a heavy case, this can be difficult.

Carriages have a white sign-board that says where the train has come from and where it is going. This is particularly useful if the train has through carriages

Fig 90 Station without platforms — this one in a village called Dorfmark. Photo: Glyn Hatherall.

(and many trains do) because the sign-boards indicate where that particular carriage is going. Thus if you are boarding a train at Munich, and most of the train is bound for Frankfurt with only a few carriages going on to Hamburg, you can see at once which carriages will be going all the way.

Most trains have two classes, First and Second, as in Britain. The First Class fare is 50% dearer than the Second. There are many types of cheap ticket, ranging from day returns to a ticket which — for a mere 3500 Mark — gives you the right to use any train First Class for a whole year. Tourists can enjoy the same facilities for a month by paying 510 Mark First Class or 380 Mark Second Class. There are also monthly seasons for a "Netz" (a wide area covering about 7000 km of track) or for a "Bezirk" (the local area with some 1000 km track). A peculiarity not known on British main lines is the "round trip" ticket, which can be made out for any journey, regardless of the number of intermediate stops, ending at the

West German railway timetables

Amtliches Kursbuch der Deutschen Bundesbahn (complete national timetable) DM 3,00
Amtliches Kursbuch Nordwestdeutschland (northern section only) DM 1,50
Amtliches Kursbuch Süddeutschland (southern section only) DM 1,50
Amtliches Omnibus-Kursbuch (post and railway bus services) DM 3,00
Auslandkursbuch (foreign services) DM 1,00
Fernkursbuch (long distance trains) DM 1,00
Reisefernfahrplan (express trains) DM 0,50
Städteverbindungen (connections between main centres)
Amtlicher Taschenfahrplan (regional timetable) DM 0,50
Amtlicher Kurzfahrplan (arrivals and departures from a single town) DM 0,20 and DM 0,30

station from which it began. The reduction on this type of ticket is less than that for a return, but is nevertheless worth having if one is making this type of tour.

Some stations offer a door-to-door luggage service; for 2,50 Mark up to 50 kg luggage will be delivered or collected from any address in the region of the station concerned. There is also an efficient system of registered luggage by which the passenger can ensure that his luggage travels on the same train as himself, if not on a faster connection. This service is, to my mind, a bargain; it also operates from London, in which case customs examination takes place at the destination.

Instead of an emergency communication cord, German trains are fitted with a pneumatic brake, which can be operated from any compartment. There is no fixed penalty for misuse, but passengers are warned that the consequences of misuse could be serious.

Restaurant cars and sleeping cars are run by the DSG (Deutsche Schlafwagen- und Speisewagen-Gesellschaft). Meals in dining cars cost pretty much the same as in British trains. The one exception is breakfast, which is more expensive in Germany. Some trains are justifiably proud of their restaurant facilities, which include wines from the DSG cellars. Many offer a corridor service for coffee and sausages — but be warned: a beaker of coffee costs 1,65 Mark!

German stations, too, frequently have excellent restaurant facilities, and the station restaurant may be one of the best in town. In large cities, the stations are central congregating points for immigrant workers, and even at midnight the Waiting Room in a city station will be quite full.

By 1980, West Germany is to have an entirely new network of links between major cities, with trains running at 150 miles per hour. Already, German progress in electrification is impressive by British standards; many of the major routes (15% of the total) are already equipped for electric trains.

Fig 91 Two symbols of progress: the network of electrification wires and the Trans-Europe-Express train. The TEE shown here is the "Parsifal" on its way to Paris. Photo: Glyn Hatherall.

East Germany

Trains in East Germany are slower than those in the West, and there is less certainty that one will arrive on time. Trains which link East and West Germany are particularly slow; one does the journey from Dresden to Cologne at an average speed of about 35 miles per hour — and it is supposed to be an express! Of the 16,200 km of track, 1095 km were electrified by the beginning of 1967.

Fares on East German trains are based on a standard rate (second class) of eight Pfennigs per kilometre. Workers' weekly seasons are particularly cheap.

East German railways have retained the name "Mitropa" (the pre-war name) for their dining- and sleeping-car organisation. Food in their dining cars is good, and prices reasonable. The railway system as a whole is known as the "Reichsbahn" — again the pre-war name.

A peculiarity of East German railways is double-decker carriages, used on local trains. The best-known branch line is that which connects Bad Doberan

Fig 92   Double-decker carriages on an East German local train. Photo: Zentralbild/Ritter.

with Kühlungsborn; the train runs through the main street in Bad Doberan! (I gather that attempts have been made to close this line, but they have met with strong resistance from the local inhabitants who refer to their little train affectionately as "Molly".)

Finally, a warning for tourists: it is not possible to buy return tickets to places in East Germany from West Germany or vice versa. Returns may, however, be bought in advance through travel agents in other countries.

The sick and the needy

In the provision of social services, the two Germanies differ sharply.

West Germany
The basic principle on which the West German health and insurance system works is that of compulsory private insurance. Health insurance is obligatory for those with an income of less than 900 Mark per month, unemployment and pension insurance for those with an income of less than 1800 Mark per month. Most of those who earn more than these sums insure privately.

The compulsory health insurance is handled by some two thousand regional or local insurance bodies, state-owned but financially independent. Four hundred of them are "local insurance institutions" with catchment areas of a single community. A further twelve hundred are restricted to a single factory or concern. The contributions average around 10% of the employee's income, and half the contribution is paid by the employer. (Privately insured patients — i.e. those with an income of over 900 Mark a month — pay the full sum themselves.)

Each quarter-year, the patient receives a "certificate of health insurance" which he gives to his doctor. He has the right to change his doctor at will, and without the formalities involved in such a move under the British National Health Service, but he is asked to stick to the same doctor for any given quarter-year. The doctor sends the insurance certificates back to the insurance institutions when he claims his fees. Because of the ease with which the patient can change doctors, many doctors are specialists in particular fields and there are fewer general practitioners than in Britain.

The health insurance also covers medicines, although there is a prescription charge of 1 Mark. Patients who are off work for ten days or more are exempt from prescription charges.

Hospital treatment is also covered by the health insurance; the hospital sends its bill to the insurance institution. But the latter can refuse payment if it can prove that the patient has been disobeying the doctor's instructions. Thus the German patient is more "under the thumb" than his British counterpart, who knows that whatever happens, the doctors' salaries will be unaffected!

In theory, the health insurance will also finance treatment at home, but in practice this is virtually precluded by the lack of doctors and nurses. (Germany needs another 25,000 nurses!)

The health insurance will also sponsor a recuperation holiday known as a "Kur", whenever it is thought necessary for the patient's well-being. This is a holiday of up to four weeks at a spa. The most famous type of Kur is the "Kneipp-Kur", named after Sebastian Kneipp, a Catholic priest in the last century who believed in walking barefoot through wet grass, water or fresh snow. In many German spas today you can see corpulent German businessmen tramping around in shallow water with their trousers rolled up. The spas of Germany are also centres of social and cultural life, as Cheltenham and Bath were in their hey-day.

Compulsory unemployment and old-age pension insurance contributions amount to 14% of wages or salary, and employer and employee each pay half this sum. There are separate schemes for manual workers and for white-collar workers, and the pensions are different. In 1964, manual workers received an average of 215 Mark per month retirement pension, white-collar workers 365 Mark per month. The widows' pensions averaged 168 and 242 Mark per month respectively. The contributions for accident insurance are paid in full by the employer, and the worker who has been injured can claim a life-long pension dependent upon the degree of incapacitation. Unemployment benefit is related to the worker's previous earnings.

East Germany

All social insurance in East Germany, including health insurance, is administered by the Trade Unions. All manual and office workers must be insured. The total contribution is 20% of the gross earnings up to 600 Mark per month, of which half is paid by the employer and half by the worker.

The social insurance covers all necessary medical treatment, including recuperation and medicaments. The patient has an "insurance book", which contains details of all treatment and benefits he has received. This book is also his certificate of insurance, which entitles him to claim benefits.

Most of the doctors now work in polyclinics or out-patient centres. The 417 polyclinics are full-scale health centres, with not less than five specialist doctors, plus a dentist, physiotherapist and dispenser. The out-patient centres are smaller units and combine the work of four general practitioners, four dentists and the specialists from the nearest polyclinic. In 1966 there were 850 out-patient centres.

Fig 93 "At the dentist's" by Förster. Reproduced from "Junge Welt".

Retirement pensions are based on the pensioner's length of service, with a basic minimum of 150 Mark per month — which would not go far. Since July 1968, a system of voluntary contributions for a supplementary pension has been in operation.

Visitors

Foreign visitors to West Germany are strongly urged to take out some sort of health insurance beforehand. This can be arranged through one's travel agent, and the cost is low considering the risk involved. Visitors to East Germany do not need special insurance, as they can obtain free treatment at the polyclinics and out-patient centres.

Armed forces

At the end of the Second World War, nobody wanted a new German army. Not even the Germans wanted a new German army. But twenty years later, West Germany's army was the fourth largest in NATO. The story is rather complicated.

Five years after the end of the War, an Allensbach survey showed that 52% of the participants were against any German contribution to European defence, 33% were in favour of Germany being invited to build up her own armed forces within the framework of a European Army, and 15% were undecided. Meanwhile, the German Government was under strong pressure from some of her allies to make a contribution towards her defence. The British and French governments were still opposed to German re-armament, but the British Opposition (under Churchill) and the USA were in favour. Those in favour were motivated by the Berlin crisis and the outbreak of the Korean War.

The first small step towards the establishment of a German army came in 1951 with the enrolment of 10,000 men as members of the Federal Border Police. Two years later, the strength of this force was doubled.

At the same time, an unsuccessful attempt was made to form a European Army. In 1950, NATO had decided to form an Atlantic Army with German participation. This decision was followed two years later by the Bonn and Paris treaties, which

Fig 94   Cartoon by Lothar Ursinus, reproduced from the Desch collection.

sought to establish the European Defence Community. But this plan collapsed in 1954 when it was rejected by the French National Assembly.

Thus the problem of a German defence contribution remained unsolved. However, action was not long delayed, and two months after the French rejection of the EDC idea, the Paris agreements admitted Germany to NATO and the Western European Union as a full member. The German constitution had already been amended to enable the Federal Government to set up an army, and as soon as the Paris agreement came into force in May 1955, plans were set in motion for recruitment. The first thousand troops were enlisted on 2 January 1956.

Public opinion, as reflected in the polls, had meanwhile changed. By November 1954, Allensbach researchers found that 45% of the population were in favour of a West German army, 37% against and 18% undecided.

So far, the West German army was still a small volunteer force. But not for long. In April 1956 a law was passed determining the legal status of the soldiers and giving the forces the title "Federal Army", and in July of the same year, the West German parliament passed the necessary legislation for conscription. The majority in the vote on this issue was 104, but according to Allensbach figures, public opinion was more evenly divided.

At first, the period of compulsory military service was 12 months, but in 1962 this was extended to 18. Many young Germans, however, prefer to sign on for

Fig 95 East German soldier on guard at the Memorial to the Victims of Fascism in East Berlin. Photo: author.

two years as volunteers, thus sacrificing an extra six months in return for much better pay and working conditions.

In 1966, just over 300,000 young men born in 1947 received their call-up papers. Of these 72% were found unconditionally fit for service, and 18% fit for certain types of work only. There were 2489 applications for exemption, of which 1206 were successful.

By 1967 the West German forces numbered 436,000 men, including the navy and air forces. They are equipped with all the latest weapons, including atomic weapons, but the "finger on the trigger" is in Washington. All the West German forces are also subject to NATO control — a fact which is frequently reiterated (and justifiably so) by German spokesmen who wish to make it clear that West Germany does not possess an aggressive army. The motto of the Federal Army is "citizens in uniform", which implies a claim that the new West German army is more democratic than that of the Nazis. But several critics have claimed that this ideal is one which originated among the politicians and was not held by the soldiers who were put in charge of the new army. Indeed, because the only experienced officers in Germany were those who had served under Hitler, the new army leaders came under fire both within Germany and abroad on the grounds that they were mainly "old Nazis".

At the end of 1966, there were three army corps headquarters, twelve army divisions, five fighter-bomber squadrons, three transport and three fighter squadrons, and two air-reconnaissance squadrons. The navy comprised two naval headquarters, three destroyer squadrons, one coastal patrol squadron, four motor torpedo boat, five minesweeper, one landing craft and two naval air squadrons. In addition, there were some 18,000 members of the Federal Border Police, and 10,000 men in the Home Defence Force. It is estimated that the number of reserves is around 480,000.

These German troops are supplemented by the forces of other NATO countries stationed in West Germany. In 1967 the magazine "Stern", quoting what it claimed to be "semi-official sources", stated that there were 225,000 US and 63,000 British troops in West Germany, compared with 258,000 Soviet troops in East Germany.

East Germany

The formation of an East German border police force began immediately after the end of the War, and by the summer of 1948 its strength had reached 9100. At the same time, the railway police force had reached 7400. In July 1948, a start was made on a "police force in barracks", which was in practice a euphemism for "army" in a state which declared itself opposed to all armies. By May 1953, it had reached a strength of 100,000.

In 1955, East Germany joined the Warsaw Pact countries, and agreed to the formation of a joint command for the forces of the participating countries. A few months later, the constitution was amended so that defence of the fatherland was officially made an "honourable national duty of citizens of the German Democratic Republic". In January 1956, the National People's Army was formed; it assimilated the "police force in barracks" a few months later.

The introduction of conscription was delayed until 1962. Cynics in the West suggest that introduction of conscription at an earlier date would merely have increased the number of emigrants to the West. In any case, considerable pressure had already been brought on members of the Free German Youth to volunteer for military service.

Two volunteer military bodies are worthy of mention at this stage. In 1952, the Society for Sport and Technics was founded as a cross between a youth organisation and a military training squad. Two years later, a start was made on the formation of "factory combat groups", which are an instrument of home defence, besides having a duty to deal with industrial unrest.

Fig 96   Cartoon by Klaus Vonderwerth, reproduced from "Junge Welt".

The East German handbooks do not give any account of the number of men in their forces. According to Western estimates, the National People's Army is 185,500 strong, the Border Police 8,000, the Alert Police 17,500, the Transport Police 8,000. The Society for Sport and Technics has some 450,000 members, the combat groups a total strength of around 320,000. There are also some 650,000 reserves.

What the East German handbooks do stress is the social structure of the People's Army. 86% of all the officers come from workers' and farmers' families. Many of the high-ranking officers were active in the anti-Nazi resistance movement during and before the Second World War. On the whole, political and ideological considerations played a more important role in the selection of Peoples' Army officers than did past military experience.

GERMANS OF THE PAST

A little history

The Germans are a collection of tribes all belonging to the Indo-European family. They first entered the historical scene when they were invaded unsuccessfully by the Romans. The latter had reached the Danube and the west bank of the Rhine (coming from France, or Gaul as it was then), but were unable to penetrate the land between these two rivers. They suffered a major setback in the year 9 AD, when the Roman army under Varus was defeated in the Teutoberg Forest by the Cheruscan leader Hermann. Hermann had served in the Roman army, and had obtained Roman citizenship; his Latin name is Arminius. The Roman historian Tacitus has described him as "undoubtedly the liberator of Germany", yet by one of those odd turns of history, it was at the hands of one of his own subjects that he met his death.

After the sack of Rome in 410, Attila's Huns swept across Germany into the heart of modern France, where Goths and Romans joined forces to repel them. They ebbed back eastwards comparatively soon, but left their mark on every tribe in their path. Once the Hunnish threat had collapsed, Gothic and Vandal tribes carried conquest to Italy, Spain, the Balkans and even Morocco. The Lombards became established in northern Italy, while the Saxons, Angles and Jutes began to colonise the coast of Britain. In between, the Franks fought their way into Gaul; they were hard-slogging foot-soldiers, less picturesque but more lasting than the Gothic horsemen. In 486 their chieftain Clovis captured the last Roman citadel at Soissons and set up his kingdom there. Some two hundred and fifty years later, it was the success of a Frankish general Charles Martel (who defeated the Arabs and Berbers at Poitiers) which determined that Europe should remain a Christian continent.

Charlemagne

Charles Martel's grandson, who became known in Germany as Karl der Grosse, and elsewhere by his French name of Charlemagne, succeeded to the Frankish throne in 762. At that time the Franks were in possession of present-day France and Northern Germany. To his kingdom, Karl added the Bavarians, the Saxons and the Lombards; he thus became the first king to unite many German tribes under one government. In the East, his kingdom stretched to the gates of Vienna; in the West, to Barcelona which he captured in 801.

In the regions he conquered, Karl set up new bishoprics and carried out a process of Christianisation. He established great schools, and encouraged scholars such as Alcuin of York and Hrabanus Maurus. Carolingian architecture is also worthy of note; an excellent example is the Cathedral at Aachen, where Karl spent much of his reign and where he is buried.

On Christmas Day, 800, Karl was crowned Holy Roman Emperor in Rome; with this event, an empire was born which was to last for a thousand years.

The Holy Roman Empire

Had Karl been given the gift of seeing into the future, I doubt if he would have been happy to know what the coming centuries would bring to his Empire. His grandsons divided it between them, and from then on the Empire became more and more a conglomeration of virtually independent kingdoms and princedoms. The Emperors frequently disagreed with the Pope, and the balance between ecclesiastic and temporal power was continually being upset. Indeed, for few of its thousand years did the Empire deserve the name "Roman", for it was more a German Empire than it was Roman; its full title was "The Holy Roman Empire of the German Nation". The title of Emperor was, in theory, one bestowed by

Fig 97   The Empire around 1100 AD

election at every vacancy, but in practice it remained hereditary for long periods in various families. From 1438 until 1806 it stayed — barring one trivial breach — with the Hapsburgs.

German mediaeval history is a particularly complicated story, but one aspect of it is worth mentioning here. This is the colonisation of large parts of what is now Poland and Czechoslovakia by German knights, monks and friars. Both North and South Germans took part, and one important result was the formation of a mixed dialect, the basis of modern High German. This colonisation is also a key factor about which Germans and Poles have argued for centuries, and upon which some German nationalists have based claims to many areas east of Germany's borders.

The Reformation

On 31 October 1517, a learned Augustan friar in Wittemberg posted a protest on the church door. By doing so he changed the course of German — and indeed of west European — history. This was Martin Luther, and although in the first instance he was protesting only against the sale of indulgences (bought pardons), his deed led to the splitting of the Church into two camps, Catholic and Protestant. For Luther's differences with the Church went deep; he laid much emphasis on the Bible and on faith, proclaiming that good works were not enough. Of the Church sacraments, he regarded communion and baptism as the only two having great importance. In 1521 he appeared before the Diet of Worms, but refused to take back what he had said. Two years later, however, he was unwilling to support the extension of a religious quarrel into the secular sphere; the German peasants staged a revolt, largely inspired by Luther's ideas, but he refused to support them. In the later years of his life, he was forced to rely on the Count of Saxony to protect him from the Emperor. In a small room in the Wartburg Castle, he worked on a translation of the Bible that (largely owing to the fact that printing had recently been invented) soon became widespread.

The remainder of the century was characterised by appalling wars fought by various German princes of Roman Catholic or Protestant allegiance. The fighting reached a climax in 1618 with the Thirty Years' War, causing incalculable devastation. The duchy of Saxony lost 900,000 men in two years and the city of Augsburg was reduced from 80,000 to 18,000 inhabitants. At the end of the war, Germany had lost a third of her population, and the Empire had almost disintegrated. The level of brutality all round can scarcely have been surpassed until the present century. The war ended with the Peace of Westphalia, which gave equality to the confessions; Germany lost Alsace to the French, and the mouths of the Oder, Elbe and Weser to the Swedes. Switzerland and the northern Netherlands formally left the Empire.

Prussia

To many Englishmen, particularly those less kindly disposed towards the Germans, the words "German" and "Prussian" are synonymous. Yet it was not until the 17th and 18th centuries that Prussia rose to power among the other German provinces. Prussia had passed into Lutheran hands at the time of the Reformation, and had amalgamated with Brandenburg in 1618. During the Thirty Years' War, when so many states were being weakened, Prussia gained in strength, and in 1701 she raised herself to the dignity of a kingdom. Her first great monarch was Frederick the Great, who ascended the throne in 1740. As a result of a harsh military upbringing, Frederick rejected as effeminate all Christian and humanitarian virtues. He saw himself as the servant of the state, and began work on a complete revision of the German Law, which he intended to make independent of the ruler. He built up an extremely efficient army and also inaugurated a civil service, the ancestor of present-day German bureaucracy (which must surely be one of the most impersonal in the world). As a result of a quarrel with Austria, Frederick became engaged in the Seven Years' War. Its outcome made no difference to Prussian territory, but made it clear to Frederick that he would be unable to extend his kingdom by force.

Prussia discreetly encouraged the forces of the French Revolution, and although drawn into the wars of royalist intervention that followed, she continued to play a less vigorous part than Britain or Austria. In the long run, however, her ruling class came into conflict with Napoleon, and suffered a shattering defeat at the battle of Jena-Auerstedt in 1806. The same year, the South and West German states joined the "Rhenish Federation" under Napoleon's protection, and the fiction of the "Holy Roman Empire" was formally ended. The Hapsburgs, however, retained the title of Austrian Emperors.

The road to unity

After 1806, the German states were largely independent, though linked in the loose confederations (the Rhenish Federation, the German Federation and the North German Federation) which succeeded each other, new federations being formed in 1815 and 1867. Real unity was not attained until it was virtually forced on the country by Prussia, thanks largely to the efforts of one man, Otto von Bismarck. He had served as Prussian ambassador to the German Federation, and in Paris, and in 1862 became Ministerpräsident. As a result of success in three wars (Danish War, Austro-Prussian War and Franco-Prussian War), Prussia's strength increased considerably. During the siege of Paris in 1871, Bismarck had the king of Prussia crowned German Emperor (Wilhelm I). He himself became Chancellor. The new Constitution gave him wide powers, and he ruled efficiently. His political career came to an abrupt end in 1890, when he disagreed with the new, young Emperor Wilhelm II and was promptly dismissed.

Whereas Bismarck had succeeded in his foreign policy and had managed to keep the peace with Russia, his successors made many enemies. The result was the First World War, which ended in 1918 with a crushing defeat for Germany and the end of the second Empire.

Chaos and dictatorship

Despite considerable loss of territory, Germany emerged from the War as a single country, albeit a poor one with a huge debt in the form of reparations. In the November Revolution of 1918 the monarchy was abolished and a republic set up. Because the constitution for this republic was adopted at a national convention in Weimar, the state itself became known as the Weimar Republic. It was a democracy, and its main fault may well have been that it took the theory of democracy too far; an abundance of political parties made effective government difficult. In its early years, it managed to suppress takeover attempts by right and left wing radicals, but the effect on Germany of the world-wide economic crisis in 1929 spelt its doom. The National Socialists (Nazis for short) had obtained only twelve seats in the 1928 elections, but by 1932 they were, with 230 seats, the strongest party.

In 1933 the Nazi leader, Adolf Hitler, became Chancellor (a title denoting a position much nearer that of Prime Minister than Chancellor of the Exchequer). The same year, he used a fire in the parliament buildings as an excuse to suppress Communist and Social Democrat organisations. The parties remaining in the parliament voted in favour of an Enabling Act, which gave Hitler much wider powers.

Fig 98   Defeat, 1945. Photo: Lex Hornsby & Partners.

156 GERMANS OF THE PAST

The period which thus began was the darkest in Germany's history. Hitler used the term "Dritte Reich" (Third Empire) to show that he was continuing the traditions of the German Empire, and called himself "Führer" (Leader). He achieved some degree of popularity by solving the country's unemployment problem; this he did by starting work on large government building programmes such as the motorway network. But the main features of Hitler's rule were uncomprising dictatorship, anti-Communism, anti-Semitism and an aggressive

Fig 99   Germany in 1945: the Zones of Occupation

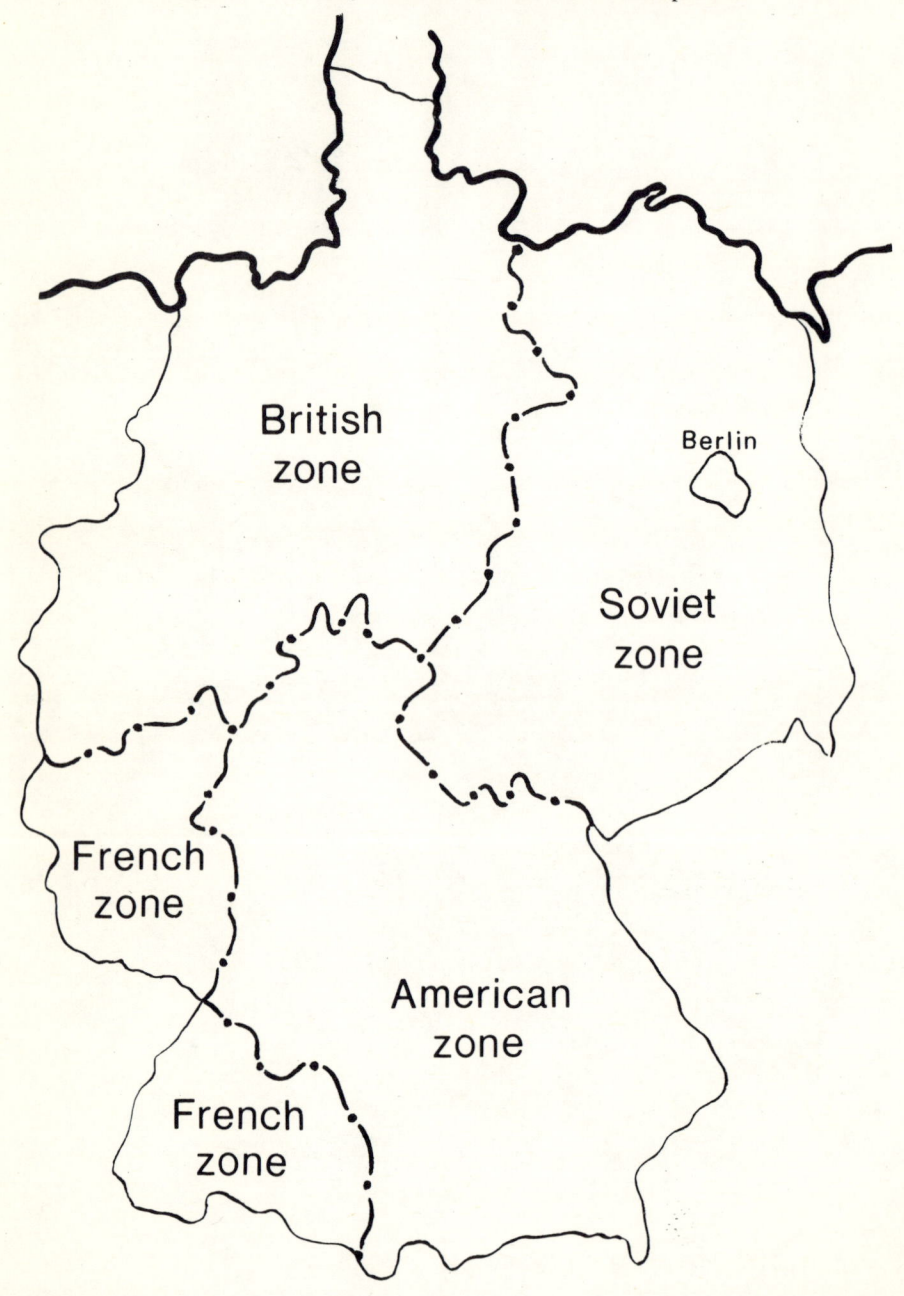

foreign policy. The mass murder of millions of Jews in the concentration camps is the worst example of attempted genocide the world has ever known.

Any opposition to Hitler had to be underground. The main resistance came from the Army generals (who tried to assassinate Hitler in 1944) and from a group of influential people around Carl Friedrich Goerdeler, a former mayor of Leipzig. A brave but futile demonstration of resistance was made by a brother and sister, Hans and Sophie Scholl, at the University of Munich. It cost them their lives.

By marching into Poland in September 1939, Hitler unleashed the Second World War. Once again, Germany was crushed, and the Third Empire ended more ignominiously than its predecessors.

East Germany, West Germany

The Second World War ended with a total surrender by Germany to the Allies who had conquered her (Britain, Russia and the USA). At the Yalta Conference in 1945, it was decided that Germany should be divided into four zones of occupation, though provision was made for "co-ordinated administration". Later the same year, an Allied Control Council was set up for the whole of Germany, and an Allied Kommandatura for the capital, Berlin.

It is now abundantly clear that the Allies had different concepts of how a future German state should be run. In the West, a capitalist economy was rebuilt with

Fig 100 West Berliners watch as the Wall which divides their city is built, August 1961. Photo: Associated Press.

NEUE ZEIT
Die führende Tages-Zeitung
YOU ARE LEAVING
THE AMERICAN SECTOR
ВЫ ВЫЕЗЖАЕТЕ ИЗ
АМЕРИКАНСКОГО СЕКТОРА
VOUS SORTEZ
DU SECTEUR AMERICAIN
CHECKPOINT
PRESS POINT
BERLIN
BERLINER BÄREN STADTRUNDFAHRT
Sightseeing Tours
BERLINER BÄREN
STADTRUNDFAHRT
APOTHEKE

Marshall Aid; in the East the economy was rebuilt on Socialist lines, beginning with a land reform in 1945. In the West, a multi-party system of democracy was established; in the East the parties united to form a common front, under the leadership of the Communists.

In January 1947 the British and American Zones were merged to form a "Bi-zone". This was intended as the first step towards a united Germany, but in practice it meant the further isolation of the Soviet Zone. The following year, as a result of Russian protests over Western reluctance to inform the Control Council of plans for the Western zones, the Control Council ceased to function. Three months later, separate currencies were introduced in East and West Germany. A Russian blockade of Berlin was overcome by a massive airlift; nevertheless, the blockade lasted from June 1948 until May 1949. Meanwhile, separate administrations had been set up in East and West Berlin.

In 1949, East and West Germany became self-governing states under the respective titles German Democratic Republic and Federal Republic of Germany. (They did not attain full sovereignty, however, until six years later.) The East German state has not so far been recognised by Western governments. In May 1955, West Germany became a member of NATO and East Germany a signatory to the Warsaw Pact.

Since the end of the War, there had been a steady stream of population movement westwards, both from East Germany and from the former German territories which had been placed under Polish and Russian administration. Those leaving East Germany (between 1949 and 1960 there were over two million) came mostly through Berlin, which was an open city. In 1961, largely as a result of enforced collectivisation in agriculture, the number of people leaving East Germany increased sharply and by July it had reached thirty thousand a month. As the East German economy could not stand such a loss of manpower, the border was sealed off on August 13 1961 with the now famous Berlin Wall. The division of Germany was complete.

Now two Germanies face each other across a barbed-wire frontier. Each has grown more hostile towards the other from year to year. Both have become adept at supplying the outsider with masses of propaganda to prove that the other side is evil.

Fig 101 A bus-load of tourists about to take a look "behind the Iron Curtain" in Berlin. Photo: German Tourist Information Bureau.

A nation of thinkers

I do not know who coined the phrase "the nation of thinkers and poets" to describe the Germans, but it is a phrase which has certainly caught on, particularly among nationalist-minded Germans. Today, fortunately, it is a phrase which is mainly used sarcastically. Yet there is some truth in it. For Germany has given the world a large number of thinkers and poets, and during the centuries has made a major contribution to Western thought. Only a few movements and names can be mentioned here.

Early Christian thought

Learning entered Germany on the heels of Christianity. Missionary bishops, urged on by Frankish monarchs, gradually set up dioceses, and throughout the country monasteries appeared which became seats of learning. History, theology, natural science and what would now be termed philosophy were at that time as inseparable as were France, Germany and the Netherlands. One of the most famous abbeys was Fulda, whose abbot Hrabanus Maurus (later Archbishop of Mainz) wrote in the middle of the 9th century a prototype encyclopaedia called simply "De Universo" ("About Everything").

As the Middle Ages evolved from the Dark, German thought was more cautiously orthodox than that of other Western European countries. The best-known thinkers of this period were Albertus Magnus (1206-80) and Meister Eckhart (1260-1327), but the former, though a pioneer in the rebirth of Aristotelian scholasticism, did not venture outside the doctrinal field, and the latter was not concerned with research but with mysticism.

The Renaissance

The dispersion of Greek libraries from captured Constantinople more or less coincided with the invention of the printing press. The result was a sudden rebirth of learning. Johann Reuchlin (1455-1522) promoted the study of Greek and initiated that of Hebrew. His followers began to popularise the works of Plato and freed those of Aristotle from the doctrinal interpretations into which they had been woven by Aquinas. Monastic colleges, meanwhile, had begun to develop into universities (though less rapidly than in countries to the south and west); the universities of Erfurt and Heidelberg were founded at the very end of the 14th century, Leipzig and Rostock early in the 15th.

Modern philosophy

The first of the modern German philosophers was Leibniz (born in 1648, later counsellor to the dukes of Brunswick-Lüneberg). He was a man of his age, and his thought was linked to that of his contemporaries in other lands, notably Descartes, Locke and Spinoza. Like Descartes, Leibniz was essentially a mathematician, but he preserved something of the "universal man" visualised in Renaissance times, being also a diplomat, economist, historian, linguist, lawyer and chemist. If we disregard differences of terminology, his concept of energy as the basis of all matter appears quite modern; though many phenomena he was able to explain away only by ascribing them to illusion.

Immanuel Kant Born in 1724, Kant was the first major thinker to emerge from the not very academic soil of Prussia, though his grandfather had been a Scottish emigrant. He spent long years as an unobtrusive teacher of mathematics and physics before publishing his famous "Critiques" of Pure Reason, Practical Reason and Judgement. These deal respectively with thought processes, morality and judgement. Though the former is the best known, it is the second treatise which contains Kant's "categorical imperative". In this, he suggests that man should always act in such a way that the principles upon which he is acting at any given moment could form the basis of a more general morality. He believed in an instinctive sense of duty, and conceded an equally instinctive sense of immortality. His "moral proof of the existence of God" shows him to be a deist rather than a liberal Christian.

Johann Fichte Born just over forty years later than Kant, Fichte developed the latter's thought to a point where it reached existentialism; thereby he revived classical concepts of pantheism. He equated a depersonalised god or "universal mind" with the total process of the phenomenal universe itself. He distinguished between the "ego" (purely subjective reasoning) and the "non-ego" (everything outside the subject), and was more reluctant than Kant had been to allow reason superiority over the material and sensual.

Georg Friedrich Hegel Though born thirty years before the turn of the century, Hegel was definitely a 19th century philosopher. He studied at Tübingen, Jena and Heidelberg, and felt above all the need to explain the turmoil of international politics that followed the French Revolution. His famous scheme of thesis, antithesis and synthesis, constantly repeating itself in all fields of life and thought, amounts to an acceptance of struggle as the supreme law of growth, with less concern for any fixed moral principles than his predecessors had felt. It became a political expedient employed both by the builders of the Prussian military state and by the more abidingly influential socialist planners, Marx, Engels and Feuerbach. Indeed, it forms the basis of Marx' dialectic. But anyone who uses it to defend a political theory in which a given state is declared perfect, has to explain away the infinite repetition inherent in the original Hegelian concepts; what claim has any given synthesis to stop the recurring process and to be immune from further antitheses?

Arthur Schopenhauer The product of an unbalanced ancestry and a disturbed childhood, Schopenhauer (1788-1860) rebelled against Hegel's drastic but willing acceptance of the struggle. He called his main work "The World as Will and Idea", constantly exalting will-power as more powerful in practice than intellect but finding nothing consoling in the world which it has created. He shrank away from any activity such as sexual procreation which tended to carry on human existence. Taking up the theme of will-power from Schopenhauer, Friedrich Nietzsche (born fifty years later) accepted the march of the masterful will-power with all its attendant cruelty. His philosophical novel, "Thus Spoke Zarathustra" is one of the most uncompromising works ever written; he glorifies the "Superman" who has overcome all human emotion.

Nationalism

German romantic interest in the other Indo-European languages was first promoted by the poet Friedrich von Schlegel (born 1772) and his brother August Wilhelm, professor of Sanskrit at Bonn University. Their keenest disciple was Karl Josias Bunsen, Prussian ambassador to London. He in turn encouraged a younger scholar Friedrich Max Müller (1823-1900), who progressed from a study of a common Aryan language to the concept of an Aryan race.

It would be unfair to stigmatise Germany alone for the abuses to which this quickly gave rise. Bunsen and Müller had English disciples, and similar ideas were taken up by some French theorists. But it was in Germany that these ideas eventually led to a viable political movement. Gustaf Kossinna, an East Prussian born in 1858, spoke of "German prehistory, a pre-eminently national science" and claimed that all evidence of advanced prehistoric culture was the work of communities related to the Germans and Scandinavians of his own time. A less unscrupulous preacher was the English-born Houston Stewart Chamberlain (no relation to the Birmingham politicians) who advocated inbreeding of the aristocracy with careful attention to environment. This theory was over-simplified by Alfred Rosenberg to form the basis for the Nazi doctrines, while Hitler, who understood even less of the original, carried aspects of it to extremes which have made the whole Chamberlain school anathema.

Socialism

Parallel and hostile to the nationalist movement, there was a social revolutionary force in literature and industry. Feuerbach and Marx were thinkers who deserve to be classed as philosophers, while their successors were content to comment on Marxist theories and work out programmes of utilitarian action. Until the last moment of 1914, German Social Democracy was outspokenly pacifist and may be given credit for putting on the brake. Bertha von Suttner published an appeal to workers of all nations at the beginning of the century, calling for passive resistance; it sold throughout Germany. Her radicalism was less fierce, however, than that of her fellow-revolutionary Rosa Luxemburg. Meanwhile, Lasalle's cautious reformist socialism was being eclipsed by more thorough plans for a complete proletarian dictatorship, of which August Bebel was the prophet. Indeed, at any time before 1917 it could have been predicted that Germany, rather than Russia, would be the home of the first successful revolution. But it was perhaps the presence of Czarist Russia on the other side which reconciled the majority of parliamentary Social Democrats to a European war.

Existentialism

Of the three major existentialists, Heidegger, Jaspers and Sartre, the former two are Germans. However, they both stress the points which separate them from the rest of the existentialist school, and it will be as well, in closing this chapter, to deal with them separately.

Heidegger Born in 1889, Martin Heidegger became Professor of Philosophy at Marburg in 1923 and at Freiburg in 1928. His main work, "Sein und Zeit" ("Being and Time") was published in 1927 — at least, the first part was published then, but no sequel has yet appeared. He is concerned with "being" and the phenomena of anxiety, care, death and temporality. He elaborated on Nietzsche's atheism by claiming that in the 20th century, God is no longer a living God. He became Rector of Freiburg University in 1933, and in his inaugural lecture welcomed the political take-over by the Nazis. Because of his political leanings, he was temporarily banned from lecturing in 1945, but since the ban was lifted his lectures have been popular, even after his retirement in 1951.

Jaspers Born six years earlier than Heidegger, Karl Jaspers studied medicine and became Professor of Psychology at Heidelberg. Later, having changed disciplines, he became Professor of Philosophy at the same university. His magnum opus is "Philosophie", written in 1932. Existence, for Jaspers, involves three things: the fact of living in a situation which, though not chosen by the individual, is nevertheless not alien to him; the freedom to choose; and the facility to communicate with others. He tries to see philosophy facing objective thought on the one hand and transcendence on the other. The situations in which we see that we must live with suffering, pain and death show us the inadequacy of philosophical and theological systems, and give us intimations of the transcendental, or of God. The Nazis sacked Jaspers in 1937, and he was not reinstated until 1945; three years later he took up a professorship in Basle. In recent years, he has turned to more practical phophecy, and has written a best-seller, "The Future of Germany". He has made a number of television appearances; one of the best known was in 1960, when he entered the field of politics by advancing the view that freedom in East Germany was more important than reunification.

The literary heritage

German literature can, for the purposes of a general book of this nature, be said to begin with the Lay of Hildebrand. Exactly when this was first composed is uncertain; the only extant manuscript dates from the end of the 8th century or the beginning of the 9th. The lay is a poem in unrhyming, alliterative verse and describes a fight between Hildebrand and his son Hadubrand. The end of the lay is missing, but we can conclude from the tragic tone that it must have described the death of one of the combatants.

The first German poet to use rhyme was Otfried von Weissenburg, whose verse "Harmony of the Gospel" was written in the latter half of the 9th century. In five books it not only tells the gospel story but also interprets each event metaphysically.

The middle of the 12th century saw the appearance of some delightful humorous epics known as the "Minstrels' Epics", though it is far from certain that they were written by minstrels. They tell, in lively terms, a series of adventure tales, each with a clear moral tone.

The courtly period

The last of the heroic epics, the Lay of the Nibelungs, was written about 1200 and combined older stories to form a whole that was then set in the milieu of the mediaeval court. It tells of the murder of Siegfried by the Burgundians and of the revenge instigated by Siegfried's widow, Kriemhilde.

At the same time, three great poets were writing what have come to be known as the Courtly Epics. Hartmann von Aue made epics from the stories of Pope Gregory, Iwein and Eric (the latter two were characters in the Arthurian legends). Gottfried von Strassburg told in verse the tale of Tristan and Isolde, using the love potion of the legend as a symbol for love itself. Wolfram von Eschenbach composed an epic based on the tale of Parsifal and the Holy Grail; he mingled exciting adventures with passages of inspired religious writing.

The courtly society for whom these epics were written also delighted in the "minne" poems, which told of unhappy love. They were written in the first person, and frequently depicted the situation of a minstrel in love with a lady at court, who always stood aloof. The greatest of the Minnesänger was Walther von der Vogelweide, who also wrote some biting political verses and some satirical attacks on the Papacy.

Mastersingers and Baroque

The mastersingers, who followed three centuries after the minnesingers, retained the same verse forms, but took their themes from religious subjects. The most

---

Fig 102   Part of Goethe's manuscript for "Faust, Part Two". This page shows Faust's final speech, in which he sees a promise of true happiness in providing new land for colonisation by building dykes. "In anticipation of such happiness, I now enjoy the finest moment" — his closing words. Photo: Lex Hornsby & Partners.

Eröffn' ich Räume vielen Millionen,
Nicht sicher zwar, doch tätig-frei zu wohnen.
Grün das Gefilde, fruchtbar; Mensch und Herde
Sogleich behaglich auf der neuesten Erde,
Gleich angesiedelt an des Hügels Kraft,
Den aufgewälzt kühn-emsige Völkerschaft.
Im Innern hier ein paradiesisch Land,
Da rase draußen Flut bis auf zum Rand,
Und wie sie nascht, gewaltsam einzuschießen,
Gemeindrang eilt, die Lücke zu verschließen.
Ja! diesem Sinne bin ich ganz ergeben,
Das ist der Weisheit letzter Schluß:
Nur der verdient sich Freiheit wie das Leben,
Der täglich sie erobern muß.
Und so verbringt, umrungen von Gefahr,
Hier Kindheit, Mann und Greis sein tüchtig Jahr.
Solch ein Gewimmel möcht ich sehn,
Auf freiem Grunde mit freiem Volke stehn.
Zum Augenblicke dürft ich sagen:
Verweile doch, du bist so schön!
Es kann die Spur von meinen Erdetagen
Nicht in Äonen untergehn. —
Im Vorgefühl von solchem hohen Glück
Genieß ich jetzt den höchsten Augenblick.

            Faust sinkt zurück, die Lemuren
    fassen ihn auf und legen ihn auf den Boden.

prolific and best-known of the mastersingers was Hans Sachs, who wrote 4300 poems and 300 plays.

The Baroque period in the 17th century brought to Germany the style of the Renaissance. Martin Opitz, an early Baroque theoretician, laid down firm rules for a new style of metre in German poetry, in which only trochaic and iambic forms were permitted; this left no room for the use of consecutive unstressed syllables. He also translated into German Sir Philipp Sidney's "Arcadia". Paul Fleming introduced a new personal element into his poems and hymns — all was based on inner experience. Andreas Gryphius combined a dogmatic faith with dreadful pictures of death and decay. Friedrich von Logau, a stylistic disciple of Opitz, assailed the brutality of the Thirty Years' War in epigrammatic verse, and Christoffel von Grimmelshausen did so more powerfully in his long novel "Simplicius Simplicissimus".

The golden age

The golden age of German literature began with Friedrich Gottlieb Klopstock. He worked for nearly thirty years on his epic poem "The Messiah". In his shorter poems, he shows a new sense of joy in living, and an enthusiastic piety.

Lessing   Gotthold Ephraim Lessing (1729-1781) has been called the "father of German literature". He introduced the "bourgeois tragedy", and showed in his play "Emilia Galotti" that tragedy need not concern itself only with the upper crust of society. In "Nathan the Wise" he made a plea for tolerance between the religions; the play shows a Jew, a Templar and a Mahommedan who discover they are related to each other.

Goethe   The importance of Goethe (1749-1832) can be seen from the wording of the question an Oxford German don put to his colleagues a few years ago. He asked, "Which ten writers besides Goethe should undergraduates study?" Goethe was an all-round genius, and dabbled in botany, geology and politics. His early novel, "Werther" is a tale of unrequited love, rather neglected today, but not without its merits. His greatest work is the drama "Faust", the second part of which is a metaphysical dramatic poem leading to the hero's salvation.

Schiller   A great friend of Goethe's, Schiller (1759-1805) wrote excellent aesthetic treatises and dramas, together with many types of poetry. His last drama, "William Tell", has sold three and a half million copies in one paperback edition alone. He was a Professor of History, and incorporated French history into his play "The Maid of Orleans", and English history in "Mary Stuart", besides writing a powerful trilogy on the native theme of Wallenstein.

Hölderlin   A writer of "difficult" poetry, Hölderlin based much of his writing on Greek models. He wrote little in the last forty years of his life, for he went insane. In a novel, "Hyperion", he portrayed the futility of human existence.

Kleist   Another contemporary of Goethe and Schiller, Heinrich von Kleist was a more violent personality. In his drama "Penthesilea" the heroine sets loose her dogs on her lover Achilles and even joins them in tearing him to pieces. Kleist also wrote some spine-chilling short stories. He ended his life with a suicide pact.

19th century writers

If the 18th century is the classical age of German literature, the 19th might be considered the most varied. For the first third of it, Goethe was still alive and writing his finest works. At the same time, the Romantic period reached its climax. It had begun in the preceding century and one of its greatest writers (Friedrich Leopold von Hardenberg, known as Novalis) died in 1801. Romanticism was an escapist movement, dreaming of an art world superior to everyday life. It was

THE LITERARY HERITAGE

closely linked with orthodox Catholicism and with the birth of nationalist pride. It expressed itself in the lyric and in the short prose form known as the "Novelle". The hero of Eichendorff's "Memoirs of a Good-for-Nothing" and Chamisso's "Peter Schlemihl" are good examples of typical Romantic heroes, living in a world far removed from our humdrum existence. The extreme of this tendency is found in the often macabre fairy-tales of the Brothers Grimm, and in the ballad-anthology "Des Knaben Wunderhorn" ("The Boy's Magic Horn") edited by Arnim and Brentano. Folk lyrics of this kind inspired Walter Scott, first as a collector and later as an original poet.

The twenty years following Goethe's death are noted for the works of a number of individualistic writers. Georg Büchner wrote dramas that show a markedly modern attitude to violence, and were it not for his tragically early death (in 1837, at the age of 24) he would probably have become one of Germany's greatest writers. At the same time Heinrich Heine was writing poems that show both satirical wit and sincerity of feeling — though it is sometimes difficult to separate the two.

Hebbel Christian Friedrich Hebbel (1813-1863) is neglected today, but in many ways he was a master of dramatic technique. He had a clear view of the need for drama to reflect the inner tragedy of man, namely his resistance to the changing world. His dramas are based on stories taken from periods of decisive change in world history (the coming of Christianity, the rise of the bourgeoisie, etc).

The latter half of the 19th century saw a gradual movement into Realism, and from Realism to its more extreme form, Naturalism. The Realists saw life as something which needed to be portrayed, rather than as something the writer should try to escape from. The realistic novelists such as Raabe and Fontane did, however, restrict the life they mirrored to those aspects of life which they felt should be mirrored, namely to that in life which was worthy. The poetess Annette von Droste-Hülshoff (an early Realist) combined precise descriptions of nature with vague portrayal of subjective impressions. The humorist Wilhelm Busch showed in verse and cartoon the funnier side of life — though some of his works

Fig 103   Max and Moritz — two famous characters created by Wilhelm Busch.

contain serious moral lessons. The Novellen of Theodor Storm show how realism can be combined with a sense of fate and destiny, whether symbolised in a water-lily or in a mysterious ghost on horseback.

Hauptmann Of the Naturalists, only Gerhart Hauptmann attained true greatness as a dramatist. The aim of the movement was to show life, not as the Realists wished to see it, but in its true drabness and misery. They were influenced by the industrial revolution, and Hauptmann's best drama ("The Weavers") depicts the weavers' uprising in Silesia during the 1840's. It is the first German drama to make a hero of a whole social class.

The present century

The early years of our century were characterised in German literature by the Expressionist period. The Expressionists attempted to show the same world as the Naturalists, namely industrial society with its misery and unhappiness, but at the same time they were concerned with the individual's power to raise the ego over the environment and overcome the suffering of the world. There is a strong sense of the supernatural in some of their work. In Werfel's "The Man in the Mirror" it is the hero's own reflection which takes on a daemonic power and wants to lead him to destruction, while a monk (appearing in several different disguises) symbolises divine intervention.

Mann The greatest German novelist of this century has undoubtedly been Thomas Mann (1875-1955). He carried into the novel Schopenhauer's concepts of Will and Idea, and demonstrated in several ways the conquest of the Will by the artistic Idea. In "Buddenbrooks", his first major work which shows striking maturity, this is reflected in the decay of a whole family, and the downfall is traced through several generations. The hero of "The Magic Mountain", however, succeeds in finding a new meaning to life through an understanding of death and decay.

Brecht What Mann was to the novel, Bertold Brecht has been to the German play. He was a prolific writer and towers above his contemporaries. He was a believer in a new type of drama, in which "alienation" is used to prevent the action appearing too real. His characters are types and often wear masks. Yet some of his greatest successes, particularly "The Good Woman of Sezuan" and "Mother Courage", occur when human characters in his drama assert themselves despite his theories. He was a Socialist, and spent the post-war years in East Berlin, where his widow took over the Berliner Ensemble theatre after his death.

As to the post-war writers, it is still too early to judge their work, since much of what they have written so far may well be seen in a new light when other works by the same writers appear. Heinrich Böll has written some excellent short stories and radio plays, and has recently turned to novels, particularly "The Clown" (1963). Günter Grass ("The Tin Drum") and Martin Walser ("The Unicorn" and "Half Time") have written some notable novels. In the world of theatre, Rolf Hochhuth has written two plays, "The Representative" and "Soldiers", which attack traditional ideas of who was right and who was wrong during the Second World War. In general, after a short period of reflection and soul-searching about the Nazi era, West German literature has turned to investigations of the role of the individual in society and his search for identity. In East Germany, the literature follows the socialist line. Erwin Strittmatter's "Ole Bienkopp" is a story about a collective farm, while Christa Wolf's "Divided Heaven" tells of a young girl who goes over to West Berlin to join her boy-friend, but decides she cannot stay there and returns to the East.

There are obviously many more authors who could have been mentioned in this

THE LITERARY HERITAGE   169

Fig 104 A scene from Brecht's version of "Coriolanus", performed by the Berliner Ensemble. Brecht's widow, Helene Weigel (not pictured here) gave a magnificent performance as Volumnia in this production. Photo: Lex Hornsby & Partners.

chapter but have been omitted for reasons of space. Moreover, I have made no reference to those authors and playwrights (notably Keller, Grillparzer, Kafka, Rilke, Dürrenmatt and Frisch) who are often included in descriptions of "German literature" but who are either Austrians or Swiss. Nevertheless, I hope the above account will do something to correct the impression, still to some extent current in England, that "German literature consists of nothing but sentimental love poems".

Art and architecture

Rather than deal with painting, sculpture and architecture separately, this chapter will take in turn the main periods of German art and mention in relation to each period the most important names from all three art forms.

The mediaeval period

The greatest German painter of the mediaeval period was Stefan Lochner (born around 1410, died 1451). His most famous work is the "Madonna in the Roses": a sweet, girlish madonna in a blue robe rather artificially arranged around her, surrounded by roses in a gold frame. The picture has a sense of precision, simplicity and pious emotion. Lochner was the leader of a group of artists in Cologne, and another of his pictures, the Adoration of the Magi, is to be seen in the Cathedral there.

In the early Middle Ages, Germany followed the Romanesque style of architecture, seen in the cathedrals of Aachen, Worms, Mainz and Bamberg. This was soon replaced by the Gothic style which the Germans came to regard as peculiarly their own. Its strong, pointed shapes reached a climax in the cathedrals of Cologne and Strassbourg. In the North, particularly in Lübeck, Bremen and Hamburg, there are examples of a uniquely German style of Gothic, using red brick and known as "Backsteingotik" ("Brick Gothic").

Sculpture was mainly limited in this period to figures designed to fill niches in churches, or to stand outside the churches. But this is not to minimise the artistry in the figures. A fine example is the "Bamberg Rider", a strong, sturdy statue at Bamberg Cathedral. And an unknown artist referred to as the "Naumburg Master" sculpted amazingly lifelike figures for the cathedrals of Naumburg and Meissen. Wood was also used for some carving, frequently painted and gilded. This style can be seen at its best in St Elizabeth's Church in Marburg.

Renaissance

The first of Germany's renaissance masters was Martin Schongauer, a 15th century artist who made elegant, detailed sketches. He compensated for a lack of colour with beauty of form and delicacy of shading.

Better known is Albrecht Dürer (1471-1528). He began with engraving and wood-cutting, and later carried over the same techniques into his paintings, which are noted for their detail and their perfection of line. He visited Venice and came under the influence of Venetian artists. A great series of his woodcuts depicts the Revelation of St John in stark and powerful tones. In contrast, he painted studies of "A Piece of Lawn" and "A Hare", and also intensive portraits, particularly of his mother and of his teacher. His best-known work is the famous "Praying Hands".

Matthias Grünewald, an early 16th century artist, is noted for the Isenheim

---

Fig 105 In Naumburg Cathedral, figures of the 13th century Markgraf (Count) Ekkehard II of Meissen and his wife Uta, carved by the unknown "Naumburg Master". Photo: Lex Hornsby & Partners.

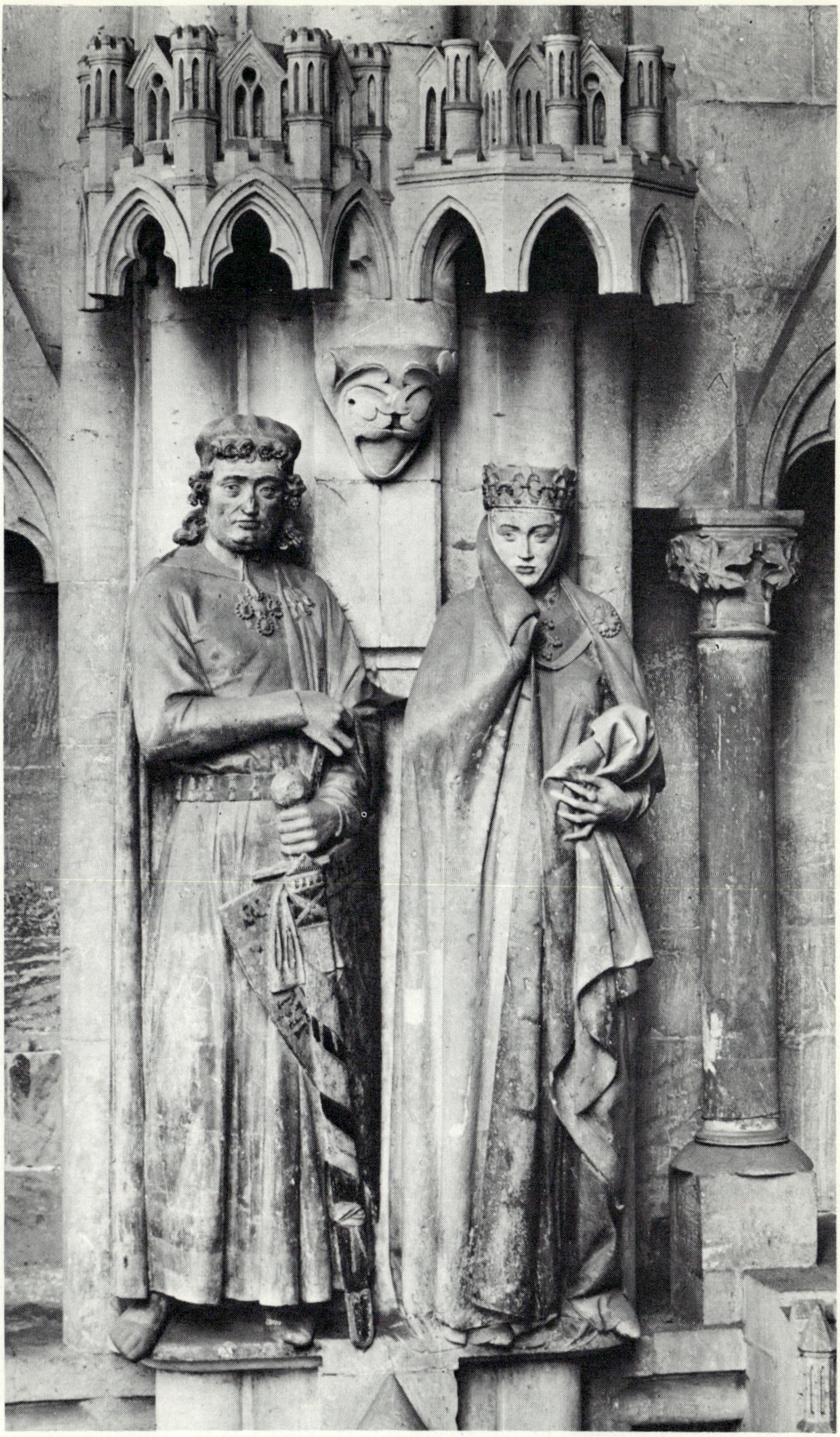

Altar in Alsace; it shows the Crucifixion with a brutal realism contrasting with the smooth lines of his Italian contemporaries. Other Crucifixion paintings by Grünewald can be seen in Basle and Karlsruhe; he makes no attempt to soften the pain and horror of the scene.

The religious paintings of Lucas Cranach (1472-1553) use landscape backgrounds, hitherto unknown. He painted the German landscape he knew rather than imagining mediterranean scenery. Later he became a court painter in Saxony, and painted mythological scenes such as the Judgement of Paris.

Albrecht Altdorfer (1480-1538) and Adam Elsheimer (1578-1610) were both painters of landscape; Altdorfer of brooding woods and monstrous trees, Elsheimer of peaceful and romantic scenes. Altdorfer was, in fact, the first European artist to paint a landscape without human figures. Much of Elsheimer's work was done in small format, mostly on copper; one of his best known pieces is a portrayal of the Flight into Egypt.

Hans Holbein the Younger (1497-1543) is best known as a portrait painter, but also did engraving, mural and glass painting. He spent thirteen of his last eighteen years in London, where he was court painter to King Henry VIII. Among his most famous portraits are those of Sir Thomas More and of Erasmus.

A contemporary of these painters was the sculptor Tilman Riemenschneider (born around 1460, died 1531). He mostly used wood, and his best-known works are the carved altars at Rothenburg and Creglingen. He carved with extreme delicacy and sympathy, and his figures are very human. He also did some work in stone, including the figures of Adam and Eve that can be seen near the south door of Würzburg Cathedral.

Architecture at this time was gradually moving away from the Gothic to the Renaissance preference for broad, round arches, classical columns and an emphasis on the horizontal rather than the vertical. A typical Renaissance building is St Michael's Church in Munich. The fortress ("Burg") was giving way to the purely residential castle, the "Schloss". (However, the picture is blurred by the fact that many fortresses carry the name of "Schloss"; thus Schloss Aschaffenburg is a

Fig 106 German architecture on postage stamps. Photo: Glyn Hatherall.

ART AND ARCHITECTURE

residential palace, but the Heidelberger Schloss is a fortress.) Another building which became popular at the same time was the Town Hall. Many were built in Renaissance style and, after seeing a few typical German Town Halls, one soon learns to identify this building when visiting a new town.

Baroque

In the Baroque period (roughly from 1700 to 1800) the work of the painters was combined with and subordinated to that of the architects, and found its expression in ceilings and panels of churches and castles. The grand model was the Palace of Versailles, and many German castles tried to better it for grandiose detail. Examples of this are the castle at Bückeburg (with its pink and white ballroom and its mausoleum with a gold mosaic roof) and the Würzburg "Residenz".

The white marble and gold heaviness of baroque gave way to the more dainty and even more elaborate Rococo. Not only the palaces of the rich, but also churches and monasteries were given this treatment, with brilliant colours and

Fig 107 While church and castle architecture was following the traditional European course through Gothic, Baroque and modern styles, village architecture pursued a style of its own. This seven-roof house is in Memmingen, Bavaria. Photo: German Tourist Information Bureau.

ornate detail. A classic example is the famous Wies Church; its exterior is rather unimposing (a neat white building set in a field), but inside it is rich with colour.

The Romantic period

Only one Romantic painter need be mentioned here: Caspar David Friedrich (1774-1840). His work is an evocation of all that one associates with Romanticism — misty landscapes, mountains, ruins by night, sunsets and solitary people gazing into the distance.

19th and 20th centuries

The last decades of the 19th century and those of our present century have seen a new flowering of German art. One of the earliest artists to show this was Lovis Corinth (1858-1925); his earlier work was mainly impressionist, his later work tended towards expressionism. He is noted for his portraits, including self-portraits and a painting of Luther. In later life he turned to scenery and painted many pictures of the Walchensee, a lake in Bavaria.

Paul Klee (1878-1940) was born in Switzerland. His father was German, his mother Swiss. He was interested in the link between art and architecture, and taught at the "Bauhaus" (which will be mentioned shortly). His paintings show a dream-world of abstract form and fantasy figures in bright colours. He believed painting, in some ways, could be truer to nature than photography. The last seven years of his life (after Hitler's rise to power) were spent in Switzerland.

Although born in New York, Lyonel Feininger (1871-1956) was of German parentage and studied and worked for many years in Germany. His harmoniously coloured paintings and delicate drawings combine cubism, impressionism and expressionism.

Emil Nolde (1867-1956) was one of Germany's leading expressionists, and his work shows an extraordinary command of colour. He painted broad, round forms in vivid hues. He is noted for his landscape and religious work.

Another expressionist, Franz Marc (1880-1916) is known for his paintings of animals. He regarded animals as symbols of innocence, and portrayed them either intimately involved in the landscape, or suffering terribly as the prey of each other. His most famous picture is "The Tower of the Blue Horses".

August Macke (1887-1914) was a pupil of Corinth, and influenced by French art. His paintings are brilliant with colour and light, and try to express the intensity of nature around us and our part in its pattern. In the last year of his tragically short life, he went on a journey to Tunis, and the paintings he did during this journey are among his most famous.

Klee, Marc, Macke and the Russian Kandinsky formed in Munich a group called the "Blue Rider" group. Their ideas were semi-religious; they wanted to bring back to art vivid colours and the forces of nature. They did not, however, attempt to create a common style.

The most important German architect of this century has been Walter Gropius. In 1919 he founded the now famous "Bauhaus" in Weimar — a centre for art, sculpture and architecture. It moved to Dessau in 1929, and was dissolved in 1933, but not before having a decisive influence on German architecture. Gropius' work can be seen in America (where he went to live in 1937) and in Berlin and Stuttgart. His design for the Fagus factory in Alfeld (1919) was an early example of what we now call "modern" architecture.

Ernst Barlach (1870-1938) was a sculptor in the expressionist style — his heavy work portrays a range of emotions, particularly sorrow and care. He portrayed "Pity" as a woman kneeling on the ground with her head covered in a cloak and

ART AND ARCHITECTURE 175

her hands outstretched, pleading. Other famous pieces by the same artist include "Singing Man" and "Hovering Angel".

Pride of place at the end of this short list of great German artists is reserved for a woman, Käthe Kollwitz (1867-1945). She is noted for her drawings, particularly those showing scenes of the city proletariat. Among the most famous are "The Weavers' Revolt" and "Peasants' War".

Fig 108 "Bread" by Käthe Kollwitz. Photo: Press & Information Office, Bonn.

Present-day interests

With such a wide range of German art, and a whole world of imported art to choose from, what art interests today's Germans? The EMNID survey in 1966 showed that only 6% of the young people questioned were interested in art at all. So the supplementary question, "Are you interested in any particular form of art?" was put to only 120 participants. Of these, 39% favoured impressionism and expressionism, 30% abstract painting and sculpture and 27% "other modern art forms". Classical art (25%), Baroque (20%) and Romanesque and Gothic church architecture (19%) were the next three on the list.

Music and musicians

Germany might be called the home of Western European music, for when one speaks of Western musicians and composers, it is mainly about German composers that one is talking. The question posed by a German journalist, "Where is England's Beethoven?" could be applied to France, Italy, Spain, and several other Western countries.

The mediaeval German singers were also the poets. They were known as "Minnesingers", and often went from court to court with their love-songs. In the 14th century, fraternities of Mastersingers sang both religious and secular songs.

The 15th and 16th centuries saw the development of choral forms along Italian patterns. The early 16th century was the great period of the German song. One of the leading composers was Heinrich Isaacs, who spent most of his life in Italy but joined the Emperor Maximilian at Innsbruck in 1496; his best-known song is "Innsbruck, I must leave you" ("Innsbruck, ich muss dich lassen").

Martin Luther stressed the importance of hymn-singing in worship, and left us many hymns, including "A Safe Stronghold" for which he wrote both text and music. From the musical needs of the Lutheran church there developed the work of

Bach Johann Sebastian Bach was born in Eisenach in 1685 and died at Leipzig in 1750. Described as "a happy, God-fearing man", he married twice, and had no fewer than twenty children. There are four main periods in his life: his singing as a choir-boy, his job as violinist in the orchestra of the Duke of Weimar, his organ-playing in the churches of Arnstadt and Mülhausen, and his position as chief musician to the court at Leipzig with charge of music in the surrounding churches. It was at Leipzig that he spent his last thirty years, and his grave now occupies pride of place in the rebuilt St Thomas's Church there. The three stages in his composition were firstly his organ works, secondly his composition for other instruments (including the Brandenburg Concerto), and finally his church compositions (St Matthew Passion, St John Passion, Christmas Oratorio, etc). He is best known for his chorales, fugues and suites. He was the most important composer in the development of German instrumental music in the early 18th century, taking Italian and French models for his work.

In the 18th century, Vienna became the focal point for German music, and the great decades of the century are often called the Vienna Period. (At that time, there was no division between Germany and Austria.) This period produced the masterpieces of Haydn, Mozart, Beethoven and Schubert: men who led the world in string quartets and symphonies.

Mozart Wolfgang Amadeus Mozart, born in Salzburg in 1756, lived only thirty-six years. He was a child genius, and at the age of six went on a concert tour with his ten-year-old sister. In later youth he lost the interest of the public, despite the fact that he was knighted by the Pope at the age of fourteen. As a member of an Archbishop's household he lived with the servants and had a rough time. He was discharged, and had to rely on the support of a few members of the nobility. He married a singer, and lived sparingly. Despite his death at an early age, Mozart wrote nearly fifty symphonies, nearly twenty operas and operettas, besides piano concertos, string quartets, violin sonatas and serenades. His work exhibits a

MUSIC AND MUSICIANS 177

Fig 109   Bach monument in Eisenach. Photo: Lex Hornsby & Partners.

classical style and pure instrumental composition. He wrote the opera "The Marriage of Figaro" at the age of thirty, "Don Giovanni" at thirty-one, and "The Magic Flute" at thirty-four. He died and was buried a pauper, his grave was unmarked.

Beethoven   Ludwig van Beethoven was born in 1770 in Bonn; his father was a tenor in the Elector of Cologne's choir. At seventeen he went to Vienna for three years, and was taught by Mozart. When he was twenty-two, both his parents had died and he settled in Vienna permanently. He never married. He received no patronage in Vienna, and was forced to rely upon the support of a body of enthusiastic amateurs. Of his nine symphonies, the best known are the Third ("Eroica"), Fifth, Sixth ("Pastoral") Seventh and Ninth ("Choral"); the best known of his nine overtures are those to Egmont, Prometheus and Coriolanus. His other work includes piano sonatas, string quartets, a Mass in D and an opera, "Fidelio". In later life he went deaf. It was his own wish that he should be called a "tone-poet", and he was conscious of the importance of "meaning" in music.

The great age of the "Lieder" was the latter part of the 19th century. This was the time when songs were written under the influence of Romanticism, including the work of Schumann, Brahms and Wolf. The Romantic spirit also produced

M

many piano works: Brahms and Schumann excelled in this field, as did Schubert and Mendelssohn.

Wagner Richard Wagner was born in Leipzig in 1813. At the age of nineteen, he wrote a symphony that was performed at one of the famous Gewandhaus concerts in Leipzig. He took on various jobs in opera houses. While visiting Paris, he wrote the opera, "The Flying Dutchman". Later he became conductor of the opera at Dresden, and while there wrote "Tannhäuser" and "Lohengrin". As a result of political unrest, he fled Dresden in 1848 and took up residence in Switzerland. He began work on "The Ring of the Nibelungs", which he was to take a quarter of a century writing. While in Switzerland, he also wrote "Tristan and Isolde" and "The Mastersingers". In later life he enjoyed the patronage of the mad king Ludwig II of Bavaria. The Wagner Festival Theatre in Bayreuth was completed in 1876, and opened with the first performance of the "Ring". Wagner's other major opera, "Parsifal", was completed in 1881. His style is unique; he took old legends and illustrated them with vigorous music. He believed in the use of a "Leitmotif", a single snatch of a tune repeated in connection with a particular character. He abandoned the traditional method of building up vocal pieces (which stressed the need for balance) in favour of a build-up from a single theme.

Our present century has seen the questioning of all musical conventions, and a new music has been developed, incomprehensible to many listeners, led in Germany by Schönberg and Hindemith. In opera, Kurt Weill is the most important name; he is best known for his collaboration with the playwright Bertold Brecht. Alban Berg's opera "Wozzeck" is worthy of note, as is the oratorio "Carmina Burana" by Carl Orff.

The contemporary scene

In March 1949, the Allensbach interviewers asked a cross-section of radio listeners whether they considered themselves "musical" or not. No less than 54% claimed to be definitely "musical", and only 11% described themselves as "not musical". This confirms the impression one gets when visiting the country. Nearly everyone one meets seems to have a knowledge of music that surprises the British visitor. In middle-class and upper-class families it is the "done thing" for children to learn to play the piano. The large towns have either opera houses or theatres that devote a lot of their time to opera. The Berlin Philharmonic under Herbert von Karajan is regarded as one of the finest concert orchestras in the world, and in recent years the German regional radio orchestras have made a name for themselves in the concert world. There are countless music festivals throughout the year, including the Berlin Festival, the May Festival in Wiesbaden, the Beethoven Festival in Bonn, the Mozart Festival in Würzburg and, most important of all, the annual Bayreuth Festival.

In the 1966 EMNID survey, 17% of the young people questioned played a musical instrument, and 57% gave "listening to music" as one of their spare-time activities. Of those who played or listened to music, 77% were interested in popular and dance music, 39% in light music, 23% in folk song and folk music, 20% in the classical composers, 15% in concert jazz and 12% in classical opera. "Modern" music appealed to only 8%, the baroque composers (including Bach) to 5% and electronic music to 4%.

Ask a German to tell you something about German "pop" music, and he will probably say there is no such thing. He will point to the large number of records and songs imported from other countries, both in translation and in the original

Fig 110   The Berlin Philharmonic. Photo: German Tourist Information Bureau.

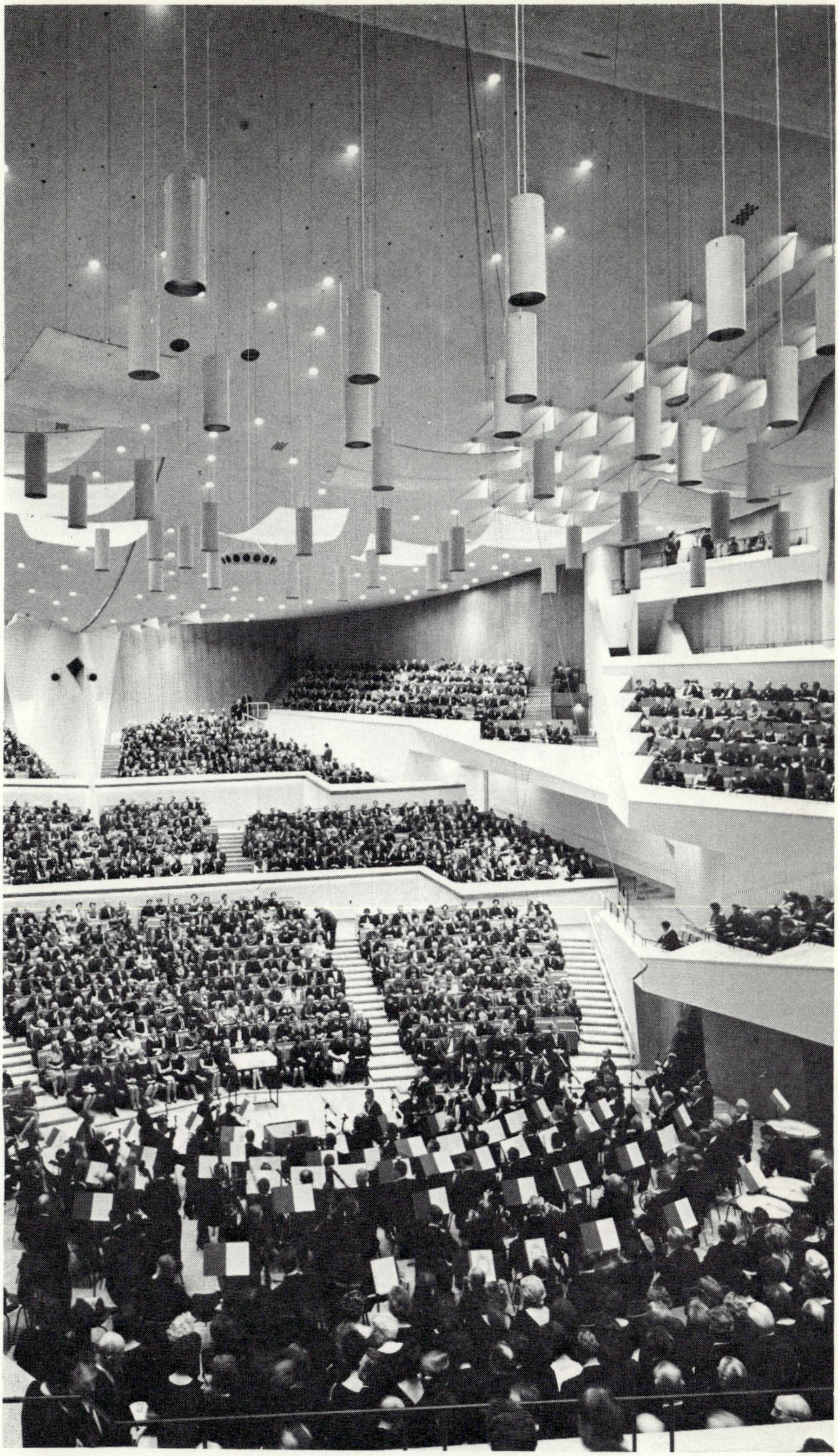

language. This is confirmed by the charts of pop record sales. Taking as a random example the "Musikmarkt" chart for February 1967, we find that among the top twenty records there are fourteen foreign titles (thirteen English, one Italian) and one foreign instrumental (the theme music from "Dr Zhivago"). The top three titles are English.

It is quite common now for foreign singers to translate their hit songs for the German market. The Beatles have recorded German versions of "I wanna hold your hand" and "She loves you", and Cliff Richard has sung many songs in German, including "What would I do?" and "Spanish Harlem".

There are, however, also German pop singers, even if some of them have deceptively English-sounding stage names like Roy Black or The Kettles. Most of their songs are sentimental, and rather old-fashioned by British and American standards. It is generally agreed among those who visit Germany that German pop music tends to be "sloppy and sentimental". Among the leading names are Freddy Quinn, Peter Beil and Udo Jürgens. Caterina Valente and Nana Musgouri also appear frequently on German television and have made many German recordings. The folk singers Abraham and Esther Ofarim have succeeded in capturing two markets in Germany by singing both folk and pop songs in German.

Fig 111 "Sssh!" Cartoon by Moese, reproduced from "Junge Welt".

Men of science

The German scientists chosen for mention here are those whose work can most easily be understood.

Chemistry

Liebig Justus von Liebig, born in Darmstadt in 1803, has been called the "founder of agricultural chemistry". He directed scientists' and agriculturalists' attention to the cycle of animal and plant life, now known as the "nitrogen cycle". He showed that the non-volatile salts in plant ash are necessary for growth and that the soil is exhausted if these elements are not returned to it by manure or natural decay. Liebig differentiated between the functions of different foods and proved that body heat comes from the chemical breakdown of food. He is best known for his discovery of chloroform, but among his other discoveries and inventions were silver-coated mirrors, a method for making unfermented bread, and techniques for analysing mineral waters.

Bunsen The name of Robert Wilhelm Bunsen will make any schoolchild learning chemistry think of the gas burner found in every chemistry laboratory today (although his Christian names may be unfamiliar). With Gustav Robert Kirchhoff, Bunsen also invented the spectroscope and used it for chemical analysis. He discovered two new chemical elements: caesium and rubidium. But his chemical work was not without its cost; it caused the loss of one eye. He also studied gases in blast furnaces, and developed new methods of gas analysis. He invented the zinc-carbon battery and ice and vapour calorimeters.

Emil Hermann Fischer (1852-1919) successfully synthesised grape sugar and caffein. Hermann Staudinger (1881-1965) worked in macromolecular chemistry, which forms the basis of today's enormous plastics industry. Another German chemist, Otto Heinrich Warburg (born in 1883) has researched into the origins of cancer, and into photosynthesis and cell respiration.

Medicine

The first great doctor in Germany called himself Paracelsus. If you wonder why he adopted this pseudonym, imagine going through life with a name like Theophrastus Bombastus von Hohenheim! Born in 1494, Paracelsus made important discoveries in pathology and psychology. Rudolf Virchnow (1821-1902), another pathologist, specialised in cellular pathology. Robert Koch (1843-1910) discovered the tuberculosis bacteria, and Emil von Behring (1854-1917) pioneered serum therapy. Local anaesthetics also began with a German discovery made by Carl Ludwig Schleich (1859-1922).

Physics and mathematics

It is in physics and mathematics that Germany has contributed most to the advancement of science. Otto von Guericke (1602-1686) demonstrated the force of a vacuum with the famous Magdeburg Hemispheres, which horses could not pull apart. Karl Friedrich Gauss (1771-1855) was an expert on many aspects of mathematics and physics, but most of his discoveries are difficult for the layman to understand. The practical results are impressive, however. For example, in collaboration with Wilhelm Werber he invented the first electromagnetic telegraph four years before Morse patented the first practical design.

Ohm Georg Simon Ohm was born in 1787, and after studying at Erlangen he became a teacher in Cologne. His name is immortalised in "Ohm's Law". All wires, he discovered in 1827, offer a resistance to electric current, and the strength of this resistance (measured in "Ohms") depends upon the nature, length and thickness of the wire. He was a careful worker, carrying out his experiments in a most meticulous manner. But it was some years before he received the recognition he deserved. In 1840 he became a foreign member of the (British) Royal Society, and the following year received its Copley Medal. In 1843 he propounded a second law, this time concerned with the production of complex tones by the combination of simple vibrations — this can be regarded as the start of the science of musical accoustics.

Fig 112 Einstein on his seventy-fifth birthday. Photo: Associated Press.

Röntgen Wilhelm Conrad Röntgen was born in the village of Lennep in 1845. While a professor at Würzburg, he experimented to see if radiation could be passed through material opaque to ordinary light. He eventually succeeded in producing rays which could be detected on a barium platino-cyanide screen some way off. He showed that these rays could pass through matter and blacken a photographic plate. Dense material absorbed more of the rays, so they showed bones in a body, or a swallowed watch, etc, by making fainter marks on the photographic plate. Röntgen called his rays "x-rays" and this is the name which has stuck in English, but in German they are known as Röntgenstrahlen. His invention caught the public's imagination, and the first dental x-ray photographs were taken five months after the discovery. But the early scientists were unaware of the effect of x-rays on living tissue and took risks which would be unthinkable today.

Einstein Albert Einstein was born in Ulm in 1789 of a Jewish family. He left Germany at an early age and became a Swiss citizen when he was twenty-one. At the age of twenty-six he published his Special Theory of Relativity. By that time he had become famous, and was a professor in Berlin. He claimed that there was no such thing as absolute speed; we can judge the speed of other objects (e.g. planets) only in relationship to our own speed or a third object. Absolutes of space and time, with one exception, are also non-existent because they are all relative to the observer. The exception is the speed of light, which is constant and is an important feature in Einstein's famous equation relating to matter and energy. He stated that the energy (E) latent in any object is equal to its mass (m) multiplied by the square of the speed of light ($E=mc^2$, where c is the speed of light). This has been proved and further developed in modern atomic research. Because of his Jewish background, Einstein was forced to leave Germany when Hitler came to power. After one year at Oxford, he emigrated to the USA, and in 1940 became an American citizen. He died in 1955. He has been described as "a gentle, modest man whose hobbies were walking, sailing and playing the violin".

Of later German physicists, Wernher von Braun is probably the best-known. He built the V2 rocket for the Nazis, then in 1945 surrendered to the Americans. He soon became one of the leading scientists in the States, and was largely responsible for the launching of America's first satellite, the Explorer, in January 1958. Gustav Hertz (born 1887) is the most prominent of the German scientists now working in the Soviet Union. Of those who remained in Germany, Otto Hahn is the most important; he has discovered new radioactive elements, and the peaceful utilisation of atomic energy owes much to his work. Rudolf Mössbauer, born in 1929, has done important work on the effects of gamma rays.

Inventors and discoverers

There remain a number of Germans whose work is known because of a single invention, or a voyage of discovery. Heinrich Goebel (1818-93) made the first electric lamp bulb from an eau-de-cologne bottle; this invention is often attributed to Edison, who was the first to make the light-bulb a commercial proposition. Johann Philipp Reis (1834-74) invented an imperfect form of telephone, and Carl von Linde (1842-1934) the refrigerator. Rudolf Diesel (1858-1915) invented the engine which we know by his name, and Gottlieb Wilhelm Daimler (1834-1900) the petrol-driven motor-car. Martin Behaim (1457-1507) made the first globe, calling it an "Earth Apple". Alexander von Humboldt (1769-1859) travelled to South America and wrote "Cosmos", a five volume summary of man's knowledge of the world. Alfred Brehm (1829-84) travelled to many lands and wrote an "Illustrated Animal Life", now a German-language classic.

THE FOREIGNER AND GERMANY

Language problems

The remaining chapters of this book are concerned with the foreigner looking at and visiting Germany, and with the relationships between Germany and the rest of the world. One problem that worries many prospective visitors is "What about the language?"

Most Germans learn English at school, but in many cases emerge with little more than the ability to pronounce "jazz" with an American accent. Consequently, although the tourist who has to rely on his native tongue should be able to make himself understood in most hotels and souvenir shops, it is a help if he is able to produce a reasonably accurate pronunciation of German place names. "Imitated prononciation" is given in most phrase books, so there is no need to try and rival them here. Instead, let us look at some of the main differences between German and English.

The German language is a member of the Indo-European family and thus shares a common root with French, Latin, Greek, Spanish, and the languages of Scandinavia and India, to name but a few. English is also a member of the same family — in fact, it is a Germanic language. Between the 5th and 8th centuries AD, German divided into two languages, known as High German and Low German. High German is the language found in modern South and Central German dialects, and in the standard written and spoken language today. Low German is found in North German dialects, as well as in Dutch and English. The distinguishing characteristic is in the consonants; while Low German retained the consonants *p*, *t* and *k*, High German "shifted" them to *pf*, *tz* and *ch*. Thus the English words "plough", "tongue" and "break" are found in German as "Pflug", "Zunge" and "brechen". (But, the observant reader will point out, modern German also has *p*, *t* and *k*. This is because the missing consonants were almost immediately replaced — but that is another story.)

However, this is not the linguistic feature that first strikes the foreigner when he comes into contact with the German language. His first question is nearly always, "Why does German have so many initial capitals?" The answer is simple: in German, all nouns are written with an initial capital. This was not always the case; the custom is only some four centuries old. But now it seems quite permanent, and attempts to rescind it, whether they have come from a learned body of philologists or from a popular weekly magazine, have proved unsuccessful.

Another feature which strikes the foreigner is "those dots". The technical term is "Umlaut", and it is used to combine the vowels *a*, *o* and *u* with an "e" sound. While English can turn "mat" into "mate" by adding a letter *e*, German achieves the same goal by putting two dots over the vowel concerned. Thus "halt!" (meaning "stop") is pronounced just as it looks to an Englishman, but "spät" (meaning "late") is pronounced "spate".

Language teachers reading this chapter may feel I am misleading the reader into thinking that the German sounds *ä*, *ö* and *ü* have exact equivalents in English. Such criticism is justified, because the sounds are not identical; my comparison is merely intended to indicate a parallel. Indeed, the sound *ü* is one which English and American students find very difficult. It is almost identical with the French *u* in "tu", and may be pronounced by rounding the lips as if to say "oo" but then trying to produce an "ee" sound.

German diphthongs present little difficulty once they have been learnt. German *ei* is pronounced like the *y* in "my", German *ie* like the *ee* in "see". The two diphthongs *äu* and *eu* are both pronounced like the *oy* in "boy", while *au* on its own is similar to the *ou* in "house".

I frequently hear the comment that "German is a harsh language". This is provoked, usually, by one sound alone: the German *ch*. It is a sound identical with that found in Scottish ("loch") and Welsh ("bach"), and is imitated by trying to pronounce a *k* and an *h* at the same time. The real problem is caused by the fact that the sound is found only after a hard vowel (i.e. after *a*, *o* and *u*) and that after other vowels the same letter combination (*ch*) stands for a different sound. This is a soft *sh* sound, and can be produced by pronouncing a *y* and then "unvoicing" it. (To get an idea of what "unvoicing" is, contrast *zzz*, which is voiced, with *sss*, which is unvoiced.)

Apart from sounds unknown in English, German also has sounds which are

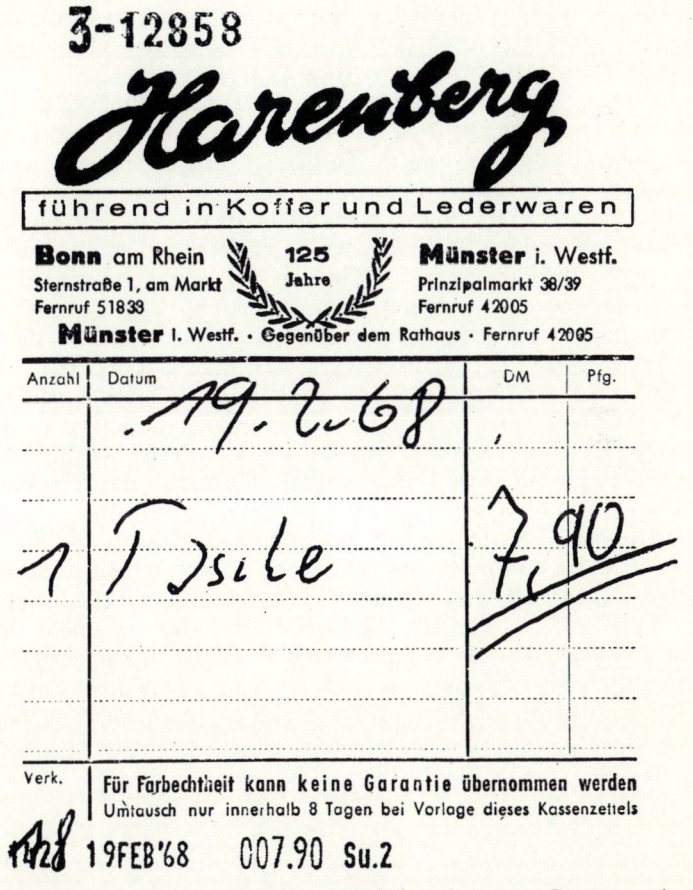

Fig 113 Foreigners are sometimes puzzled by the way Germans (and other continentals) write their figures. On this bill for a wallet, note the figure 1 in the date, and the "crossed" 7 in the price. Legend has it that during the Second World War a British spy impersonating a German officer gave himself away by forgetting to write figures the "continental" way.

represented in writing by letters which English uses for something entirely different. Thus the word "ja" (meaning "yes") is pronounced "ya", and "zu" (meaning "to") is pronounced "tsoo". But these are differences which foreign students of German quickly master.

Even after one has learnt to pronounce German, and acquired a good vocabulary, there are still some big obstacles to be overcome. One of the strangest is the German word-order, which, under certain circumstances, sends the verb to the end of the clause or sentence. This is best illustrated by giving a word-for-word translation of a German sentence, such as the following from Böll's novel, "End of a Journey":

"The trial (of) Gruhl took in the smallest of the three available standing rooms before ten onlookers place, who almost all with the accused, witnesses, experts, lawyers or other with the trial concerned persons related were."

German handwriting and printing have come into line with the practice in other countries during the last half century, and the old-fashioned "Gothic print" and almost illegible Sütterlin handwriting are now out-of-date (though the Frankfurter Allgemeine Zeitung still uses the former for headlines). One rather strange printers' convention in Germany is that if the combination ck has to be divided because the end of a line has been reached, the *c* is changed to a *k;* thus if the word "Wecker" ("alarm-clock") has to be split, it is written as Wek-ker.

There are many more differences between German and English that I have omitted from this outline. As it is, the reader may be feeling that German is an impossibly difficult language to learn. This is not the case; indeed, many Englishmen find it easier than French, because the pronunciation comes more easily to English ears. There are, of course, many different ways of learning a language, and each has its advantages and disadvantages. The best, though the most expensive, is to take six months' holiday with a German family in Germany; also effective, though far from cheap, is a course of lessons from a good private tutor. The private tutor has an advantage over the language class, because the individual pupil has more work to do each lesson and has more practice. But this is not to deny the first class work being done by language schools and evening classes all over the world, although schools differ tremendously in quality, as do teachers within any given school. Language record courses, with the exception of the most expensive, have a limited range and cannot take the learner much beyond the stage of "Can I buy a cup of coffee at the station?" When one of these courses assures the prospective customer that he will speak German "fluently" within, say, three weeks, I want to ask *how much* German will he be able to speak. Moreover, one should be wary of courses which claim to have "done away with all formal grammar learning". They seldom have. (In any case, I am firmly convinced that a small amount of grammar, sensibly explained, can be an aid to language learning.) In the long run, the value of a course depends far more on the quality of the material it contains, or of the person teaching it, than on any particular "method".

Looking at the map

In a way, this chapter should have been entitled "Looking at two maps". By this, I am not referring to the division into East and West Germany, but to two different ways of looking at a country. We can look at the physical divisions, the mountains, rivers, scenery etc. Or we can look at the political divisions, the different regions and their industries, the main centres of population. We can, of course, try to combine the two, but in a country already divided by an arbitrary frontier, this would lead to further confusion.

Let us therefore take the two maps separately, looking first at the natural divisions, then at the political divisions.

Natural divisions

There are three main regions in Germany: the North German Plain, the Central Mountains and the Alpine region.

The North German Plain This is an extension of the Flemish Lowlands, and in the east it merges with the Central European Plain. The soil is sandy or loamy and there are many lakes. The region includes the Cologne, Münster and Saxo-Thuringian bays, which cut into the Central Mountains.

This region attracts fewer tourists than south Germany, but it would be wrong to imagine it as monotonous. Apart from the lakes, there are marshes, moors and woods. In the far north, Schleswig-Holstein is a peninsula with fjords, bays and lagoons.

Off the northern coast are many islands. There are three main groups. Firstly, the East Frisian Islands off the North Sea coast of Lower Saxony, which are a continuation of the West Frisian Islands belonging to Holland. Secondly, the North Frisian Islands (including the holiday paradise of Sylt) which lie in a belt of shallows off the North Sea coast of Schleswig-Holstein. Thirdly, the islands in the Baltic, including the East German holiday island of Rügen.

The Central Mountains This is a region of great variety, with woods, plains and hills, not to mention rivers and streams of every description. The Central Mountains form a barrier between north and south, and have been largely responsible for differences in temperament and dialect which can still be found today. At the same time, they have increased the importance of the Rhine as a north-south highway.

This area includes the Eifel (a continuation of the Ardennes), the Harz mountains, the Thuringian Forest and the Black Forest — all areas popular with visitors.

The Alpine Region The Alpine foothills, known technically as the Swabian-Bavarian Plain, have an average height of some 1500 feet. The top-soil is made up of moraines and broken stones, formations left by glacial snows and glaciers. As one travels southwards across the plateau, one sees the peaks of the Alps themselves looming up on the horizon: an unforgettable sight. They are separated from the plateau by a ridge of sandstone foothills.

The alpine scenery is characterised by woods, meadows, snow-capped mountains and lakes. The lakes are often very deep, and in summer unusually blue.

188 THE FOREIGNER AND GERMANY

Fig 114   Physical division of Germany

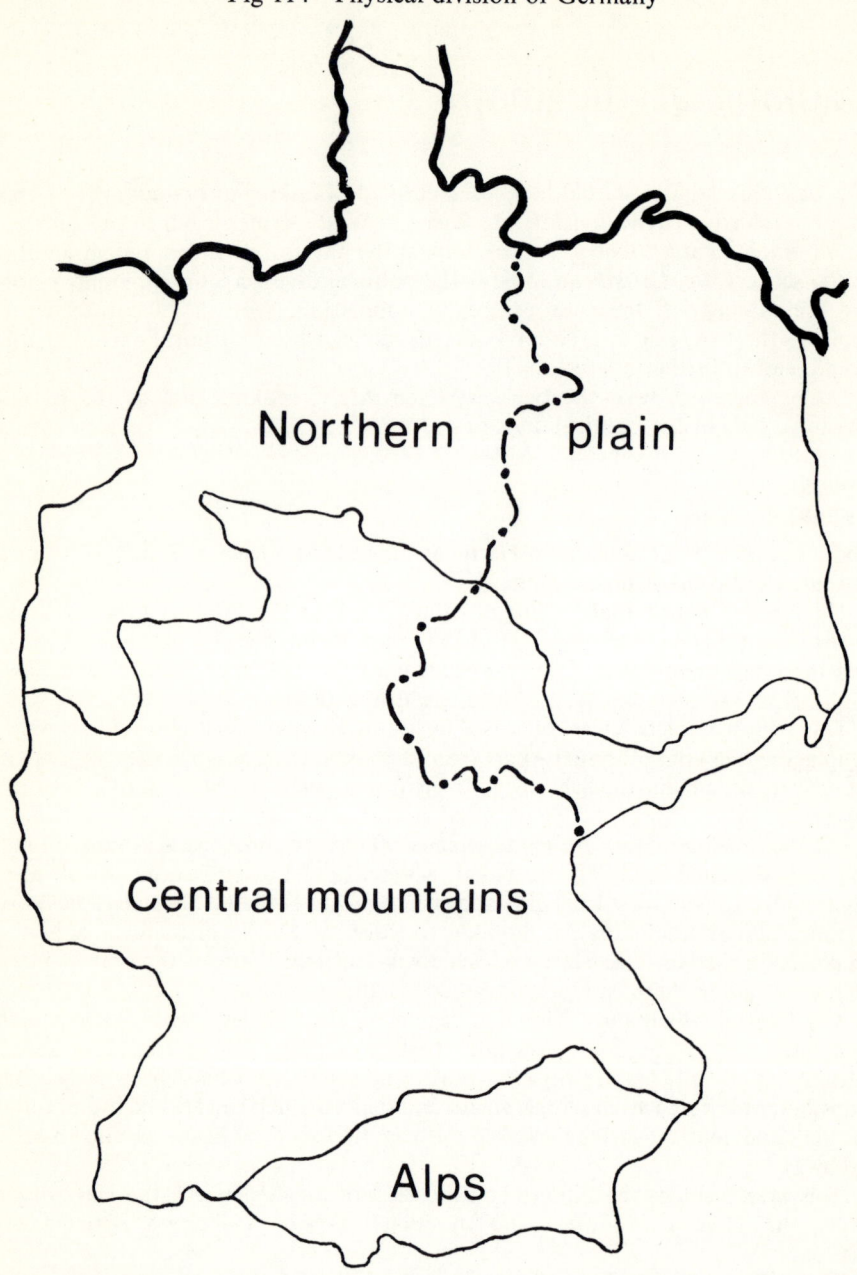

Rivers   Cutting across the main natural divisions are the big rivers. With the exception of the Danube, all the main rivers flow from south to north. The Ems and Oder are lowland rivers for most of their course; the others link the Central Mountains and the Northern Plain — and the Rhine even penetrates the Alpine region.

Linking the rivers are the canals, of great importance economically. The longest, the Mittelland Canal, has a total length of 202 miles.

LOOKING AT THE MAP

Fig 115 Major rivers

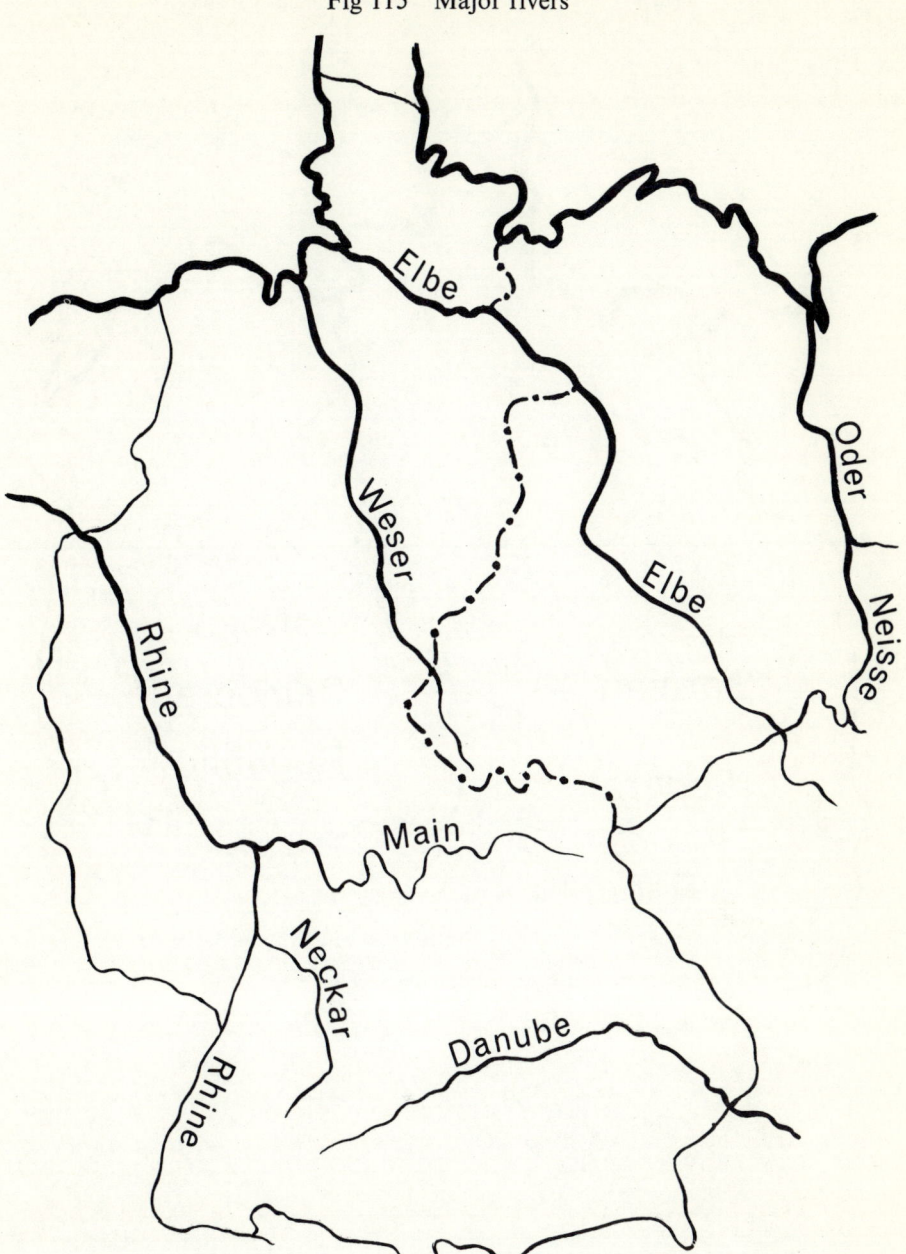

Political divisions

For purposes of administration, Germany is now divided into three regions. These are the German Federal Republic (West Germany), the German Democratic Republic (East Germany) and West Berlin.

The Federal Republic This was formed in 1949 from the British, French and American Zones of Occupation. It experienced an "economic miracle" in the

190 THE FOREIGNER AND GERMANY

Fig 116   Political divisions of Germany 1968

nineteen-fifties, partly due to massive financial aid from the USA, partly due to skilled management and hard work.

The Democratic Republic   Founded in 1949 from the Soviet Zone of Occupation, the GDR is sometimes referred to as the "so-called German Democratic Republic" because the Western governments have refused to recognise it diplomatically. In

Figs 117 and 118 Two states, two symbols: the eagle for West Germany, the hammer and dividers for East Germany.

practice, it is a one-party Socialist state; all aspects of life are permeated with Socialist doctrine.

West Berlin At the end of the War, Berlin was treated as the responsibility of the Four Powers jointly, but the four-power control gradually collapsed. Joint control ended in 1948 but, until the building of the Berlin Wall in 1961, the city was still to some extent a single unit. Now East Berlin is in practice part of the East German state. According to the "Berlin Constitution" of 1950, which in practice applies only to West Berlin, Berlin is a "Land" of the Federal Republic, but all laws passed in the Federal Republic require formal adoption by the Berlin House of Representatives, and Berlin deputies have no voting rights in the West German parliament. Despite this theoretical independence, however, most West Germans and West Berliners regard West Berlin as a part of the Federal Republic.

Other areas West German maps also show other areas to the east of the German Democratic Republic. These are the former German territories put under Russian, Polish or Czech administration after the last war. In practice, they are now part of Russia, Poland and Czechoslovakia; but the West German government insists that they are still German, pending a formal peace treaty between Germany and those who fought against her between 1939 and 1945.

Regional administration

West Germany is divided into ten "Länder" of which two, Bremen and Hamburg, are autonomous cities. The others are:

Bavaria Known in German as Bayern, the largest of the Länder with an area of over 70 thousand square kilometres. It is also the most romantic, and thrives on its tourist trade. Its boundaries are historical, and give the Bavarians a sense of "belonging" to Bavaria rather than to Germany as a whole. A large proportion of the energy produced comes from hydro-electric power, but it was also the first of the Länder to have a nuclear power station. The chief industry is farming, particularly dairy farming. Besides the regional capital, Munich, the main towns are Nuremberg, Augsburg, Regensburg and Würzburg. It is a predominantly Catholic area, the ratio being 7:3.

Baden-Württemberg According to the Baden-Württemberg authorities, this is a traditional home of liberal and democratic ideas. It is the most highly industrialised of the Länder; the industries are concerned with processing and finishing, for there are few raw materials. It is also the Land with most craftsmen and small farmers. Partly as a consequence of the tourists (attracted by the Rhine and Danube valleys, the Black Forest and the Casino in Baden-Baden) the roads are particularly crowded. The main towns are Stuttgart, Mannheim, Karlsruhe, Freiburg and Heidelberg.

Fig 119   Administrative regions of West Germany (the "Länder")

Saarland   A predominantly Catholic area, which became German as late as 1957; until then it was French. A quarter of the workers are employed in the coal or steel industries. The only large town is Saarbrücken.

Rhineland-Palatinate   An area under Roman occupation for four centuries, now dominated by agriculture. Vegetables, fruit, tobacco, hops, sugar beet and barley are produced here, but 20% of the agricultural yield is wine. This is the great Rhine and Moselle wine area. The main towns are Ludwigshafen, Mainz and Koblenz. Tourists are attracted to the Rhine and Moselle valleys and to the

LOOKING AT THE MAP   193

many health resorts. The climate is particularly mild, and many almond trees actually bear fruit — something rare in Germany's climate.

Hesse A Land of great variety, with an agricultural area in North Hesse, industry in the Rhine and Main valleys, and a mixture of both in the valleys of the Lahn and Dill. It has natural resources of crude oil, soft coal, iron ore and natural gas; its best-known industrial product is the Opel car, made at Rüsselsheim. Hesse is a particularly progressive Land in the educational field, and university students from all over the world study in the romantic university town of Marburg. The main towns of Hesse are Frankfurt, Wiesbaden, Kassel, Darmstadt and Offenbach.

North-Rhine-Westphalia This is the most populous of the Länder with 16,846,900 inhabitants (1966). It is also the most important in the industrial field, producing a third of West German output. Pit coal is found in the Ruhr and near Aachen, and iron ore in the Siegerland and Sauerland. These have combined to give a flourishing iron and steel industry. A textile industry has also been developed, originally in order to give employment to the wives of men working in heavy industry. North-Rhine-Westphalia is predominantly Catholic, particularly in the Rhineland. It has the largest number of towns and villages — 16,000 in all, of which twenty-four are officially classed as "major towns" (including Cologne, Essen, Düsseldorf, Bochum, Münster, Aachen and Bonn).

Fig 120   Germany's industrial heart — the Ruhr

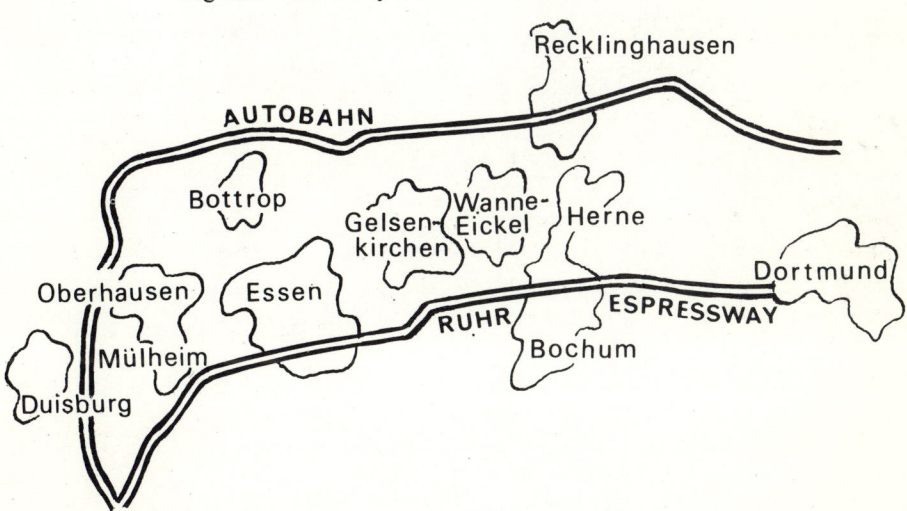

Lower Saxony A Protestant area, and a Land rich in natural resources (rock- and potash-salts, crude oil, natural gas, turf, soft coal and iron ore). In the post-war years there has been much development of the ship-building and other industries but 71% of the population still lives in rural areas. The main agricultural products are horses, cattle, pigs, turnips, potatoes and grain. The most important towns are Hanover, Braunschweig, Osnabrück, Salzgitter, Wilhelmshaven and Oldenburg. Tourists find this area less attractive than others, but some do visit the Lüneberg Heath.

Schleswig-Holstein This is the most northerly and most Protestant of the Länder; it also had the highest percentage of refugees after 1945. It is the nearest Land to Scandinavia and this is clearly visible, not only in the scenery, but in the appearance of the inhabitants. The main industries are shipping, agriculture, oil, quarrying and building materials. The Land is bisected by the Kiel Canal, under which a road tunnel has been built. Since 1963, the railways boast an "As-the-crow-flies-line" comprising a bridge over the Fehmarn Sound and a ferry to Denmark. The climate is mild, the effect of the sea being noticeable. Agricultural produce includes cattle, vegetables and fruit; there are also many nurseries for trees. The only large towns are Kiel and Lübeck; tourists enjoy Lübeck's "old-town" atmosphere and visit the off-shore islands, notably Sylt.

East Germany

In East Germany, the five Länder which formerly made up the country (Mecklenburg, Saxony, Thuringia, Brandenburg and Sachsen-Anhalt) were abolished in July 1952. In their place, fourteen "Bezirke" were created.

Fig 121   Administrative regions of East Germany (the "Bezirke")

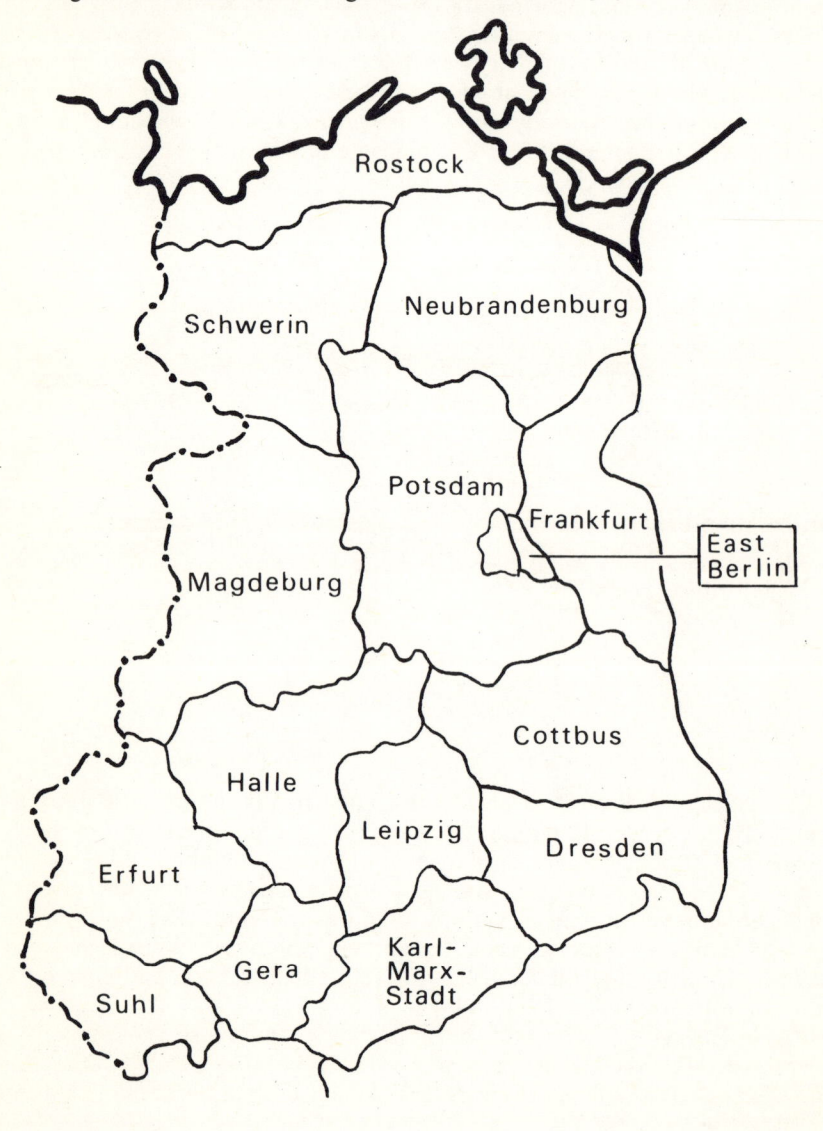

LOOKING AT THE MAP 195

Rostock The chief industry is agriculture, but the shipbuilding industry has been developed considerably during the last few years, and is now quite important. A third industry is fishing. The main towns are Rostock, Stralsund and Wismar.

Schwerin Primarily an agricultural area, the industry being limited to the processing of agricultural produce. The only large town is Schwerin itself, where some clothing manufacture takes place.

Neubrandenburg Agriculture is again the main occupation, but there are also some foundries and hardware industries. There are no large towns. Neubrandenburg, the town which gives the Bezirk its name, has only 38,000 inhabitants.

Magdeburg An area of both agriculture and industry, with many raw materials (potash, rock-salt, iron ore, pyrites and limestone). The industries are concerned with the processing of agricultural products, with chemicals, and with machine production, vehicles and goods made from iron and steel. The only large town is Magdeburg itself.

Potsdam Primarily an agricultural region, but with some industries, particularly machine production, iron and steel works, locomotive and optical industries. The only large towns are Potsdam and Brandenburg, the latter having some textile and leather industries.

Frankfurt Another agricultural area, but producing steel, chemicals and building materials. The main towns are Frankfurt-an-der-Oder, Schwedt and Eisenhüttenstadt. The latter is a new town begun in 1951 — but in spite of its newness a rather lifeless place.

Erfurt Noted for vegetable farming, mechanical and optical industries, and the manufacture of vehicles and machines. The main raw material is potash. The chief towns are Erfurt itself (with a variety of industries) and Weimar, the home of German classical literature.

Halle One of the leading Bezirke for both industrial and agricultural production. The natural resources include copper, potash and lignite, and a thriving chemical industry has been developed. This area is East Germany's main source of electric energy and of cement. The two most important towns are Halle and Dessau.

Cottbus The main income is from the production of lignite. Far behind this come food, chemicals, ceramics and textiles. The only large town is Cottbus itself, which boasts a technical college specialising in the building industry.

Leipzig A wide range of industries include lignite mining, foundries, leather and fur goods, and printing. The only large town is Leipzig, the former centre of the German book trade and still important for its publishing houses and library (two and a half million books).

Suhl The most important occupation is the metal industry (including electrical engineering). Potash and iron ore are mined, and many glass, ceramic and wooden articles are produced. There are no large towns.

Gera Textiles are the leading industry, followed by iron and steel, chemicals

---

English versions of some German geographical names

English	*German*	*English*	*German*
Bavaria	Bayern	Lake Constance	Bodensee
Cologne	Köln	Lower Saxony	Niedersachsen
Hamelin	Hameln	North Rhine-	Nordrhein-
Hanover	Hannover	Westphalia	Westfalen
Moselle	Mosel	Rhine	Rhein
Munich	München	Rhineland-	Rheinland-
Nuremberg	Nürnberg	Palatinate	Pfalz

and foodstuffs. There are two large towns, Gera and Jena. The latter is noted for its optical goods (Zeiss) and glassware.

Karl-Marx-Stadt Until 1953, this area was known as Chemnitz, and West German books still refer to it as such. It is the most highly industrialised and most populous of the Bezirke. A wide range of industries is based on the products of the Ore Mountains (including cobalt, lead, tin, zinc, silver, nickel and uranium). There is also some coal mining and many processing industries, including textile and vehicle manufacture. The main towns are Karl-Marx-Stadt (formerly known as Chemnitz), Plauen and Zwicken.

Dresden A highly industrialised area, producing many different articles including electrical and metal goods, optical instruments, leather work, paper, textiles, chemicals and articles made of wood. A characteristic of the area's industry is the concentration on small firms. The two main towns are Dresden and Görlitz.

Places worth seeing

This book does not set out to be a detailed travel guide. However, for the benefit of the reader who is contemplating a holiday in Germany, here is a brief list of places worth considering for a visit, with notes about the most interesting items to see (and, where appropriate, some personal comments).

West Germany

Aachen Known in French as Aix-la-Chapelle, a reference to the 9th-Century Imperial Chapel later enlarged to form the present Cathedral. Charlemagne lived at Aachen for many years, and his Bible and other relics are on view in the Cathedral treasury. In the upper section of the Cathedral is his marble throne. The present Town Hall is an imposing Gothic building, but two towers remain from an earlier Carolingian palace on the same site. Aachen has been a spa since Roman times, and the Kurhaus and Kurgarten offer typical spa atmosphere.

Augsburg Home of the oldest social settlement in the world, built in 1519 to house deserving families; the rent has remained the same at 1.71 DM (the equivalent of one Rhenish Florin in those days) per year! The Cathedral contains the oldest stained glass in the world, and altar paintings by Hans Holbein the Elder. The Maximilianstrasse is claimed to be Germany's finest Renaissance street.

Baden-Baden An internationally famous spa with two castles (ingeniously known as the Old Castle and the New Castle) and a richly-decorated Casino. Those who come for health reasons enjoy all the facilities of an ultra-modern 7-storey building completed in 1965; on its sun-roof terrace it has a thermal therapy pool.

Bad Kreuznach A radium spa, centre of a wine-trade area. The most picturesque of its relics are the 15th-century houses built on the bridge over the Nahe.

Bamberg An interesting Mediaeval town with narrow streets and an old town hall built in the middle of a bridge over the River Regnitz. The most important building is again a Cathedral, built in the 11th century. It contains the statue of the Bamberg Rider, chiselled in stone around 1230 by an unknown master.

Bayreuth World-famous as the home of the annual Wagner festival that takes place in the theatre Wagner himself designed. Wagner was anxious that the acoustics of the theatre should be perfect, and there was no money left to make the building elaborate. Three miles outside the city is Eremitage, a rococo-style park with two castles and elaborate fountains.

Berchtesgaden An important tourist centre set in excellent scenery, also popular as a winter sports resort. It also boasts a castle-palace which used to be an Augustinian abbey, a woodcarving school and a salt-mine. Not far from Berchtesgaden is Kehlstein, Hitler's former "eagle's nest" which affords excellent views of the Alps from a height of over 6000 feet.

Berlin (West) Somewhat less of a "boom town" than some reports would have us believe; I found the famous Kurfürstendamm (shopping street) rather disappointing. At the Western extreme of the city there are some wonderful parks and lakes, one of which includes "Peacock Island", a delightfully peaceful spot reached by a small ferry. In the centre, the rebuilt Kaiser Wilhelm Memorial Church is worth seeing, though the exterior is less successful than the interior.

198 THE FOREIGNER AND GERMANY

Fig 122   Places of interest in West Germany (A-H)

Nearby is the Europa Centre (restaurant and shopping complex) which can be recommended to all who have money to burn. Further sights of the city include a television mast rather like the Eifel Tower, the stadium built for the 1936 Olym-

---

Fig 123   The Europa-Center in West Berlin. Photo: German Tourist Information Bureau.

DGB
VORSORGE
STOTZ
HAUS DER NATIONEN
Schultheiss
Schultheiss
PHOTO-PORST

pics, and the Hansa Quarter, a new housing estate built as the result of a competition in which architects from all over the world competed.

Bernkastel   One of the better known villages on the Moselle, and worth seeing on account of its beautiful half-timbered houses.

Bonn   The capital of West Germany and formerly a dreamy university town on the banks of the Rhine. Narrow streets converge on a central square containing a statue of Beethoven in front of an elaborate post office. Beethoven's birthplace is interesting, much better than Shakespeare's in Stratford. The university is housed in an old palace, and has its own park. The new parliament buildings were once a teacher-training college; besides the debating chamber they contain a first-class restaurant. A Rhine promenade extends from here to the "Alter Zoll", a mighty bastion overlooking the Rhine.

Bremen   Now surpassed in importance by Hamburg, Bremen is Germany's oldest port and thirteen thousand ships dock here each year. The Cathedral dates from the 11th century and contains the Silbermann Organ on which Bach played. Opposite the Cathedral is a colourful Town Hall built of rose-coloured bricks with a green roof; the style is Renaissance. Bremen has two famous statues, the statue of Roland (a three-times-lifesize mediaeval knight) carved in 1404, and the statue of the Bremen Town Musicians (a donkey, a dog, a cat and a rooster) erected in 1955 and based on an old folk tale recorded by the Brothers Grimm.

Brunswick   The bronze lion which stands in the Burgplatz (Castle Square) dates from 1166 and symbolises Henry the Lion, who built the city's cathedral. Also of interest is the Old City market, with half-timbered houses in Gothic and Renaissance styles.

Cologne   A city about which I cannot comment objectively, because I know it too well. The cathedral has been criticised by some, but I find its Gothic interior most impressive (if one looks over the heads of the hundreds of tourists who are continually "doing" the place). The river Rhine is not at its most beautiful here except when the sun catches it on a Summer evening. I can strongly recommend the evening boat trips on the river; the boats are floating restaurants and there is a musical background. An excellent piece of modern architecture is St Columba's Chapel, built in 1950 in the ruins of an old church. Among the many remains of Roman Cologne, the best is the Dionysus Mosaic.

Dinkelsbühl   A town with a thousand years of history behind it, an authentic example of mediaeval construction. It has been described as "a museum in itself", and as "a mediaeval town that has drifted off to sleep". The annual Children's Tribute was described in an earlier chapter.

Dortmund   A leading industrial centre of the Ruhr, Dortmund boasts several large breweries. Considering the industrial nature of the area, Dortmund's "Westphalia Park" is exceptionally beautiful, and contains a lakeside stage and restaurant, the latter offering outstanding value for money.

Düsseldorf   A large, spacious town on the banks of the Rhine. The mile-long "Königsallee" is a famous shopping street, alleged to be a fashion-leader; it also contains many fine cafés. The Old Town houses some quaint inns and restaurants; one of the more unusual is "Hühner Hugo", specialising in roast chicken (which, as all over Germany, is eaten with the fingers).

Frankfurt   Better known as a business centre than as a tourist attraction, Frankfurt has not only two international trade fairs each year, but also many specialised exhibitions, such as the Book Fair, the Poultry Show and the Automobile Show. The Old Town contains the "Römer", a group of three Gothic buildings whose gables rise in steps. St Bartholomew's Cathedral is built in red sandstone, a universal building material in old Frankfurt. The New Town is not

PLACES WORTH SEEING

as modern as its name suggests, for the name dates from 1333! It is now more commonly referred to as the Inner Town; it contains the traffic centre "An der Hauptwache", at which eight roads converge. Frankfurt Zoo is noted for its young animals, and although it lost many animals and buildings during the war, a new collection has been built up under the direction of Dr Bernhard Grzimek.

Freiburg im Breisgau A university town for over five hundred years, Freiburg is also the gateway to the Black Forest. Despite extensive war damage, Freiburg Cathedral was left standing; it is best known for its open lacework steeple, 370 feet high. One of its eight bells weighs five tons and was cast in the thirteenth century. This bell is officially called "Hosanna", but is better known as "Susanne". Sharing the same square as the Cathedral is the Kaufhaus (Department Store), a most impressive building; four great arches at its base curve over the pavement, and above them are four statues of Hapsburg monarchs. Tiny windows peer out from the slope of the steep roof, and at the corners are two pulpit-like excrescences wearing conical hats. A cable-railway leads from Freiburg to Schauinsland — a name meaning "Look into the countryside" — and from a height of 4200 feet one does indeed have a magnificent view over the Black Forest and Rhine Valley.

Furtwangen A health and winter sports resort in the Black Forest, with a fascinating clock museum.

Füssen A picturesque Bavarian spa in beautiful surroundings, with mediaeval buildings. Three miles south-east are the castles of Hohenschwangau and Neuschwanstein; the latter is a fairy-tale castle built for Wagner's patron, the mad king Ludwig II.

Fig 124 When you visit a German town, ask for its official leaflets, which give a lot of useful information. Nearly all towns issue them. Photo: Glyn Hatherall.

Garmisch-Partenkirchen The best known of the winter sports resorts, dominated by Germany's highest mountain, the Zugspitze (whose peak, incidentally, is in Austria). Not far from Garmisch is another of Ludwig II's castles, Linderhof, which has a giant fountain.

Hamburg A warning: save the botanical gardens "Planten un Blomen" for the end of your stay, or you may miss everything else in the city by spending too much time in this one place. I myself saw it at the time the International Botanical Exhibition was held there in 1963, but I gather it is worth seeing at any time. In the evenings, fountains of coloured water play to musical accompaniment. Near the gardens is the Reeperbahn, a night-club and amusement centre; most of the clubs offer harmless fun and should not be confused with the brothels in the adjacent back-streets. Hamburg is Germany's leading port, with the first underwater tunnel in Europe, built in 1911. In the city centre, the Alster Lake is divided into the Inner Alster and the Outer Alster by the Lombard Bridges. The Town Hall is built in Renaissance style, and has a high clock tower, a fine festival hall, a vaulted ceiling and elaborate doorways. A view over the whole city can be obtained from the top of St Michael's Church.

Hamelin Home of the Pied Piper Legend, Hamelin has many fine mansions, including the Pied Piper's House. It lies, as most Englishmen will be aware from the poem, on the River Weser.

Hanover (Written in German as "Hannover") To house its annual industrial fair, Hanover has the largest and most modern fair grounds in Europe. There are three fair buildings, twenty-two exhibition halls and a vast open-air exhibition area, all on one site in the south-east of the city. The centre was badly damaged in the war, but has been restored and reconstructed. Thus there are now two City Halls, the Old City Hall having been rebuilt forty years after the building of the New City Hall. The Herrenhausen Gardens in the northwest of the city are particularly beautiful; they contain fountains, cascades, an orangerie and a baroque theatre.

Heidelberg A romantic university town on the banks of the Neckar, popular with tourists (particularly Americans) in Summer. Somewhat over-commercialised — souvenir shops all round the church — but nevertheless worth a visit. A cable railway takes tourists up to the Castle, in whose grounds one can see a 40,000 gallon cask. Down in the town there are romantic student inns, some containing a variety of notices from all over Europe.

Hildesheim Described as "a real treasury of old architecture", though much had to be rebuilt after war damage. The Cathedral was begun in 852.

Kassel An industrial centre where locomotives, machinery, and optical instruments are manufactured. An excellent centre for touring the Hesse region, Kassel contains a fine new shopping centre around the long Königsstrasse. From this, streets lead off in the form of long flights of steps. The town contains many parks, notably the Wilhelmshöhe, a hillside park crowned by a colossal statue of Hercules.

Kempten Capital of the Allgäu district in Bavaria, an old Roman town. Besides well-preserved remains of the Roman buildings, the town is noted for its baroque church of St Lorenz.

Kiel An important port, but nevertheless clean and a good centre for touring Schleswig-Holstein. A walk along the promenade is worth-while, particularly in the evening. Boats take tourists out to the naval monument at Laboe. The Kiel Week in June is an international regatta.

Koblenz Where the Rhine and the Moselle converge, Koblenz is an important centre for the wine trade. The fortress of Ehrenbreitstein, overlooking the Rhine,

PLACES WORTH SEEING   203

is the scene each August of a fireworks display linked with the illumination of the other castles in the area. A good way to view the whole spectacle is from a boat on the river.

Königswinter A commercialised village at the foot of the Drachenfels, Europe's most-climbed hill. As you go up the hill, you pass many restaurants, whose price increases with their height. From the top, there is a fine view of the Rhine valley (if it is clear weather, a phenomenon which I have rarely encountered in several visits to the Drachenfels).

Fig 125   Places of interest in West Germany (K-Z)

Konstanz An historic old town on the lake which, in English, bears the same name (though in German it is known as the Bodensee). It boasts a Romanesque cathedral and a Renaissance Town Hall. Nearby is the Island of Mainau, with subtropical vegetation, besides 12,000 iris plants, 15,000 dahlias and two million roses.

Limburg The seven-spired Cathedral seems to grow out of the cliff on which it stands; inside there are excellent murals. Near Limburg the Autobahn crosses the River Lahn by means of an impressive high bridge.

Lindau Built on an island on Lake Constance, Lindau has road and rail connections with the mainland. It has many quaint old streets, and an abbey with a painted ceiling. There is also a small but well-appointed casino.

Lübeck An old Hanseatic (trading) city with many "patrician" buildings, the best-known being the Buddenbrooks House, which provided the background for the famous novel by Thomas Mann, himself a native of Lübeck.

Lüneburg An old town on the Heath of the same name. It contains many brick houses from the 15th and 16th centuries, together with excellent half-timbered houses. The Town Hall has beautifully decorated beams.

Mainz This centre of the Rhine wine trade celebrated its two thousandth anniversary in 1962. It is a university town, and the birthplace of Gutenberg (inventor of the printing press). Visitors are attracted by its annual wine festival, its Romanesque cathedral and the Rhine promenade.

Fig 126 Nymphenburg Castle, Munich. Photo: German Tourist Information Bureau.

Marburg Another university town, this time in the middle of Hesse, situated on the Lahn. There are several narrow streets and half-timbered houses. The town is dominated by a Castle, worth climbing up to if only for the excellent view over the surrounding countryside. There are several student inns offering good value for money.

Maria Laach A beautiful abbey in the middle of nowhere, on the banks of its own lake. Its domed basilica has been described as the Rhineland's finest example of Romanesque architecture, and worth the detour necessary to reach it.

Mittenwald Besides being an alpine village with painted house façades and a baroque church, Mittenwald is the centre of a flourishing violin-making craft. Violins have been made here since the 17th century.

Munich The capital of Bavaria, and scheduled host for the 1972 Olympics. It has two universities and a student and artists' quarter in Schwabing, where artists sell their work on the pavements. The twin-towered Frauenkirche was rebuilt after the war, and from the north tower (which is ascended by a lift) the view on a fine day stretches to the Alps. Munich is noted for its beer, and there are many fine beer-cellars, the best known being the Hofbräuhaus. The City Hall's animated clock goes into action every morning at eleven. In the north-west of the city is Nymphenburg Castle, set in a huge park which contains several small castles and pavilions besides.

Münster The town centre is mediaeval, and the Romanesque cathedral has a portal hall with 13th-century carved figures of the apostles and saints. Southwest of Münster is Nordkirchen, with a group of castles on an artificial island surrounded by a moat.

Nuremberg Best known as the city of the Mastersingers, Nuremberg's Old Town has many mediaeval buildings. The castle-fortress has a round watch-tower which offers an excellent view over the city.

Oberammergau Known all over the world for the Passion Play performed every ten years in obedience to an oath. Now a great tourist centre, much commercialised. However, in all fairness I must admit that after seeing the Play I felt I wanted to take home as many souvenirs as I could afford. Specialist shops offer excellent wood-carvings, but they are expensive.

Ravensburg A mediaeval city with fortified gates and towers. Nearby, at Weingarten, is Germany's largest baroque church.

Regensburg Originally a Celtic settlement on the Danube, Regensburg was taken over by the Romans two thousand years ago. It has a stone bridge, and a Gothic cathedral linked by an arcaded courtyard with the Baroque St Stephen's Church.

Rothenburg-ob-der-Tauber The finest of the mediaeval towns, with walls and sentry walk. It is a tourist centre, with quaint inns and hotels.

Rüdesheim The most popular of the Rhineland villages, now frowned on by many Germans as being over-commercialised. Just right for foreign tourists who want to go somewhere lively. The narrow "Drosselgasse" is composed almost entirely of inns and souvenir shops. A chair-lift to the Niederwald Monument (a colossal statue of Germania) carries visitors over the vineyards. Many wine cellars welcome tourists, as does the Asbach cognac firm.

Stuttgart An important city set in beautiful surroundings. It boasts two castles and a monument to the poet Schiller, who was born there. This century, many well-known architects have worked in Stuttgart, including Gropius and Le Corbusier. The 700-foot television tower offers panoramic views. Of the town's area, 50% is taken up with parks, vineyards, orchards, gardens and fields, and a further 25% by woodland.

Fig 127 Apart from the play, Oberammergau has much to offer the sightseer. Painted houses, for instance, like this one with its Red Riding Hood mural. Photo: David Kedgley.

Titisee One of the leading tourist centres in the Black Forest, with an enormous camping site. Half an hour in a pedal-boat on the lake of the same name is great fun but hard work.

Triberg A popular resort in the Black Forest, noted for its waterfall; the water drops 535 feet in seven steps.

Trier The only German town to claim Assyrian ancestry; traces of human occupation have been found going back over four thousand years. The Romans left a bridge, two bathing establishments, an amphitheatre and the Black Gate. The latter is a massive edifice, dating from the 4th century.

Tübingen An old university town on the Neckar; some famous German intellectuals have studied here. Besides a castle and a Gothic church, the town has many gabled half-timbered buildings. The houses surrounding the market-place are particularly good examples of the latter.

Ulm Another old town, this time on the Danube. It is noted for its 528-foot cathedral tower, the highest church tower in the world. A 16th-century astronomical clock can be seen in the Town Hall.

Wiesbaden The largest of the German spas, set in attractive countryside. The suburb of Biebrich contains a baroque castle on the banks of the Rhine. Among the town's attractions are a casino and an annual international drama festival. Germany's oldest cable railway takes visitors to a Greek Orthodox chapel on the Neroberg.

Würzburg Prehistoric remains show that this area was inhabited by man 120,000 years ago. The town is dominated by a fortress, in whose courtyard is the St Mary's Church, one of the oldest in Germany, built in 706. Elsewhere in the town are several examples of rococo architecture; not, however, the gilded rococo found elsewhere, but a white rococo. Würzburg University is over five hundred years old.

East Germany

The reader should not be misled by the brevity of this section in comparison with the lengthy description of tourist centres in West Germany. It is not meant to indicate a lack of places of tourist interest in East Germany, but is based on the practical consideration that only a small minority of readers will want to tour East Germany. The list is therefore restricted to the main centres.

Berlin (East) Most visitors start with the museums, dealt with in the next chapter. But like its Western half, East Berlin is also rich in lakes and streams, making a boat trip worth-while. The Karl-Marx-Allee has been rebuilt in Russian style, and was for many years the country's show-piece. At the Alexanderplatz, a new "House of the Teacher" has been built, with a gaudy mural on the outer walls. More successful is the new State Council Building, on the Marx-Engels-Platz. On the outskirts, the Treptow Park with the Russian War Memorial is a

Fig 128 Alexanderplatz, East Berlin, showing the "House of the Teacher" (with mural). Photo: Lex Hornsby & Partners.

popular spot with sightseers. The newly-built Müggelturm Tower offers a good view over the lakes and over parts of the city. Contrary to information sometimes supplied by official bodies in West Berlin, there is no visa charge for tourists wishing to spend less than 24 hours in East Berlin.

Dresden Formerly one of Germany's finest cities, Dresden is now being rebuilt after extensive war damage. The "Zwinger", which houses a number of museums, is an "open air festival hall" with delightful fountains and surrounds. Nearby is the new restaurant complex "Am Zwinger", which includes a self-service restaurant and a dance-café. The Catholic Cathedral is, at the time of writing, being restored. White steamers take tourists eastwards to the two palaces at Pillnitz (set in a beautiful garden) and northwestwards to Meissen, where Meissner Porzellan (Dresden China) is made.

Fig 129   The Zwinger at Dresden. Photo: Lex Hornsby & Partners.

Eisenach Dominated by the Wartburg Castle, where many of Germany's mediaeval minstrels stayed, and which in recent years has been the scene of many cultural gatherings. Luther and Goethe also "slept here".

Erfurt An important industrial centre with an attractive cathedral, also the home of the East German International Horticultural Exhibition each summer.

Halle A university town on the Saale River, birthplace of Handel. The Gothic cathedral has a separate bell-tower.

Jena Another university town, but also an industrial centre. The original Zeiss factory is here, and visitors are recommended to see the Zeiss Planetarium. The university is named after Friedrich Schiller, who was Professor of History.

Leipzig Best known for its spring and autumn trade fairs, which gave the town priority in the post-war building programme. The fair buildings are mostly in the town centre, but the technical fair-ground is on the outskirts near the monstrosity which commemorates the Battle of Leipzig (1806). Auerbachs Keller is a well-known restaurant, where Dr Faustus is reputed to have been a frequent guest.

Fig 130   Auerbach's Keller in Leipzig is given a spring clean before the Fair visitors arrive. Photo: Lex Hornsby & Partners.

o

Fig 131   Places of interest in East Germany

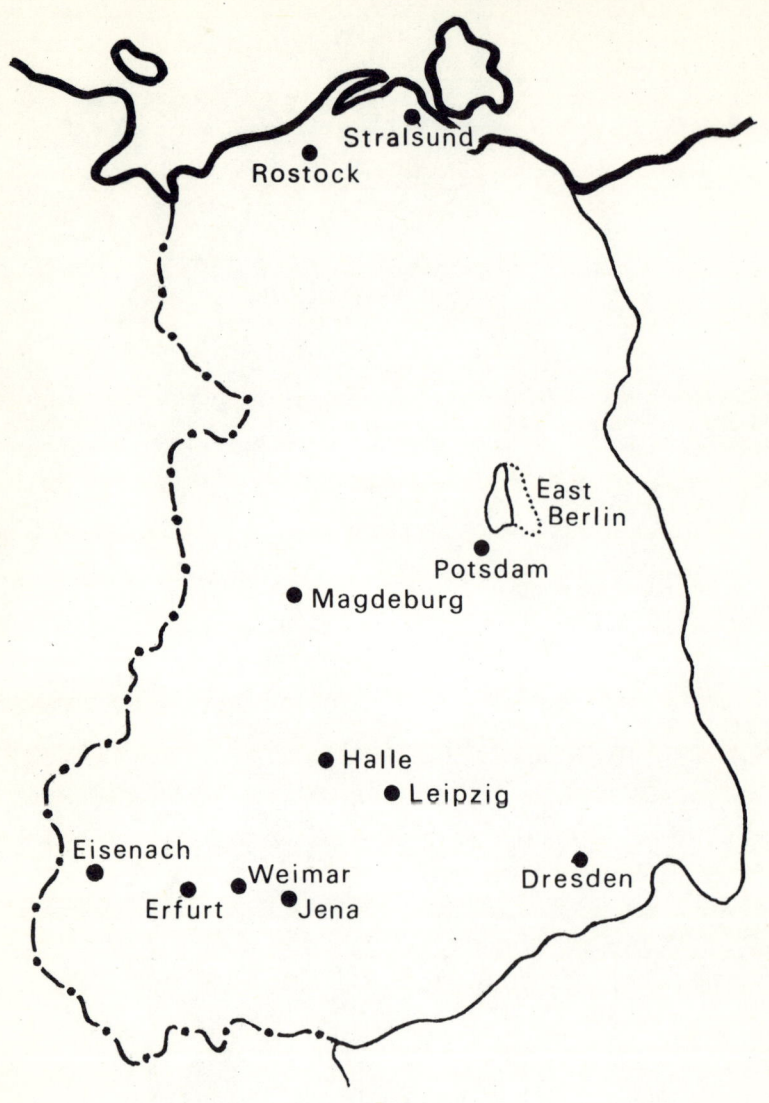

Magdeburg   An industrial centre on the Elbe with a history of over a thousand years. The Cathedral was the first church in Germany to be designed from the beginning in Gothic style; it was begun in 1209. After the Second World War it had to be restored, and this was made possible by a Government grant of two million Mark. The statue of the Magdeburg Rider, built in the 13th century, is now in the Museum for Cultural History, but until 1945 it stood in the open air in front of the Town Hall.

Potsdam   The name is best known in connection with the Potsdam Agreement of 1945, but the town's tourist attraction is the palaces of Sanssouci, Cecilienhof and Charlottenhof. Sanssouci, in particular, has magnificent gardens reminding one of Versailles; there is also a modern open-air stage with over 2000 seats.

Rostock An important port and shipbuilding centre, which like Kiel is more attractive than this description suggests. The Town Hall is a combination of Gothic and Baroque architecture, most attractive when illuminated at night. The main shopping street is the Long Street — though "wide" would be a more appropriate adjective. Nearby is Warnemünde, a leading seaside resort.

Fig 132   Rostock's Town Hall. Photo: Lex Hornsby & Partners.

Stralsund A quaint though rather grubby old town with many old houses and inns. The Town Hall is a good example of the style known as Brick Gothic. A service bus runs between Stralsund and Altefähr, a little village on the Island of Rügen, from which one can look back at a panorama of Stralsund. The ride across the Rügendamm Bridge linking Rügen with the mainland is, however, rather bumpy.

Weimar Germany's Stratford: the home of her great poets, Schiller and Goethe, and of Franz Liszt. Nevertheless, the town is almost completely uncommercialised and gives the impression of a sleepy village. All the building in recent years has been in the outer areas, and the centre does not seem to change. The homes of the great poets are worth a visit, as is the park by the River Ilm. The town is rich in statues — almost anyone who has lived there has a statue somewhere, and there is even a statue of Shakespeare who most probably never heard of Weimar (he lived before the town achieved fame).

Serious and not-so-serious museums

One hesitates to say that any country is more "museum conscious" than another. Yet the British visitor to Germany is more conscious of the existence of museums than he is at home. Moreover, the schools take a greater interest in organised visits to museums as a normal part of the timetable.

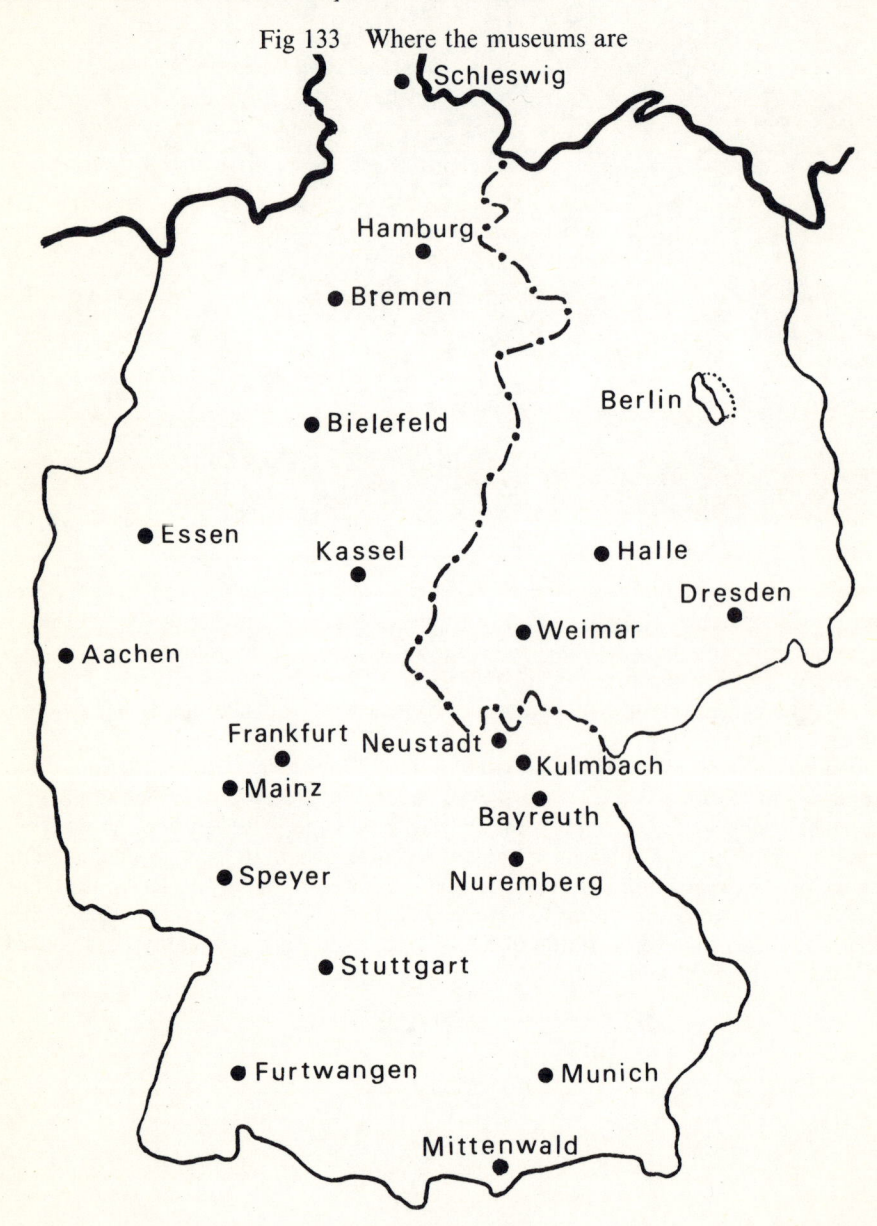

Fig 133 Where the museums are

West Germany

According to official statistics, there were in 1963 a total of 431 public museums in West Germany. Of these, no less than 88 were in Bavaria — and these Bavarian museums alone were visited by nearly three million visitors. (Presumably any visitor who went to two museums was counted twice.)

West Berlin The West Berlin museum is in Dahlem, in the South of the city, near the University. Its best-known treasure has been described by a guide book as "the celebrated bust of Queen Nefertete", and dates from 1370 BC. The colours can still be seen, despite its age.

Munich The capital of Bavaria has many museums, among them the German Museum, concentrating on science and technology, and the Pinakothek, which contains paintings by Dürer (the world's largest collection of his works), Van Dyck, Rembrandt and Holbein.

Nuremberg The German National Museum here has many interesting exhibits, among them the original manuscript of Wagner's opera "The Master Singers" and Behaim's globe (referred to in the chapter on scientists).

Essen The new Folkwang Museum at Essen specialises in 19th and 20th century paintings, including work by van Gogh, Renoir, Cezanne and Gauguin.

Frankfurt has made a museum out of the poet Goethe's home, and in Bonn the birthplace of Beethoven is worth seeing. It contains some of his ear-trumpets.

Bremen The Overseas Museum in this port contains exhibits from all over the world, including boats from the South Pacific and costumes from China and Japan.

Fig 134 Mask and hut from New Ireland (until 1918 the German colony of Neumecklenburg) in the Overseas Museum at Bremen. Photo: Glyn Hatherall.

Schleswig The castle museum houses a magnificent collection of old Anglo-Saxon exhibits, including a complete boat (the Nydam Boat) from the 4th century.

Not all museums in West Germany are devoted to such items of artistic or archeological interest. There are many which one might term "off-beat" museums. Mainz boasts two such museums: one is concerned with the history of printing, and the other with the manufacture of German champagne ("Sekt"). In Aachen, there is a museum of old newspapers. It contains over a hundred thousand editions from all over the world, and includes the world's largest (51 x 35 inches) and smallest (3½ x 4½ inches).

In Hamburg, the German Hydrographic Institute contains a collection of messages sent in bottles. From the case-histories of such bottles, much information has been gathered about the movements of winds and tides. At Sparrenburg Castle near Bielefeld there is a collection of playing cards, including 2,000 complete packs and nearly 80,000 individual cards.

Kassel has the only museum in the world devoted entirely to wallpaper, and also a museum concerned with the Brothers Grimm. For the more technically minded, the Daimler-Benz museum at Stuttgart shows the development of the motor-car from 1883 to the present day.

The Black Forest area is noted for its clocks, and there is a museum at Furtwangen containing nothing but historical clocks. The exhibits include not only the work of local craftsmen, but also many items from other countries. Mittenwald, in Bavaria, has been famous for its violins for many years, and many old instruments are kept there.

In Speyer, there is a museum devoted to the history of wine. Presses, glasses and flasks are on display, together with a complete wine tavern. In Bayreuth, there is a museum for old typewriters.

The Nymphenburg Castle in Munich incorporates the Marstallmuseum, a collection of old coaches, including the elaborate state coach of the mad king Ludwig II of Bavaria. In another palace in Munich, the Residenz, is a collection of 300,000 coins, medals and cut stones.

At Neustadt, near Coburg, there is a German Costume Doll Museum, with over a thousand costume dolls from all over the world. At Kulmbach, in the Plassenburg Castle, is a collection of tin soldiers.

East Germany

Go to the tourist office in any East German town and ask what there is to see, and the chances are they will recommend firstly the local museum. However poor

Fig 135   The Pergamon Altar, East Berlin. Photo: Lex Hornsby & Partners.

SERIOUS AND NOT-SO-SERIOUS MUSEUMS 215

the collection may be — and I have wasted time in some very poor local museums — the town will be proud of it.

But the large museums in East Germany are excellent. East Berlin alone boasts several. The best-known is the Pergamon Museum; this houses the Pergamon Altar, one of the finest pieces of Greek art still visible today. The Museum of German History shows the whole history of the country interpreted from a Marxist-Leninist standpoint. At the National Gallery, the work of Käthe Kollwitz is worthy of special attention.

In Dresden, the world-famous Zwinger houses collections of painting, porcelain and pewter. The best-known exhibit is Raffael's "Sistine Madonna". Dresden also has a most interesting Hygiene Museum, with a "glass woman" and a "glass horse" which can be used for biology lectures.

Fig 136 Raffael's "Sistine Madonna" attracts visitors from all over the world. Photo: Lex Hornsby & Partners.

The houses of Goethe and Schiller in Weimar have both been turned into museums, and attract many visitors. Of the two, Goethe's house is far more rewarding. Halle has a museum of Prehistory, and finally the collection of Dutch paintings in Schwerin is worthy of mention.

Question time

This chapter is a rag-bag of often-asked questions not dealt with elsewhere in the book. Some of the questions can be answered only with subjective opinions.

Faults "What are the Germans' main faults?"

Fortunately, this provocative question can be answered tactfully by referring to faults which the Germans themselves admitted to in an Allensbach poll taken in December 1957. (It is a pity the poll has not been repeated, but it may still be regarded as valid, for people's natures change little in ten years.) The most commonly admitted fault, given by 44%, was "too nervous, easily flustered" — this was mostly admitted by women (50%) rather than by men (36%). "Too yielding" was mentioned by 30%, and "a little stubborn, unyielding" by 29%; this defies the opinion often expressed by foreigners that the Germans are a thoroughly stubborn race. A further 29% felt that they too often let others feel their bad moods, and 23% "make a resolution to do something, to give up smoking or drinking, for instance, and then fail to do it".

Humour "Isn't one of the Germans' main faults their lack of a sense of humour?"

The cartoons in this book may already have given the lie to this favourite criticism. Indeed, there is hardly an area of Germany which does not have its own brand of humour. Many of the jokes are told in dialect, and the point is often lost when they are "translated" into High German. In Hamburg, a "stock character" for local jokes is Little Erna, a young lady whose age seems quite flexible and varies from one joke to the next. One day she went to the doctor's with a long tale of woe. She and her husband were gradually coming to the conclusion that theirs would be a childless marriage. The doctor decided that an examination was called for, and asked her to undress. "Oh, er, um . . ." Erna began to stutter, "I really wanted my *first* child to be my husband's."

In Cologne, the stock comic figures are the red-haired Tünnes (short for Anton) and his sombre, rather slow-witted friend, Schäl. "You know, Schäl", Tünnes said on one occasion, "every time I see you, you remind me of Hubert Schmidt." "Why, do we look so alike?" "No, but he owes me five Mark too."

It is easy to generalise about the different varieties of humour. For example, some Germans maintain that Berlin humour is the most pointed and irreverent, while Munich humour is the coarsest. But such generalisations do not take account of the fact that many jokes wander and become attached to the local stock figures in each city. Indeed, I have frequently told what I thought was a Cologne joke, only to be greeted with the comment, "Oh, that's an old one. The version I know is about a Scotsman and a Welshman . . .". Jokes about the Scots, by the way, are quite popular in Germany.

Formality "Admitting the Germans have their own brand of humour, aren't they still a formal nation? Why do they stick to surnames so long?"

The Germans make a clear distinction between friends ("Freunde") and acquaintances ("Bekannten"). The friends are close friends, addressed by their Christian names and with the pronoun "du". Everyone else is an acquaintance, addressed by surname and "Sie". Some foreigners — fortunately only a few — insist that "du" is the equivalent of the English "you", and use it for all and sundry. As well as being linguistically incorrect ("du" is really "thou"), this line of thinking shows an unfortunate disregard for other people's customs and is liable to cause offence. Apart from relatives and close friends, "du" is used for small children and animals, or if one wants to be particularly derogatory. (This is true of High German, though not of all the dialects.) The use of surnames and "Sie" is not formality; it is just habit and linguistic usage.

Gambling "Do the Germans go in for football pools?"

Far less than they used to. According to Allensbach figures, the number who regularly go in for football pools dropped from 17% in 1955 to a mere 4% in 1961. The reason for this decline is the increased popularity of number lotteries. These were introduced in 1955, and spread over the whole country by 1958. By 1963, Allensbach pollsters found that 30% of their sample regularly bought these "Lotto" tickets, and a further 24% did so from time to time. The idea is to pick six numbers from a possible forty-nine. Every Saturday night, the winning numbers are selected by a sophisticated form of tombola drum in the Munich television studios. The top prize is a half a million Mark. The Länder authorities take 20% of the stake for financing social, cultural and sports facilities.

Prostitution "One hears about Hamburg's night-life and vice rings. Is the German attitude towards prostitution different from that of British authorities?"

Prostitution is legal in West Germany, provided the prostitutes submit to regular health checks and do not "offer themselves for immoral purposes publicly in an obvious way, or in a way liable to annoy individuals or the public in general". But the interpretation of "obvious" is rather different from the provisions of the British Street Offences Act. Every large West German city has its prostitutes, who go about their business quite openly in clearly-defined areas, often in streets from which "young people" are prohibited. In some cities (notably Stuttgart, Düsseldorf and Hamburg) there are authorised brothels, run like hotels and with rules for the prostitutes' protection. Since 1964, prostitutes have been liable for income tax. Living off immoral earnings (i.e. off someone else's immoral earnings) is illegal. In East Germany, prostitution has been officially abolished as an "unnecessary remnant of bourgeois society"; in practice it has merely gone underground.

Old Nazis "Is it true that West Germany is still run by old Nazis?"

This is an allegation continually being made by Communists and left-wingers all over the world. It ignores the fact that anyone who was thirty years old or over in 1933 (the year in which Nazi Party membership became a prequisite for promotion) would now have passed his sixty-fifth birthday. Most former Nazis in West Germany are now harmless old men. Another group will be those who genuinely supported Hitler in the 'thirties but saw the error of their ways when details of the gas-chamber horrors came to light.

But there will also be those who can never lose the spirit of Nazism, and there are those guilty of crimes against humanity which can never be forgiven. Statistics of how many of these Nazis have been punished are difficult to come by. In 1961, the Federal Ministry of Justice announced that under German law, a total of 12,715 former Nazis had been tried, of whom 5372 had been sentenced (including 12 death sentences and 68 of life imprisonment). In addition, Allied courts in the Western zones of occupation convicted 5025 former Nazis, of whom 806 were sentenced to death. Many of the sentences, however, were later reduced in severity.

There is a further group of people who, while not directly responsible for any crime, worked with the Nazis or in Nazi ministries. These include the Federal Chancellor, Kurt-Georg Kiesinger, together with many industrialists, doctors and lawyers. It is a matter of opinion whether or not such people should be allowed to hold public office.

It was not until 1958 that the Länder judiciaries set up a Central Agency for the Investigation of National Socialist Crimes. Since then, this office in Ludwigsburg has continued to track down a number of war criminals who have been pursuing harmless occupations at home and abroad. But by 1965, Allensbach pollsters found that 52% of the population felt that Germany "should cease trying people now for crimes they committed years ago".

An East German government publication in 1964 claimed that since 1945, Soviet and East German authorities had convicted a total of 12,807 former Nazis, including 118 death sentences. But former Nazis who embraced the cause of Socialism were welcomed with open arms by the new National Democratic Party (provided they were not guilty of any major crime). West German authorities claim that a number of leading state functionaries in East Germany are former Nazis (though not war criminals).

New values "Has the introduction of Socialism in East Germany brought any new values to the foreground?"

It is impossible to assess to what extent new Socialist values have been accepted by the population as a whole, since public opinion testing is an almost completely neglected science in East Germany. Some West German sources claim that they can build up a picture of East German thought from the views of refugees, tending to ignore the fact that those who leave a country must inevitably be an unrepresentative (and particularly unsympathetic) sample.

As to the attitudes of party and youth organisation members in East Germany, some indication of these may be obtained from a study of the columns of the youth newspaper, "Junge Welt". Some new values do seem to be emerging, at least among the more devoted party members. Based on an intense loyalty to the party and state, there is a tendency to view all work in terms of its usefulness to the community. The idea of the "collective", be it in a school class or at work, seems to have caught on, and the collective groups assume responsibility for the welfare of each individual member. In court cases, the accused's collective will stand bail. Many personal decisions, such as movement from one part of the country to another for reasons connected with work, are viewed in the general context of serving the state interest. Competition between individuals and collectives is instigated by means of decorations and financial incentives. Most important of all, the loyal party member insists on taking an interest in politics at all times, even when on holiday; he feels he must be "up to date" with the news.

Germany and the world

"Friend or foe?" An old challenge, and particularly applicable to the post-war Germans. Both East and West Germans now have to deal as friends with those who learnt to hate them as a nation during the years immediately preceding 1945.

Everyone will have his own opinion as to whether or not his own nation regards the Germans as friends. Those who have visited the country will also have their own opinion about how they were received. In this chapter my comments are more subjective than elsewhere in the book, and the reader should bear in mind that I move mostly among those who have a special interest in Germany and a favourable bias towards her.

Attitudes towards individual Germans are easier to describe than attitudes towards the Germans "as a race". Individual Germans are welcome almost everywhere. The number of exchange groups and international cultural events with Germans as participants has never been so great. Seldom does one hear now of a German having "hostile experiences" in a foreign country. A British journalist tried not long ago to prove that there was still considerable anti-German feeling in Britain and France. He went about in both countries posing (effectively) as a German. The report of his experience was the opposite of what he intended — while insisting to the last that anti-German feeling does exist, he had to admit that he himself had been treated cordially everywhere he went.

Nevertheless, I have met many people outside Germany who draw a distinction between "Germans I have met" and "Germans as a race". Individual Germans, they assure me, were charming and courteous. But the Germans "as a race" are "militaristic, conceited, over-efficient, too ready to be dominated, and untrustworthy". The one thing which is generally admitted as a German virtue is hard work. Indeed, in the post-war years, West German efficiency has become proverbial. But there is still a latent fear of the Germans in some quarters, particularly in Poland and Czechoslovakia. Even Polish "specialists" on Germany have told me that they will never be able to forgive or forget what the Germans have done during the war.

To some extent these hostile views are limited to the older generation. Young people who travel to Germany on exchange visits have more favourable impressions, and even young people who have never been to Germany have a generally friendly attitude towards the country.

Attitudes towards East Germany are too often based on ignorance. It is regarded, if only subconsciously, as "part of Russia". More than once I have been asked if I spoke to East Germans in Russian. Many young people — not only left-wingers — are now in favour of recognising the East German regime, though West Berlin is still regarded as an "island of freedom". The situation is not helped by the mainly hostile articles which appear from time to time in Western magazines.

How they see us

In 1959 the Allensbach pollsters asked the question, "Which country do you consider to be Germany's best friend?" 49% named the USA, 9% France, 6% Britain, 5% Austria, 3% Switzerland, and 2% Holland.

But political considerations will doubtless have played a large part in the answering of this question, and it will not reflect attitudes towards the foreigners concerned as individuals. In September 1962 the pollsters found that 66% of those questioned thought the British were "proud of their fatherland", 39% that they were "enterprising", and 39% again that they were "cultivated and refined". Only 10% regarded the British as "natural, unprejudiced, sincere" and again only 10% as "gay, cheerful". As to faults, 33% regarded the British as "arrogant, conceited" and 25% as "pig-headed, obstinate".

At the same time, a similar poll was conducted with regard to the Americans. They were regarded by 62% of the participants as "modern, progressive", by 54% as "enterprising", by 50% as "placing personal freedom above all else" and by 48% as "energetic, venturesome". As to the debit side, 38% felt the Americans were "wasteful, place too much value on money", 23% "pampered, spoiled" and 20% "boastful, show off too much". Only 6% regarded the Americans as "modest, unassuming".

The Germans on the other side of the "Iron Curtain" have little opportunity of seeing an Englishman or an American unless they live in East Berlin, which is frequently visited by tourists. But these tourists are more interested in seeing the Pergamon Altar than in talking to the East German populace. An East German girl told me that many of her countrymen regard it as an honour, and are flattered, when an Englishman or American is their guest. But sometimes this hospitality is rewarded by an incredible lack of consideration, based on ignorance of many of the little courtesies which help life go smoothly, and which vary from one country to another. All East German books and newspapers give a biased view of the West, and I have never read praise of any Western country in anything published in East Germany.

APPENDICES

The value of money

The following table shows approximately the par values of the West German Mark after the 1967 sterling devaluation.

West German Mark	Sterling	US dollars
0,50	1s 0½d	0.13
1	2s 1d	0.25
3	6s 3d	0.75
5	10s 5d	1.25
10	£1 0s 10d	2.50
20	£2 1s 8d	5.00
50	£5 4s 2d	12.50
100	£10 8s 4d	25.00
1000	£104 3s 4d	250.00

For the tourist visiting East Germany, the above table will also serve as a rough guide to the value of East German currency, because his exchange rate will differ only marginally from that operating in West Germany. Other exchange rates for East German currency were explained in the chapter on "The value of money".

How to get there

From Britain
The shortest sea crossing is via Dover-Ostend (about four hours), but you may prefer to travel overnight and use the longer Harwich to Hook-of-Holland crossing, which gives you a proper night's sleep on board. Most of the connecting trains at the Hook-of-Holland allow time for a leisurely breakfast before you disembark.

By car, the most popular sea ferry is again Dover-Ostend, though many tourists making for Southern Germany prefer to go via France (Calais or Boulogne). Private firms operate car ferries from Tilbury to Rotterdam, and from Harwich and Hull to Bremerhaven.

By air, there are direct flights from London to all the major cities in Germany, and from Manchester and Birmingham to Düsseldorf. There is an air ferry for cars from Southend to Ostend and Rotterdam.

From North America
Most American tourists now fly to Europe. Lufthansa, Pan Am and TWA have frequent services to Frankfurt, and the Lufthansa planes go on to Hamburg and Stuttgart. Lufthansa also operates between New York and Cologne/Bonn, New York and Munich, Chicago and Frankfurt, Chicago and Stuttgart, San Francisco and Frankfurt, Montreal and Frankfurt. TCM operates between Canada (Toronto and Montreal) and Frankfurt, via Brussels. West Coast residents can also take the polar route to London, and get connecting flights from there to Frankfurt.

For those who want the more leisurely sea crossing (five to eleven days, depending on route and speed), there are various alternatives to choose from. You can sail from New York to Bremerhaven or Cuxhaven (for Hamburg), or from Quebec and Montreal to Bremerhaven. It is advisable to book early — some ships have their tourist-class accommodation booked six months in advance.

East Germany
From the West, East Germany may be entered at the following points:
Sassnitz (by ferry from Sweden)
Warnemünde (by ferry from Denmark)
Herrnburg (by rail from Lübeck or Hamburg)
Schwanheide (by rail from Hamburg)
Horst (by road from Hamburg)
Oebstfelde (by rail from Hanover)
Marienborn (by road and rail from Brunswick and Hanover)
Wartha (by road from West Germany)
Gerstungen (by rail from Frankfurt and Cologne)
Probstzella (by rail from Nuremberg)
Juchhöh (by road from Hof)
Gutenfürst (by rail from Hof)
Berlin-Schönefeld (by air from various places in the world, including London)
Berlin, Friedrichstrasse Station (by rail or underground from West Berlin)
Berlin, Friedrichstrasse/Zimmerstrasse (by road or on foot from West Berlin; this crossing is known as "Checkpoint Charlie").

Tourists wishing to enter East Berlin on foot are recommended, if they have no luggage, to enter via "Checkpoint Charlie", where formalities normally take less time. But if you have a heavy suitcase, take the underground to Friedrichstrasse Station, where you stand a better chance of getting a taxi.

There are direct flights to East Berlin from many East European cities, also from Paris, Brussels, Amsterdam and London. The East German airline "Interflug" also has direct services to Africa and the Middle East. For the Leipzig Fair, there are special services connecting many European capitals with Leipzig.

Further reading

Several new books on Germany and the Germans appear each year, and it is difficult to keep up to date. The following list is restricted to books I have found valuable and readable, published since 1960. An excellent bibliography of earlier books will be found in the volume by Terence Prittie, listed below. Books published in East Germany are marked with an asterisk. Authors are named first, or publisher if author not known.

In English

Atlantik-Brücke: Meet Germany (new editions appear regularly)
  A good introductory survey, written by a team of experts, mostly about political and economic aspects of West Germany. Unsympathetic towards the East.
Atlantik-Brücke: These Strange German Ways (1965)
  A lively booklet full of amusing cartoons. Covers with extreme simplicity many aspects of German everyday life. Written for American servicemen stationed in Germany.
Board of Trade: Hints to Businessmen Visiting the Federal Republic of Germany and West Berlin (reissued periodically)
  Clear, concise information on matters affecting trade visits. Full of statistics, addresses, etc.
Fodor, E: Germany (Fodor's Modern Guides, reissued regularly)
  A most readable guide book for tourists. Tells you the date the Town Hall was built, also recommends hotels, restaurants and shops.
Hangen, W: The Muted Revolution (Knopf, New York, 1966)
  A journalist's account of East German politics, personalities, etc. Tries hard to be fair, but often gives the impression that sensational writing is more important than informing the reader.
Heidenheimer, A J: The Governments of Germany (Cromwell, USA, 1961; University Paperbacks, UK, 1965)
  A scholarly, objective yet readable account of the political and economic growth of both East and West Germany.
Hornsby, L: Profile of East Germany (Harrap, in collaboration with Zeit im Bild, 1965)
  Informative and full of details about East German institutions. The chapters are written by individual experts. The editor's firm acts as public relations agent for the East German travel information office in London.
Hubatsch, W: The German Question (Herder Book Center, USA, 1967)
  Factual, informative guide to the political development of East and West since 1945. Heavy-going in places, but a good reference work.
Latham, P: The German Federal Republic (Blackie, 1964)
  Has been described as "an awesome collection of facts". Separate sections for students and businessmen. By far the most informative book on German trade and education.
Leonhardt, R W: This Germany, the Story since the Third Reich (Penguin, 1966)
  German politics and everyday life described by a former Cambridge don, now one of Germany's top journalists. Delightfully amusing and most informative,

though one could wish the author were more informative about his sources.

Loewenstein, Prince Hubertus: A Basic History of Germany (Inter Nationes, 1962)
   Clear and concise account of German history since Roman times, though not always the traditional interpretation. Somewhat over-patriotic when dealing with the Holy Roman Empire.

Mander, J: Berlin — Hostage to the West (Penguin, 1962)
   In some ways a standard work, though short. Clear account of the division of Germany in its Cold War context.

Dr Oetker: German Home Cooking (Ceres-Verlag, 1963)
   A good cook-book for all who want to try out some of the German specialities themselves. Plenty of illustrations.

Pounds, N J G: Divided Germany and Berlin (Nostrand, USA, 1962)
   A hard-hitting book by a British professor in the USA. The author is a well-known geographer, and shows a thorough knowledge of German economics and politics. Not a re-hash of traditional arguments.

Press and Information Office, Bonn: Germany Reports *and* Facts about Germany (both reissued periodically)
   Handbooks published by the West German government. Less readable than their British equivalents, but full of facts. Official government policy (including non-recognition of the Oder-Neisse Line) throughout. The shorter version, "Facts about Germany", is livelier and gives better coverage of some fields (notably the health services).

Prittie, T: Germany (Seymour Press, 1967)
   This book has appeared in both the "Sunday Times World Library" and in "Life World Library". Clear account of German politics and economics, and many excellent colour pictures. The author was "Guardian" correspondent in Bonn for many years. Good bibliography.

Stahl, W: The Politics of Post-War Germany (Praeger, 1963)
   A serious tome, containing much sound information. Particularly informative on some of the more important controversial issues, especially the treatment of war criminals.

Tempel, G: Speaking Frankly About the Germans (Secker & Warburg, 1963)
   Originally a set of newspaper articles, so rather lacking in continuity. Nevertheless, an excellent autobiographical account of life in Germany from 1935 to 1950.

Thonger, R: A Calendar of German Customs (Wolff, London, 1966)
   The author acknowledges that most of his information, and all the illustrations, are taken from Heidi Lehmann's book (see below). But he has succeeded in adapting the original to form a most readable English version.

Verlag Zeit im Bild: Meet the GDR (1966)*
   An official handbook on East Germany, containing data favourable to the GDR.

Magazines

Encounter, April 1964
   A collection of great names, including Toynbee, Muggeridge, Erich Heller and Ralf Dahrendorf. Thought-provoking articles, often humorous (e.g. Goronwy Rees' description of East Germany as Kafkaland).

Holiday, October 1964
   Less sophisticated than the "Encounter" issue, but again a wealth of talent in the writers — Postgate, Trevor-Roper, Tynan, etc. Many good pictures.

The Economist, 15 October 1966
  A perceptive supplement on the structure of the German banks and industry, drawing some conclusions that might be adopted in Britain. Sold out almost immediately.

In German

Apel, H: Ohne Begleiter (Wissenschaft und Politik)
  Conversations with East Germans, which read as though reported accurately. To my mind the best book on life in East Germany.
Bertelsmann-Verlag: Deutschland, das Land in dem wir wohnen (1966)
  Full of pictures, charts, etc. Has been criticised for right-wing bias.
Bundesministerium für gesamtdeutsche Fragen: Die SBZ von A bis Z (reissued annually up to 1966, new edition due Autumn 1968)
  Reference book produced by the West about the East. Factual.
Deutsches Institut für Zeitgeschichte: DDR — 300 Fragen, 300 Antworten (last published 1965)*
  An official East German view.
Dietz-Verlag: Grundriss der Geschichte der deutschen Arbeiterbewegung (reissued periodically)*
  The official East German history of the German working-class movement, and of post-war Germany. Pure party-line stuff.
Dönhoff, Leonhardt and Sommer: Reise in ein fernes Land (Naumann, 1964)
  Three West German journalists report on a trip through East Germany. Most readable, particularly Leonhardt's section on entry formalities.
EMNID-Institut: "Junge Menschen 1964"
  Public opinion polls showing young people's views on everything from politics to sex.
Engelmann, B: Deutschland-Report (Exlibris, 1965)
  A provocative book pointing out the flaws in West Germany and some of the advantages of life in the East. Each chapter supported by documents, but some of the criticism is not as fair as it would appear on the surface.
Gatzke, Köppen, Plückebaum: Deutschlandfibel (Metzner, reissued periodically)
  Concise information about West German institutions with many charts and drawings. Short, hostile chapter on the East.
Haller, C: Der gute Ton im Umgang mit Menschen (Südwest Verlag, 1960)
  Excellent value for money; a complete guide to "good manners" in the office, at meal times, when visiting, etc. Alphabetical arrangement.
Hubatsch, W: Die deutsche Frage (Ploetz, 1964)
  The German original of "The German Question" (see above).
Leonhardt, R W: X-mal Deutschland (Piper, 1964)
  Contains some information omitted from the English version of "This Germany" (mentioned above).
Mayn, H: Massenmedien in der Bundesrepublik Deutschland (Colloquium-Verlag, 1966)
  Thorough analysis of press, radio and television, with four informative pages on East Germany.
Presse- und Informationsamt der Bundesregierung: Deutschland Heute *and* Tatsachen über Deutschland (both reissued periodically)
  German originals of the English books mentioned above; new editions appear in German long before the translations are ready.

Tempel, G: Deutschland — aber wo liegst du? (Rowohlt, 1963)
  A German translation of "Speaking Frankly" (see above). Would make a good reader for advanced students of German.
VEB F A Brockhaus: Reiseführer DDR (reissued periodically)*
  Comprehensive but stodgy travel guide to East Germany.

Some useful addresses

In Britain

Embassy of the Federal Republic of Germany
Chesham Place, London S W 1

Anglo-German Association
2 Henrietta Street, London W C 2

German Tourist Information Bureau
61 Conduit Street, London W 1

BDI Secretarial Office (Federation of German Industry)
33 Bruton Street, London W 1

Curzon Publicity Ltd (public relations consultants to the German Embassy)
31 St James's Place, London S W 1

Berolina Travel Ltd (travel information office for East Germany)
19 Dover Street, London W 1

KFA Ltd (East German Chamber of Foreign Trade)
27 Albermarle Street, London W 1

German Institute (lectures, concerts and library)
51 Princes Gate, London S W 7

The Wiener Library (German politics since 1933)
4 Devonshire Street, London W 1

Scottish-German Society
3 Park Circus, Glasgow C 3

In the USA

Embassy of the Federal Republic of Germany
4645 Reservoir Road NW, Washington DC 20007

German Information Center
410 Park Avenue, New York, NY 10022

German-American Chamber of Commerce
666 Fifth Avenue, New York, NY 10019

German Tourist Information Office
500 Fifth Avenue, New York, NY 10036

German Cultural Institute Boston
535 Boylston Street, Boston, Massachusetts 02116

In West Germany

Inter Nationes (many different services to foreign individuals and organisations interested in Germany)
532 Bad Godesberg, Kennedyallee 91-103

British Council (including Central Library)
5 Köln, Hahnenstrasse 6

Deutsch-Englische Gesellschaft
53 Bonn, Remigiusstrasse 1

German Student Travel Service
53 Bonn, Kaiserstrasse 71

Institut für Auslandsbeziehungen (Institute for Foreign Connections)
7 Stuttgart 1, Charlottenplatz 17

British Embassy
53 Bonn, Friedrich-Ebert-Allee 77

British Travel Association
6 Frankfurt, Neue Mainzer Strasse 22

Federation of British Industry
5 Köln, Apostelnstrasse 3

Deutsch-Englische Austauschstelle (Anglo-German Exchange Service)
6 Frankfurt, Hochstrasse 37

Deutsch-Amerikanischer Wirtschaftsverband (German-American Economic Association)
6 Frankfurt, Börsenstrasse 10

United States Embassy
532 Bad Godesberg, Mehlemer Aue

Amerika-Gesellschaft eV
2 Hamburg 13, Tesdorpfstrasse 1

Atlantik-Brücke (many publications on Germany)
2 Hamburg 64, Sanderskoppel 15

Federation of German American Clubs
7 Stuttgart O, Richard-Wagner-Strasse 14

United States Travel Service
6 Frankfurt, Grosse Callusstrasse 1-7

American Chamber of Commerce in Germany
1 Berlin 12, Fasanenstrasse 4

In East Germany

Reisebüro der DDR (official tourist office, includes visa department)
104 Berlin, Friedrichstrasse 110/112

Kammer für Aussenhandel (Chamber of Foreign Trade)
108 Berlin, Unter den Linden 40

Deutsch-Britische Gesellschaft
108 Berlin, Ernst Thälmann Platz 7-8

INDEX

Entries are listed in alphabetical order. Main entries are followed by sub-headings where a breakdown of the main subject might be useful. Page numbers are given first, then any figure numbers. A single-page number refers to a mention of the subject on that page or to a whole chapter or section starting on that page. Two-page references (e.g. "Advent 91–2") indicate that the subject is dealt with in a passage starting on the first page and continued on the second page. Three-page references (e.g. "American aid 157–9") mean that a figure occupies the middle page.

German expressions For the benefit of teachers and students, many German expressions defined or explained in the book are listed in the index (e.g. "Amtsgericht"), even if the reference is not long enough to otherwise merit indexing.

Names with "von" German names with "von" ("of") are listed according to conventional German practice in two ways:

Kleist, Heinrich von Otfried von Weissenburg
Schiller, Friedrich von Wolfram von Eschenbach

This is not inconsistency. Wolfram, a mediaeval poet, had no surname and was known simply as "Wolfram of Eschenbach". Later, the "von" became a sign of nobility, which has led many people (Germans included) to assume incorrectly that all the German mediaeval poets were noblemen. Some English catalogues do not distinguish between the two types of name and would list Wolfram as "Eschenbach, Wolfram von".

Aachen 197
 museum 214
"Abitur" 103
Added Value Tax 63
address
 envelope 120
 form of 64
Adenauer, Konrad 97
adultery 18
Advent 91–2
advertising 65, Figs 37, 38, 39
 advisers 69
 attitudes to 65
 East Germany 69, 127
 law 65
 methods 65
 newspapers 122, 127
 products advertised 65
AFN 130
agricultural production cooperative 54
agriculture
 collectivisation 54
 East Germany 54
 size of farms 52
 West Germany 52
Albertus Magnus 160
alcohol and driving 138–9
Alcuin 151
Allensbach Institute 8

Alps 187
 customs 95–6
Altdorfer, Albrecht 172
American aid 50, 157–9
Americans
 attitudes to 221
"Amtsgericht" 114
Anabaptists 108
"Angestellter" 61
"Apotheke" 40
appearance 11
architecture 170, Figs 106, 107
army Figs 94, 96
 East Germany 149, Fig 95
 West Germany 147
Arnim, Achim von 167
arrogance 10
art 170
 interest in 175
Ascension Day 91
Attila 151
"Aufsichtsrat" 52, 63, 113
Augsburg 197
"Autobahn" 137, Fig 85

Bach, Johann Sebastian 176, Fig 109
Baden
  customs 94
Baden-Baden 197
Baden-Württemberg 191–2
Bad Kreuznach 197
Bad Schandau Fig 53
balconies 12
Baltic 87
Bamberg 197
  Bamberg Rider 170
banks 134
  East German 135
  hours of business 134
Barlach, Ernst 174–5
Baroque architecture 173, Fig 70
basket ball Fig 48
"Bauhaus" 174
Bäumler, Hans-Jürgen 124
Bavaria 191
  beer 33–4
  costume 24
  customs Fig 5
entertainment 70
  "Enzian" 34
  museums 213
  politics 97
  religion 111
  tourists 81
  wood-carving 57, Fig 31
Bayreuth 197
beach baskets Fig 52
"Beamter" 61
Bebel, August 162
bed-linen 14
beds 13–14
beer 10, 33–4, Figs 13, 16
beer-mugs Fig 57
Beethoven, Ludwig van 177
Behring, Emil von 181
Berg, Alban 178
Berlin
  Alexanderplatz Fig 128
  beer 34
  blockade 159
  cycle race Fig 46
  East 207–8
  Europa-Center 198, Fig 123
  in 1945 22
  museums 213, 215, Fig 135
  music 178, Fig 111
  Pergamon Altar Fig 135

  political status 191
  theatres 73, 74–5
  tourists Fig 101
  Wall 159, Fig 100
  West 197–200
Berchtesgaden 197
Bernkastel 200
"Berufsaufbauschule" 104
"Berufsfachschule" 104
"Berufsschule" 104
"Bezirke" 194, Fig 121
BFBS 130
Bielefeld
  museum 214
birthday
  celebration in office 60
birth-rate Fig 6
Bismarck, Otto von 154
Bi-zone 159
Black Forest
  morning snack 29-30
  museums 214
  spirits 34
  tourist attractions 81
  wood carving 57
blazers 22
"blue letters" 103
"Blue Rider" Group 174
boat trips 70
"Bocksbeutel" 31
Boehme, Jakob 108
Böll, Heinrich 168
Bonn 200
books 44, 125
  East Germany 128
book-shelves 13
bookshops 38, Fig 81
brandy 34
  East Germany 35
Braun, Wernher von 183
bread 29
bread rolls 26
bread saw 14
breakfast 26–7, Fig 10
Brecht, Bertold 168. 178, Fig 104
Brehm, Alfred 183
Bremen 200
  museum 213, Fig 134
  ragout 30
Brentano, Clemens 167
Brethren of the Common Life 108
Brick Gothic 170

British
  attitudes to 221
Bruns, Ursula 45
Brunswick 200
Büchner, Georg 167
"Bundesgerichtshof" 114
"Bundesrat" 97
"Bundesstrassen" 137
"Bundestag" 97
"Bundesverfassungsgericht" 114
bureaucracy 61, 154
"Burg" 172
Busch, Wilhelm 167, Fig 103
buses 139

cabarets 73
  East Germany 75
cameras 56, 58
camping Fig 20
  day camps Fig 24
carnival 89–90, 96, Figs 55, 56
CDU
  East Germany 100
  West Germany 97
censorship (East Germany)
  newspapers 127
  post 121
Central Council of the Advertising Trade 65
Central Mountains 187
cereals, East Germany Fig 29
chairs 13
Chamberlain, Houston Stewart 162
  champagne 70–2
  museum 214
Chamisso, Adalbert von 167
Chancellor 97
Charlemagne 151
Checkpoint Charlie 223–4, Fig 101
cheese 29
chemical products 56
chemist 40
chemistry 181
Chemnitz 196
china 15, 58, Figs 4, 32
chips 30
Christian Democrats
  East Germany 100
  West Germany 97
Christian Socialists 97
Christmas 92, Figs 58, 59
  in the office Fig 75
  roundabout 58, Fig 33
church 108, Figs 70, 71
  East Germany 112
  membership 111
  tax 112
cinema 44, 73, Figs 43, 44
  advertising 67
  behaviour 46
circulars 67
"citizens in uniform" 149
Civil Law Book 113
clocks 40
Clovis 151
coffee
  and cakes 29, Fig 12

East Germany 30
  grinder and filter 14
  how made 27
  mentioned 19, 26
Cologne 200
  artists 170
  beer 34
  fritters 30
Communist Party
  East Germany 100, 159
  West Germany 99
company, types of 63
confirmation 19, 111–2
conscription
  East Germany 149
  West Germany 148–9
consumer magazines 66
contracts 113
Corinth, Lovis 174
Corpus Christi 91
correspondence 64
cosmetics 23, Fig 8
  teenagers 25
Cottbus 195
Council of Ministers 101
courts
  East Germany 115
  West Germany 114
Cranach, Lucas 172
credit transfer 134
crime rate
  East Germany 115, Fig 72
  West Germany 114
Criminal Law Book 113
crosswords 11
crucifixes Fig 69
CSU 97
currency 222
  East Germany 135
  West Germany 133–4, Fig 84
Currency Reform 133, 135, 159
curtains 12, 14

Daimler, Gottlieb Wilhelm 183
Daimler-Benz museum 214
dancing 44
  lessons 45
dating 45
DBD 100
death penalty 114
debts 113
DEFA 75
dentist (cartoon) Fig 93
Deutsche Welle 130
Deutschlandfunk 130
DFB 101
DFU 98–9
d'Hondt, Victor 97
Diem, Carl 76–7
"Diener" 36
Diesel, Rudolf, 183
Dinkelsbühl 200
  Children's Tribute 95
direct mail advertising 67, Fig 38
discipline (home) 19
divorce 18
  East Germany 19–20
DKB 101
DM 133–4
doctorate 105
dogs 10
dolls, museum of 214
Dortmund 200
Dresden 208
  Bezirk 196
  china 42, 58, Fig 32
  museums 215, Figs 129, 136
dress 21
  East Germany 25, Fig 9
  expenditure 38
  ladies' clothes 22
  men's clothes 21
  suitability for occasion 21, Fig 7
  theatre 70
drink 31
  customs 35
  East Germany 35
  expenditure 38, 40
  non-alcoholic 34–5
  opening hours 35
  quantity 31
"Drogerie" 40
Droste-Hülshoff, Annette von 167
DTSB 79
Durbridge, Francis 131

Dürer, Albrecht 172
Dürkheim
  sausage fair 93
Düsseldorf 200, Fig 36
  Opera House Fig 40

Easter 90
  East Germany 96
eau-de-Cologne 56
Eckhardt, Meister 108, 160
education 102
  expenditure 38
  East Germany 105–7
  general knowledge 11
  technical 104
Eichendorff, Josef 167
"Einfuhrumsatzsteuer" 63
Einstein, Albert 183, Fig 112
"Einwohnermeldeamt" 113
"Eisbein" 27
Eisenach 208, Fig 109
Elbe Fig 53
election day 99
electrical goods 40, 56
Elsheimer, Adam 172
emblems Figs 117, 118
emigration (East Germany) 115, 159
EMNID Institute 8
Ems 188
engagements 17
entertainment 70
  expenditure 38
entry points (East Germany) 223
envelopes 64
"Enzian" 34
Erfurt 208
  Bezirk 195
Erhard, Ludwig 97
Ernst Thälmann Pioneers 46–7
Erzgebirge
  wood carvings 58, Fig 33
Essen
  museum 213
European Economic Community 55
Europe Student Travel 45
Evangelical Church 108
Existentialism 162
exports
  East Germany 57–8
  West Germany 55–6
Expressionism 168
"Exquisit" 41
Extended High School 105

"Fachschule" 104
factory combat groups 150
Fair of the Master-Craftsmen of Tomorrow 49
family 17
  monthly budget 38
  strength in East Germany 20
father 18
  Father's Day 91
faults 217
FDGB 101
FDJ 46-9, Fig 23
  in Parliament 101
  newspaper 127, 219
FDP 98
Federal Republic of Germany 159, 189
Feininger, Lyonel 174
festivals
  local 93, Fig 60
  national 89
Feuerbach, Ludwig 162
Fichte, Johann 161
figures, how written Fig 113
films
  East German 75
  imported 74
  West German 73-4
first communion 19, 111-2
First World War 154
Fischer, Emil Herman 181
fish 28
flans 29
  mentioned 19
flats 12, Fig 1
Fleming, Paul 166
flowers 37
  pot plants 12, 37
flower shops 38
"Flur" 12
food 26
  East Germany 30
  expenditure 38
  meal prices 83
  quantity eaten 26
  regional dishes 29-30
football 78, Fig 47
foreigners
  attitudes to Germany 220
  German views on 220-1
foreign trade
  East Germany 57
  West Germany 55

fork 27
formality 217-8
Franconia
  wine 31
Frankfurt-am-Main 200-1
  museum 213
  trade fairs 68
Frankfurt-an-der-Oder
  Bezirk 195
Frederick the Great 153
Free Democrats 98
Free German Youth 46-9, Fig 23
  in Parliament 101
  newspaper 127, 219
Freiburg-im-Breisgau 201
Friedrich, Casper David 174
Friends of God 108
furniture 13, Fig 2
Furth
  Dragon's Fight 95
Furtwangen 201
Füssen 201

gambling 218
games 43
Garmisch-Partenkirchen 202
Gauss, Karl Friedrich 181–2
geographical names 195
geography 187
GDR 99, 159, 190
  recognition 99
Gera 195–6
German Peace Union 98–9
German Student Travel Service 45
German Youth Ring 45
gifts
  as adverts 67
  for host 37
giro 135
glass 58
Goebel, Heinrich 183
Goethe, Johann Wolfgang von 166, Fig 102
going steady 45
Golden Plan 77
Gottfried von Strassburg 164
Gothic architecture 170
Grass, Günther 168
Grimm, Jakob and Wilhelm 45, 167
Grimmelshausen, Christoffel von 166
Grünewald, Matthias 170–2
grocer's shop Fig 18
gross national product 50
GST 79, 84, 149
Guericke, Otto von 181
"guten Morgen" 36
"Gymnasium" 102

Hahn, Otto 183
Halle 208
  Bezirk 195
  museum 216
Hamburg 202
  museum 214
Hamelin 202
"Handelsorganisation" 41
hand-shaking 36
handwriting 186
Hanover 202
  trade fair 68
Hapsburgs 153, 154
Hartmann von Aue 164
Harz
  tourists 87, 82
hats
  ladies' 22–3
  men's 22
Hauptmann, Gerhart 168
health insurance
  East Germany 146
  West Germany 145
Hebbel, Christian Friedrich 167
Hegel, Georg Friedrich 161
Heidegger, Martin 162
Heidelberg 202
  customs 93
Heine, Heinrich 167
Hermann 151
herrings 28
Hertz, Gustav 183
Hesse 193
  religion 111
Higher Criticism 109
High German 184
Hildebrand, Lay of 164
Hildesheim 202
hiring service 41, Fig 20
history 151
Hitler, Adolf 154, 162
HO 41
Hochhuth, Rolf 168
"Hock" 31
Holbein, Hans 172
Hölderlin, Friedrich 166
holidays 81
  East Germany 84
  favourite areas Fig 49
  ideal venues 81
  ships 84
Holy Roman Empire 151–3, Fig 97

homes 12
  cleanliness 13
  East Germany 16
  influence 19
  survey 12–13
hotels
  breakfast 27
  cartoon Fig 51
  East Germany 30, 87
  photo Fig 54
  West Germany 83–4
house building
  cost 12
  rate 16
household goods
  expenditure 38
house-names 12
Hrabanus Maurus 151, 160
Humboldt, Alexander von 183
Hummel figures Fig 19
humour 11, 89, 217

identity card 113
illegitimacy
  East Germany 19
imports
  textiles 22
  West Germany 55
industrial standards 113–4
industry 50
  growth rate, East German 52
  raw materials Fig 27
  size of firms 50, Fig 26
  state-owned 52
insurance book 146
intellectuals 99–100
"Intendant"
  broadcasting 130
  theatre 72
intercourse, premarital 17–18
"Intershop" 37, 42
Isaacs, Heinrich 176

jackets 22
Jaspers, Karl 162–3
Jena 208
  glass 58
judges
  East Germany 115
June 1953 54

Kant, Immanuel 161
Karl der Grosse 151
Karl-Marx-Stadt 196
Kassel 202
  mince 29
  museum 214
Kästner, Erich 45
Kempten 202
keys 14
Kiel 202
Kiesinger, Kurt-Georg 97, Fig 62
Kilius, Marika 124
"Kirmes" 91
"Kirschwasser" 34
kitchen gadgets 15
"Klassenarbeiten" 103
Klee, Paul 174
Kleist, Heinrich von 166
Klopstock, Friedrich Gottlieb 166
Kneipp, Sebastian 145
"Knicks" 36
knife 27
Knigge, Adolf Freiherr von 36
"Knirps" 22
Koblenz 202–3
Kollwitz, Käthe 175, Fig 108
"Konfliktkommissionen" 115
Königswinter 203
Konstanz 204
"Korn" 34
Kossinna, Gustaf 162

"Labskaus" 28
Länder 97, 102, 191, Fig 119
  East Germany 194
"Landgericht" 114
language 184
law 113
  East Germany 115
  war crimes 218–9
LDPD 100
leather 40
Leibniz, Gottfried Wilhelm 160–1
Leipzig 208
  Auerbach's Keller Fig 130
  Bezirk 195
  hotel Fig 54
  inventors' exhibition 49
  trade fair 69, Fig 39
leisure time 70
"Lesezirkel" 67
Lessing, Gotthold Ephraim 166
letter-boxes 12
Liberal Democrats 100
library (cartoon) Fig 79
Liebfraumilch 33
Liebig, Justus von 181
"Lieder" 177
Limburg 204
Lindau 204
Linde, Carl von 183
literature 164
  youth 44–5
local government taxes 64
Lochner, Stefan 170
lodgers 20
Logau, Friedrich von 166
Loreley Fig 51
lorries 138
Lower Saxony 193
Low German 184
LPG 54
Lübeck 204
luggage 143
lunch 27
Lüneburg 204
Luther, Martin 108, 153, 176
Luxemburg, Rosa 162

Macke, August 174
"Made in Germany" 55
magazines
  advertising 66
  "Bunte Illustrierte" 124
  "Christ und Welt" 124
  "Constanze" 66
  "Das Neue Blatt" 66
  "Der Spiegel" 66, 97–8, 100, 124
  "Die Zeit" 66, 124
  "DM" 66
  East Germany 127–8
  "Eulenspiegel" 128
  "Heim und Welt" 66
  in English 125
  libraries 67
  "Neue Beliner Illustrierte" 30, 127
  "Neue Illustrierte" 124
  "Pardon" 100
  "Quick" 66, 124
  "Revue" 124
  "Stern" 66, 124
  West Germany 124
  "Zeit im Bild" 127
Magdeburg 210
  Bezirk 195
Mainz 204
  museums 214
Mann, Thomas 168
manners 36
Marburg 205
Marc, Franz 174
Margate jugs 55
Maria Laach 205
Mark der DDR 135
Markgrönningen
  Shepherds' Race 93–4
marriage
  East Germany 19
  West Germany 18
Marshall Aid 50, 157–9
Martel, Charles 151
Marx, Karl 161
Marxism-Leninism 107
mass organisations 101, 127
Mastersingers 176
May, Karl 44
May Day 90–1
  East Germany 96
meat 27
  butcher's shop 38, Fig 17
  East Germany 30

"Mehrwertsteuer" 63
"Meissner Porzellan" 58
milk 38
mini-skirts 23
Minnesänger 164, 176
Mittelland Canal 188
"Mittelschule" 102
Mittenwald 205
  museum 214
"Mittlere Reife" 102–3
money order 119
"money postmen" 119
Moselle
  tourists 81
  vineyards Fig 14
  wine 31
Mössbauer, Rudolf 183
mother 18
  Mother's Day 91
  working mothers 18, 20
motor vehicles
  cartoon Fig 89
  East Germany 140
  exported 56, Fig 30
  loading equipment Fig 39
  production 50
  registration plates 137
  Volkswagen 56, Fig 30
  Wartburg Fig 28
Mozart, Wolfgang Amadeus 176–7
Müller, Friedrich Max 162
Munich 205
  customs 95, Fig 61
  museums 213, 214
  Nymphenburg Castle Fig 126
Münster 205
  carnival Fig 56
  St Lambertus' Day 93
  theatre Fig 42
museums 212, Fig 133
music 176, Figs 110, 111
  festivals 178
  interests 178
  piano lessons 13
  musical boxes 40

National Democrats
  East Germany 100
  West Germany 99
National Front 54, 101, 127
nationalism 161–2
National Reconstruction Scheme 54
National Socialists 154
  former 149, 218–9
NATO 148, 149
Naturalism 167
Naumburg Master 170
NAW 54
Nazis 154
  former 149, 218–9
NDPD 100
Neubrandenburg 195
Neustadt
  museum 214
newspapers
  advertising 65–6
  "Berliner Zeitung" 127
  "Bild-Zeitung" 65–6, 122
  "BZ am Abend" 127
  "Die Welt" 122–3
  East Germany 69, 126–7
  "Frankfurter Allgemeine Zeitung" 122–3
  local 122, Fig 78
  museum 214
  "Neues Deutschland" 127
  special edition 78
  style 122
  "Süddeutsche Zeitung" 122–3
  West Germany 122, Fig 77
New Year's Eve 92
Nibelungs, Lay of the 164
Nietzsche, Friedrich 161
Nolde, Emil 174
"Norm" 54
North German Plain 187
North Rhine-Westphalia 193
North Sea 82
notepaper 64
Novalis 166
NPD 99
Nuremberg 205
  museum 213
  soup 30
nursery schools 102

Oberammergau 205, Fig 127
"Oberlandsgericht" 114
"Oberschule" 102
Oder 188
office building Fig 36
office routine 60, Figs 34, 35
Ohm, Georg Simon 182
Olympic teams 79
opera 176, 178, Fig 40
Opitz, Martin 166
optical equipment 56
Orff, Carl 178
Otfried von Weissenburg 164
out-patient centres 146
overcoats 22

Paczensky, Gertvon 130
paperbacks 126
Paracelsus 181
parcels 119
parents, course for Fig 68
Paris Agreements 148
pensions
  East Germany 146
  West Germany 145–6
People's Chamber 100
People's Universities 104
philosophy 10–11, 160
physical divisions 187, Fig 114
Pietism 108–9
"Pils" 33, 35
playing cards
  museum 214
"Plumeau" 13
pocket money 44
police
  blood tests 138–9
  cartoon Fig 88
  powers 113
  signals 138
political divisions 189, Fig 116
politics 97
  East German 100
  influence on broadcasting 130
  interest 99
  main issues 99
"Polterabend" 18
polyclinics 146
Polytechnic High School 105
"pop" music 178–180
post 116
  East Germany 121
  guide numbers 118–9, Fig 74
  offices 40, Fig 73
  rates 116
  savings 135
  stamps 121, 116, Fig 73
posters
  commercials 67
  political 99, Fig 37
Potsdam 210
  Bezirk 195
precedence (etiquette) 37
President 97
press advertising 65–6
prices 42, 51
primary schools 102
printing 186
  museum 214

prostitution 218
Prussia 153
public holidays 96
public transport
  East Germany 140
  West Germany 139
punctuality 60
punishments 114

qualities looked for in men 10
queue, reluctance to 10, 140

radio 129, Fig 82
  advertising 66
  East Germany 131
  programmes 130
  sets produced 50
Radio Free Europe 130
Radio Liberty 130
railways 141, Figs 90, 91, 92
  cheap tickets 142–3
  East Germany 144, Fig 92
  fares 141, 144
  timetables 141, 142
  types of train 141
raincoats
  East Germany 25
Ravensburg 205
Realism 167
"Realschule" 102
Reclam 126, Fig 80
Reformation 153
Reformed Church 108
"Reformhäuser" 40
refrigerators 50
refugees 115, 159
Regensburg 205
Reis, Johann Philipp 183
religion 108, Figs 69, 70, 71
  belief 111
  division 111
  East Germany 112
  schools 104
Renaissance architecture 172
rent
  East Germany 16
  West Germany 12, 38
resistance to Hitler 157
restaurant cars 143, 144
restaurants
  East Germany 30
  good manners 37
  on motorways 139
  on stations 143
  with music 70
Reuchlin, Johann 160
reunification 99
Rhine 188
  wine 31
Rhineland Fig 50
  religion 111
  tourists 81
  wine festivals 93
Rhineland-Palatinate 192–3
RIAS 130

Riemenschneider, Tilman 172
rings 17
rivers 188, Fig 114
road accidents 136
road building 137
road signs Fig 87
road traffic 136
  driving habits 10
  East Germany 140
  Highway Code 137
  right of way 137–8, Fig 86
  speed limit 138, 140
Rococo architecture 173–4
Romanesque architecture 170
Romanticism
  art 174
  literature 166–7
  music 177–8
Röntgen, Wilhelm 183
Rostock 211, Fig 132
  Bezirk 195
Rothenburg-ob-der-Tauber 205
"Roulade" 27
rubber plant Fig 3
rubber stamps Fig 35
Rüdesheim 205
Ruhr 193, Fig 120
Ruwer
  wine 31

Saar
  wine 31
Saarland 192
Sachs, Hans 166
St Martin's Day 91
St Nicholas' Day 92
salad 28
salt-pot 14–15
"Sammeltassen" 15
sauerkraut 10, 28, Fig 11
sausages 27–8, 38, Fig 11
savings 134
savings banks 135
Saxon Switzerland 87, Fig 53
"Schiedskommission" 115
"Schiedsrichter" 114
Schiller, Friedrich von 166
Schlegel, Friedrich and August Wilhelm 161
Schleich, Carl Ludwig 181
Schleswig
  museum 213
Schleswig-Holstein 187, 193–4
"Schloss" 172–3
"Schnaps" 34, Fig 13
"Schöffen" 114
  East Germany 115
Scholl, Hans and Sophie 157
Schongauer, Martin 170
schools 102, Figs 65, 66, 67, 68
school uniform, lack of 23
Schopenhauer, Arthur 161
"Schützenfest" 91
Schweitzer, Albert 99
Schwerin
  museum 216
science 181
Second World War 157
SED 100
"Selters" 35
Seven Years' War 154
shirts 22
shoes 22
shops 38
  courtesy and service 38
  dress shops 22
  East Germany 40–1
  hours open 38
shorts, leather 24–5
signature 64
singing 70
slogans Fig 63
slums 16

small ads 122
smoking
 cinema 73
 expenditure 38
Social Democrats 98
Socialism 107, 162, 219
Socialist Unity Party 100
social services
 East Germany 146
 West Germany 145
Society for Sport and Technics 79, 84, 149
"Soljanka" 30
Sorbs 96
soup 27
souvenirs
 East Germany 42
 West Germany 40
Soviet Companies 52
specialisation (schools) 103
Spener, Philipp Jakob 108
Speyer
 museum 214
spirits 34
sports 76, Figs 45, 46, 47, 48
 associations 76
 East Germany 79-80
 time spent on 44
 winter sports 82
Springer, Axel Cäsar 122
stainless steel 40
State Council 101
stations (railway) 143, Fig 90
 foreign exchange banks 134
Staudinger, Hermann 181
"Steinhäger" 34
stereotype 10
stew 28
Storm, Theodor 168
stoves, tiled 13, Fig 2
Stralsund 211
Strauss, Franz-Josef, 97, Fig 62
strikes 50-1
Strittmatter, Erwin 168
students 104
 duelling 104-5
 East Germany 107
 help with harvest 54
 political activity 100
Stuttgart 205
 museum 214
Suhl 195
suits (men's) 22

Sunday 112
 breakfast 27
 dress 22
supervisory council 52, 63, 113
supper 29, Fig 13
Supreme Federal Court 114
Suso 108
Suttner, Bertha von 162
sweets 28-9
Sylt 82

table, how laid 27
tabloids 124
"Tanzcafe" 70
"Tartar" 27
"Tauchsieder" 14
taxes 63
tea 27
telegrams 121
telephones 120
 alphabet 121
 cartoon Fig 76
 directory 121
teleprint 121
television 130–1
 advertising 66–7
 cartoon, Fig 83
 East German 131–2
 "Hello, Neighbour" 100
 "Panorama" 100, 130
 political criticism 100
 programmes 131
 sets produced 50
 time spent watching 45
theatre 70, Figs 40, 41, 42
 East Germany 74
 good manners 37
 programmes 70
 repertoires 73
 subsidies 72
 ticket Fig 41
Thirty Years' War 153
"three K's" 18
Thyssen Building Fig 36
ties 22
tipping
 East Germany 88
 West Germany 83–4
Titisee 206
tourist attractions 81–2, 87, 197,
 Figs 122, 125, 131
tourist literature Fig 124
tourists 81, Fig 101
 East Germany 85
town halls 173
tractors
 East Germany 54
 West Germany 52
trade fairs
 East Germany, 69
 West Germany 68
trade unions
 East Germany 52, 84, 101, 146
 West Germany 51–2

traffic lights 138
trams 139
translations (foreign books)
 East Germany 128
 West Germany 125
transport, expenditure on 38
travel agents 84
trial procedure 113
Triberg 206
Trier 206
trousers 22
Tübingen 206
Tucholsky, Kurt 19

Ulbricht, Walter 101, Fig 64
Ulm 207
umbrellas 10, 22
"Umlaut" 184
universities 104
 East Germany 107
 foundation 160
UTP 107, Fig 67

Varus, Publius Quintilius 151
VEB 52
vegetables 28
violin-making Fig 26
Virchnow, Robert 181
visas 87
visiting 19, 37
visitors in offices 61
vodka 35
Voice of America 130
"Volkshochschule" 104
"Volkskammer" 100
"Volksschule" 102
voting system
 East Germany 101
 West Germany 97

wages
　East Germany 54
　West Germany 51
Wagner, Richard 178
waiters 83
Walther von der Vogelweide 164
Warnemünde Fig 52
"Weckewerk" 29
Warburg, Otto Heinrich 181
Wartburg
　Castle 153, Fig 28
　car Fig 28
water bowl (on table) 27
weight 29
Weill, Kurt 178
Weimar, 211
　museums 216
　Shakespeare Festival 74
Weimar Republic 154
Werfel, Franz 168
Westphalia
　ham 30
　Peace of 153
Wiesbaden 207
Wies Church 174
window displays 38
windows
　double glazing 12
　shutters 12
wine 31, Fig 14
　at grocer's 40, Fig 18
　East Germany 35
　festivals 93
　grapes used 31
　label Fig 15
　museum 214
　shops 40
　vintages 33
winter sports 82, Fig 21
Wolf, Christa 168, Fig 44
Wolfram von Eschenback 164
wood carving 57, 58, Fig 31
word-order 186
work
　"hard-working Germans" 10, 60
　hours worked 60
works council 52
Würzburg 207

youth 43
　Dedication Ceremony 112
　dress 23
　free time 44
　jazz club Fig 22
　leisure time Fig 25
　organisations 45, 46–9, 84, 101
　Protection Law 73
　respect for elders 19
　Sports Festival Fig 48
　television preferences 131
　working teenagers 19

ZAW 65
Zones of Occupation Fig 99

Anglo-German Songbook

Compiled and translated by Alan G Jones BA FIL

A sing-song is almost sure to start when English- and German-speaking friends are gathered together in a relaxed mood. The songs favoured on these pleasant occasions are folk songs and student songs, simple in theme, strong in melody, rich with tradition and national flavour.

The singing goes so much better if each party knows the words and meaning of the other's songs. This is the purpose of the Anglo-German Songbook. It contains the lyrics of 34 of the German and English songs most popular for community singing.

A literal verse-by-verse translation (not for singing) is given alongside the original words. A brief introductory note in the appropriate language mentions a few points of interest about each song.

This Songbook will help to make Anglo-German occasions go with a real swing and is a delightful gift for each of your guests to take home as a souvenir (probably full of host signatures and addresses). It also makes a refreshingly different "reader" for language students, of special interest before and after an exchange visit.

Price in UK: 7/6. 6/- each for 10 or more. Outside UK: US$ 1.25 or DM 5,-. US$ 1.00 or DM 4,- each for 10 or more. Prices include postage.

— and the tunes on tape

The first verses of the songs in the Anglo-German Songbook are available as tape-recordings so that students and others can hear the tunes also.

There are two tapes, sold separately. One is for English listeners and is a recording of the German songs with announcements in English. The songs are sung in German by a male solo voice to a guitar accompaniment. The tunes can be easily learned by listening to this recording, which is also a guide to pronunciation of the German words.

The other tape is for German listeners. On it the English songs are sung by children in an English secondary school.

Each recording is on standard $1/4$ inch tape, playing speed $3\tfrac{3}{4}$ inches per second, supplied on a 4 inch diameter spool. Only half the tape width is used so that the whole recording can be played on a twin-track recorder without stopping to reverse the tape. The spool box contains a list of the songs in the order they are heard on the tape.

Both tapes are available by post, direct from Pond Press only. They can be ordered with the Songbook or independently. Price £2 or US$ 5.00 or DM 20,-, post free. Priority is given to orders sent with cash. These tapes are NOT supplied "on approval".

Published by **POND PRESS**
46 St Augustine's Avenue, Ealing, London W5